VIOLENT MEN

An Inquiry Into The Psychology of Violence

Revised Edition

HANS TOCH

American Psychological Association
Washington, DC

First printing July 1992
Second printing June 1993

First edition published 1969 by Aldine Publishing Company. Revised editions published 1980, 1984 by Schenkman Publishing Company. Revised edition published 1992 by the American Psychological Association.

Copies may be ordered from
APA Order Department
P.O. Box 2710
Hyattsville, MD 20784

In the U.K. and Europe, copies may be ordered from the American Psychological Association, 3 Henrietta Street, Covent Garden, London WC2E 8LU, England.

This book was typeset in Palatino by Easton Publishing Services, Inc., Easton, MD

Printer: BookCrafters, Chelsea, MI
Cover designer: Michael David Brown
Technical/Production Editor: Olin J. Nettles

Library of Congress Cataloging-in-Publication Data

Toch, Hans.
    Violent men : an inquiry into the psychology of violence / Hans Toch.—Rev. ed
        p.   cm.
    Includes bibliographical references and index.
    ISBN 1-55798-172-8 (acid-free paper)
    1. Aggressiveness (Psychology)   2. Violence.   I. Title.
    [DNLM: 1. Men.   2. Violence.   BF 575.A3 T631v]
    BF575.A3T6   1992
    155.2'32—dc20
    DNLM/DLC
    for Library of Congress   92-10715
                                                                   CIP

To the memory of FRITZ REDL
My teaching partner
And teacher.

Contents

Foreword

Violence is a troubling reality of the human condition, about which none of us wants to think. But not to think about what troubles us most is a guarantee of misunderstanding, mishandling, and ever-worsening problems. That the problem of violence in our society is misunderstood, mishandled, and increasingly problematic is evidenced by even a cursory reading of any newspaper.

Psychologists and psychiatrists avoid understanding violence; they delegate it to the police and then condemn the police for not coping with it adequately. As Mortimer Bard once said, "There are psychologists and psychiatrists who think aggression is upper-middle-class people saying unpleasant things to each other in group therapy. But there are people out there who beat each other up, stab each other, shoot each other, kill each other." When I go to conferences in psychology, psychiatry, or corrections where violence is discussed, I always hope to learn something of value, but in most cases I am disappointed. What is presented are theories, thinly disguised, but gleaned from detective stories (which are not really sources of information about violence but about enjoyable violent fantasies), or coping measures that won't work, or medications that can only be used, because of their unpleasant effects, on unwilling individuals in situations where they can be coerced— and which frequently don't work even then.

Why is so much useless information presented? Because there is so little real information, despite the fact that no issue is of more importance to people who have to deal with troubled people, whether criminal or mental patients, whether in hospitals, residential facilities, outpatient treatment, or jail. Indeed, even those people working in schools and other institutions of normal society with supposedly normal people are confronted with the problem of coping with violence. And although mental health professionals, practitioners as well as researchers, avoid thinking about violence, nothing concerns

them more than avoiding, preventing, or preventing the re-
currence of violence when they are forced by events to cope
with it.

Violent Men is an unusual book. It is based on real research
and is packed with useful information. It is the only book that
psychologists, social workers, parole and probation officers,
juvenile workers, and ward staffs have ever spontaneously
reported to me as being useful in understanding and coping
with violent people in the course of their work.

Dr. Toch assumes that if you want to understand violence
in human beings, you must talk to the human beings who are
violent. Even more, he assumes that violence is a problem for
all human beings, not just for the investigators, not just for
the victims, but for the violent person as well. He utilized the
unique method of a joint research team of professionals and
of violent men to investigate violence, knowing that both "scientific" investigators and violent individuals understand things,
but not the same things, and have biased perceptions, but not
the same biases. Furthermore, he knew that people talk openly
to people like themselves, but that they do not talk openly to
people whom they perceive as likely to look down on them.
He studied violent criminals and violent police officers and
found that the sources and meaning of individual violence
generalized. Interestingly enough, his technique of including
violent individuals in the collaborative study of their own and
others' violence turned out to be a potent technique not only
of gathering information and insight, but also of enabling violent individuals to understand and master their violence. Especially insightful is his description of the pressures that lead
police officers to unnecessary violent encounters, both against
the police officers and by the police officers, and some of the
relatively simple procedures that police officers themselves
originated to help other officers learn how to avoid unnecessary violence.

Despite its simplicity of expression, this is a sophisticated
book, making use of relevant theories and empirical findings
from a number of disciplines, but only when they clarify the
meaning of the findings. The discussion of collective and social
violence, although not directly related to these samples, would
in itself justify reading the book.

Dr. Toch once jokingly confronted me with many of the inadequacies of psychoanalytic theories, knowing that these theories guide my own research and practice. But, I pointed out, no one who really did not value a set of theories could possibly have his detailed knowledge of them. "Moreover," I said, "I know that you encourage your students to read August Aichhorn's *Wayward Youth*."

"August Aichhorn," he said, "was not a psychoanalyst; he was a human being."

Dr. Toch is a psychologist and a human being who has helped us begin to understand the most troubling part of what it means to be human.

BERTRAM P. KARON
MICHIGAN STATE UNIVERSITY

Preface

Books are defined by readers, and readers are tuned by settings. The essayist Macaulay traces Byron's rapid transformation from youth-hero to poet, and Johnson's demotion from lionized critic to public grouch. Such changes in public opinion face the most humble of us, and we ignore them at our peril.

The book *Violent Men* appeared in 1969, in the year of the National Commission on the Causes and Prevention of Violence, in the heyday of public concern with street violence, in a time of crisis. In 1969, violence meant assassinations, race riots, police riots, student riots, hijackings, runaway crime statistics, and an unjust war.

Today, in 1992, race riots, alarming crime statistics, and police use of violence against civilians are again in the headlines, and so is internecine warfare, at home and abroad. Teenage shooting death rates in our inner city streets have been dubbed a "national health crisis." The picture is not very encouraging: We have much more experience with violence in 1992 than we had back in 1969, but we are no closer to understanding it, or knowing how to control it.

For a scholarly book on violence, a climate of this kind is at best a mixed blessing. On the one hand, books on crisis-relevant subjects sell, which (for the author) is nice. On the other hand—and less nice—is the freight that is imposed by the public's "need for meaning," by people's desire for formulas that offer a handle on complex issues and a concise strategy for reform. More modest goals—efforts to make sense of a circumscribed segment of a problem—are distorted or found wanting. This means that, even in the best of circumstances, a book rides the crest of its popularity under false colors.

All this is difficult enough to deal with, but in 1969 there was more. For one, there was hope of formulating integrating conceptions in the social sciences, including in our understanding of violence. The classic treatise on violence published in the sixties was subtitled *Towards an Integrated Theory of Criminology.*[1] Though my book was merely called *An Inquiry into the Psychology of Violence,* there was pressure (very tempting pressure) to ignore or strain this boundary.

The revised *Violent Men* is still, first and foremost, about aspects of violence that are in the domain of the psychologist—meaning that the book is concerned with the personal motives, attitudes, assumptions, and perceptions of persons who are violent. This exploration does not claim to shed light on such aspects of violence as the impact of social institutions or the patterning of violent behavior in large human aggregates. There is also no implication that these or other aspects of violence are not important or relevant.

This book deals with the subject of headlines—police uses of force, acts of criminal violence, and participation in riots—because it deals with persons who become involved in such acts. To the extent to which violence, however organized or collective it may be, of necessity involves individuals as participants, psychology as perspective is relevant to its understanding.

The book is strictly concerned with individuals—all male—who are in some way involved in the criminal justice system, who have *recurrently* done physical harm to other people, and who can be said to have a "propensity" for violent conduct. In dealing with such people, I do not mean to play down other violence-linked problems, such as those caused by peddlers of defective tires, dispensers of pollutants, or oppressors of the poor. I believe it is axiomatic that a student does not need to depreciate the importance of one social problem when he elects to study another.

Obviously, however, I also believe (among other things) that examining violent men as defined in this book is scientifically and socially important. I believe it is scientifically important because it illuminates continuity and patterning in human per-

---

[1]M. E. Wolfgang and F. Ferracuti, *The Subculture of Violence: Towards an Integrated Theory of Criminology* (London: Tavistock, 1967).

sonality.[2] And I think it is practically important because (1) recurrent violence is a predictor of future violence, and because (2) in settings in which we face high rates of violence, it is repetitively violent individuals who commit most of the violence we face.[3]

The approach to violence in this book is *social* psychological. This means that the violent act is always seen in relation to the situation that inspires it. It means that violence is viewed as interpersonal, as a form of social conduct comparable to other forms of social conduct. By the same token it is assumed that repeated violence is personally syntonic, that it is a characteristic personal reaction, and that it is invoked by some people with the same consistency that persuasion, or retreat, or self-insulation, or humor, or defiance, is employed by others. I feel that violence is linked to human personality in such a way that the study of one can teach us about the other. The exercise of violence can be viewed as a clue, a symptom, a calling card, which, if properly read, could expose the central motives and concerns of violent men.

I also feel that the study of violence must not be circumscribed by legal or socioeconomic classifications. It must be viewed in the context of taverns and school rooms, in prison cells and living rooms; it covers brawls and killings, riots and revolts. One's statements must be both general and specific. They must link the contexts in which violence occurs; they must also isolate their distinguishing properties.

One of the universals that is probably still of importance today is the link between police and ghetto violence. Colin McGlashan of the *London Observer* has written that

> The black kids and the white cops—their pride, their fear, their isolation, their need to prove themselves, above all

---

[2]G. W. Allport, *Pattern and Growth in Personality* (New York: Holt, Rinehart & Winston, 1961).

[3]M. E. Wolfgang, R. Figlio, and T. Sellin, *Delinquency in a Birth Cohort* (Chicago: University of Chicago Press, 1972); P. W. Greenwood (with A. Abrahams), *Selective Incapacitation* (Santa Monica, CA: Rand Corporation, 1982); M. Wolfgang, T. Thornberry, and R. Figlio, *From Boy to Man, From Delinquency to Crime* (Chicago: University of Chicago Press, 1987).

their demand for respect—are strangely alike: victims both, prisoners of an escalating conflict they didn't make and can't control.

Some aspects of this problem are examined in the following pages. In examining them, attention has been paid not only to commonalities but also to differences. For I feel that in some important respects the warring parties in the ghetto live in different worlds. While they are "prisoners" of the same dilemma, they will have to be freed differently. The same holds true for inmates and guards, discordant spouses, and for felonious assaulters and their victims.

But in essential respects the focus of this book is on common denominators in violence. The research deals with chronically violent men. It tries to understand them as individuals, and to sort them into groups. It tries to link them to the rest of humanity, while separating them for their violent acts. I feel that both aims are important. This means that if the reader emerges from the experience sensing the humanity of violent men, as well as their uniqueness, the book will have accomplished its mission.

HANS TOCH

Acknowledgments

I remain much indebted to J. Douglas Grant, a longtime partner and colleague. Grant's thinking permeates so much of *Violent Men* that it is difficult for me to determine which ideas in the book are his and which I can claim as mine.

The NIMH Center for Studies of Crime and Delinquency (now renamed) paid for most of the work on which this book is based. Our relationship transcended that of sponsorship. I am grateful to the NIMH Center and its former director, Saleem Shah, for their support and encouragement.

Fred Seiler and Alex Morin encouraged me to write this book and believed in the integrity of the enterprise from its inception. I am mindful of this act of faith, and that of Alfred Schenkman, who gave *Violent Men* new life in its first revised edition. As for the present version, the publisher is the message. I originally wrote the book for psychologists, hoping to advance the discipline and assist our profession. My hope then was to gain some measure of acceptance by my peers. I am indebted to Julia Frank-McNeil for resuscitating this hope through APA publication of the book.

1

Violence in Psychological Perspective

Psychology has a lot to say about violence. In saying it
psychologists prefer to use the word "aggression"—a term
that draws attention to assaultive conduct, but also denotes
"forceful action" or "encroachment." This preference for mod-
erate language reflects a tradition of studying behavior with
scientific neutrality. If we opt for stronger language (as we
shall do), we acquire undesirable surplus baggage, but we also
sharpen the focus of our discourse. A book entitled *Aggressive
People* could easily refer to intrusive techniques of salesman-
ship, competitive drivers, or New York pedestrians. The nuances of "violence" (such as illegitimacy, explosiveness, injury
to victims) preclude generalizing across a broad spectrum of
human behavior, but, with regard to the restricted subject of
our inquiry, such nuances are not misleading. For the behavior
we shall deal with *is* injurious, is rarely planned, and almost
invariably is affect-laden.

Psychologists often talk of "instrumental" and "hostile"
aggression to differentiate violence that is deployed for gain
from undiluted expressions of revenge or destructiveness.[1] In
the world of violence we must view, dispassionateness and
vengefulness are rare. Real-life encounters tend to yield eclectic

---

[1]S. Feshbach, "The Function of Aggression and the Regulation of Aggressive Drive," *Psychological Review* (1964), 71: 257–272.

admixtures, composites of goal and rage, purpose and hate, reason and feeling, rationality and irrationality. Instrumental and hostile violence are not only *kinds* of violence, but also violence qualities or *components*. To tease out these components may not help us to describe violent acts, but does help us to understand and explain them.

When we talk of "hostile" violence-components we refer to a person's capacity for explosiveness, for reacting to frustration with a stance of bitterness and hate. The assumption is that most of us, most of the time, monitor and control our explosive reactions. In "violent men" this potential may be *undercontrolled*,[2] meaning that such persons allow themselves to attack or retaliate under circumstances where the rest of us would sulk, complain, or retreat. Psychologists talk of such behavior in stimulus–response terms. They also talk of a capacity for cumulated resentment that welcomes opportunities of release. This image is apt, but its emphasis suggests a surplus of affect where the problem may be a deficit in self-control.[3]

Hostile violence is of interest to all sorts of psychologists, ranging from laboratory scientists to clinicians. Physiologists have a field day tracing hostile violence to its presumed source or explaining differences in thresholds of explosiveness.[4] Such violence is also of concern to ethologists and biologists, who assume that it exists among lower organisms, who have learned to control unfettered aggressivity in the course of evolution.[5] Freud's contribution to our understanding of violence was threefold: (1) he observed his conflicted patients struggling against (among other things) primitive bloodthirstiness; (2) he

---

[2] Violent behavior by one-time exploders is sometimes *overcontrolled*, which means that overly rigid defenses cumulatively collapse. These contrasting types of violence have been documented and described by E. I. Megargee in "Undercontrolled and Overcontrolled Personality Types in Extreme Antisocial Aggression," *Psychological Monographs* (1966), 80: 3, Whole No. 611.

[3] See R. W. Novaco, *Anger Control* (Lexington, MA: Heath, 1975); C. Travis, *Anger: The Misunderstood Emotion* (New York: Simon & Schuster, 1982). For a review of earlier insights into the problem, see H. Toch, "The Management of Hostile Aggression: Seneca as Applied Social Psychologist," *American Psychologist* (1983), 38: 1022–1026.

[4] K. E. Moyer, *Violence and Aggression: A Physiological Perspective* (New York: Paragon House, 1987).

[5] K. Lorenz, *On Aggression* (New York: Harcourt Brace Jovanovich, 1966).

highlighted traumatic experiences as the root of personal conflicts, which often included a repressed desire for revenge
against past victimizers; and (3) he pointed to the "control
functions" of the ego (personality) and suggested that deficits
can occur in our ability to check our drives, including our
aggressive drives.[6]

Freud's practice dealt with neurotics and borderline psychotics (for whom aggression is transformed into obsession,
anxiety, or psychosomatic symptoms) and he had little to say
about patients who act out their aggressions. The task of studying such persons fell to Freud's students and in particular to
August Aichhorn, the director of an institution for delinquents.[7] Aichhorn discussed the role of destructive child-rearing practices in building reservoirs of aggressiveness and in
creating unconscious assumptions about a hostile or uncaring
world. Aichhorn demonstrated that such bitterness translates
into violence, but that it can be "disconfirmed" through love
and reassurance in a nonretaliatory institutional environment.

This work was extended by Fritz Redl and David Wineman,
who (like Aichhorn) centered on developmental deficits in aggressive children's personalities. Like Aichhorn, Redl and
Wineman showed that hostile children can combine effective
defenses against change (delinquent egos) with difficulties in
modulating feelings and impulses (weak egos).[8]

Psychoanalysis was merged with learning theory to create
the "frustration aggression hypothesis," which hypothesizes
an invariant tendency for frustration (the interference with a
person's achievement of prized goals) to lead to retaliatory

---

[6]In English translations, the German word for "drive" is often translated
as "instinct," and Freud's views thus acquire connotations that Freud never
intended. See H. Toch and F. Redl, "The Psychoanalytic Perspective," in
H. Toch (Ed.), *Psychology of Crime and Criminal Justice* (New York: Holt,
Rinehart & Winston, 1979).

[7]A. Aichhorn, *Wayward Youth: A Psychoanalytic Study of Delinquent Children,
Illustrated by Actual Case Studies* (New York: Meridian Books, 1955).

[8]F. Redl and D. Wineman, *Children Who Hate: The Disorganization and
Breakdown of Behavior Controls* (New York: Collier Books, 1962). For another
excellent clinical account, see V. L. Agee, *Treatment of the Violent Incorrigible
Adolescent* (Lexington, MA: Heath, 1979).

violence or displaced attacks.[9] Though the postulated link between frustration and aggression is not as inflexible as was initially assumed, studies of laboratory aggression still depend on the fact that if subjects are harassed they will behave more violently than comparable persons who are left alone. Such paradigms are short-term counterparts of longer-term processes revealed through psychoanalysis.

"Instrumental" components of violence have been studied by social learning theorists—most notably by Albert Bandura and his associates.[10] While hostility experts discuss violence in terms of propensities (aggressive drives) that are checked or expressed, Bandura describes violence as a wide range of behavior that is built up through past experience, is meaningfully related to the context in which it occurs, and is maintained because it makes sense to the person who is behaving violently. One way in which violence is learned is by observing it, especially in situations in which violence pays, or where the "model" who deploys it is respected. Violence is used when it is deemed appropriate. This sometimes includes situations in which the person feels he has been provoked. It always includes situations in which the consequences anticipated from the violence are desired and valued. Violent behavior continues as long as violence is somehow rewarding. Though the rewards can be material, they more frequently consist of such intangible commodities as status, approval, discontinuance of discomfort, or retributive justice. Justice is different from vengeance (the hostile-component version) in that the goal is to balance books rather than to express hatred. Similar distinctions cover situations where violence does *not* occur. Bandura does not see restraint as resulting from built-in controls, but as abstinence from violence where it makes no sense in terms of assumed consequences.

Social learning theory (unlike other views of learning) makes

---

[9]J. Dollard, L. Doob, N. Miller, O. Mowrer, and R. Sears, *Frustration and Aggression* (New Haven, CT: Yale University Press, 1939).

[10]A. Bandura, *Aggression: A Social Learning Perspective* (Englewood Cliffs, NJ: Prentice-Hall, 1973); A. Bandura and R. H. Walters, *Adolescent Aggression* (New York: Ronald Press, 1959).

provision for man-as-actor. The view includes portraits of moral perspectives and standards which prescribe or proscribe behavior. "At one extreme," writes Bandura, "are persons who have adopted behavioral standards and codes that make aggressive feats a source of personal pride. Such individuals readily engage in aggressive activities and derive enhanced feelings of worth from physical conquests. . . . Lacking self-reprimands for hurtful conduct, they are deterred from cruel acts mainly by reprisal threats. Idiosyncratic self-systems of morality are not confined to individuals or fighting gangs. In aggressive cultures where prestige is closely tied to fighting prowess, members take considerable pride in aggressive exploits."[11] This view draws attention to premises that attenuate (or circumvent) self-restraints and can undergird violent acts. It also assumes that such premises can be shared, which anticipates (in summary form) one theme of this book.

The Shape of Violence

Patterns of Violence

The hostile-component view of violence assumes that human beings are reservoirs of destructiveness but maintains that civilization equips most people with the means of discharging their hatreds judiciously and selectively. Unfortunately, there are instances in which this effort fails. Some persons are disposed to remain unchecked in their aggressiveness, so that they become quite consistently violent upon slight provocation. Empirical evidence for this view includes excellent longitudinal studies which show that aggressive children—schoolyard bullies, for example—tend to become aggressive adults and to have aggressive offspring.[12]

---

[11] A. Bandura, "The Social Learning Perspective: Mechanisms of Aggression," in H. Toch (Ed.), *Psychology of Crime and Criminal Justice* (New York: Rinehart & Winston, 1979), p. 226.

[12] D. Olweus, "Stability of Aggressive Reaction Patterns in Males: A Review," *Psychological Bulletin* (1979), 86: 852–875; L. R. Huesman, L. D. Eron, M. M. Lefkowitz, and L. O. Walder, *The Stability of Aggression Over Time and Generations* (Victoria, British Columbia, Canada: International Society for Research on Aggression, 1984).

One problem with centering on hostile violence, however, is that even a cursory review of violent conduct suggests that violence is not blind and random. We know, for instance, that members of fighting gangs are frequently nonviolent when separated from their companions; that many extremely dangerous people seem to specialize in certain categories of victims—women or business competitors; that individuals recurrently violent in the street may be model prisoners when incarcerated (or vice versa), and that there is sometimes a relationship between being violent and being socially inept.

Violence takes place predominantly in certain circles, in certain settings, and on certain occasions.[13] If we want to witness a stabbing, we can best do so by locating a family squabble in a slum late on a Friday or Saturday evening. We might also frequent taverns in the same neighborhood, or the street corners inhabited by drug-trafficking gangs. If violence is really blind and random, it is hard to understand why we should find so much of it in specific types of situations. Is the "localization" of violent acts a result of opportunity or climate? Does a man assault his wife rather than someone else simply because she happens to be available? Are bars simply fashionable locations for brawls?

It appears as if violence cannot be equated with angry explosiveness. There is shape and form to violence. Patterns of destructiveness show consistency, and they vary reliably from person to person. For each of us, violence seems tied to a restricted range of life situations. It seems to reflect purpose, and it implies the presence of hidden (if perverted) meanings. But what needs does violence satisfy? How is it provoked? What values and dispositions does it reflect? How do violent people become involved in violence? We must have the answers to such questions if we are to face the problem of regenerating violence-prone persons.

---

[13] R. C. Bensing and O. Schroder, *Homicide in an Urban Community* (Springfield, IL: Charles C Thomas, 1960); M. E. Wolfgang, *Patterns in Criminal Homicide* (Philadelphia: University of Pennsylvania Press, 1958); M. E. Wolfgang and N. A. Weiner (Eds.), *Criminal Violence* (Newbury Park, CA: Sage, 1982).

The World of Violent Men

The remainder of this book reports on the results of an effort to search the minds of recurrently violent individuals (Violent Men) for whatever sense and purpose they contain. Violence is both the focus of inquiry and the object of explanation. Our assumption is that if we want to explain why persons are driven to acts of destruction, we must examine these acts, and we must understand the contexts in which they occur. We must know how destructive acts are initiated and developed, how they are conceived and perceived, and how they fit into the lives of their perpetrators.

We must also assume that we can *not* make sense of violent acts by viewing them as outsiders. Ultimately, violence arises because some person feels that he or she must resort to a physical act, that a problem he or she faces calls for a destructive solution. The problem violent persons perceive is rarely the situation as *we* see it, but rather some dilemma they feel they find themselves in. In order to understand a violent person's motives for violence, we must thus step into his or her shoes, and we must reconstruct his or her unique perspective, no matter how odd or strange it may be. We must recreate the world of the violent person, with all its fears and apprehensions, with its hopes and ambitions, with its strains and stresses.

Another safe assumption is that violence is often a two-person game. Even where the victim does no more than appear at the wrong time and place, his or her contribution is essential for the consummation of his or her destruction. And usually more than mere physical presence is involved. Common sense and law are attracted to the image of passive victims mauled by spontaneously malevolent aggressors. In the world of violence, however, the situation is rarely that simple. As Von Hentig has eloquently pointed out,

> the relationships between perpetrator and victim are much more intricate than the rough distinctions of criminal law. Here are two human beings. As soon as they draw near to one another, male or female, young or old, rich or poor, ugly or attractive, a wide range of interactions, repulsions as well as attractions, is set in motion. What the law does

is to watch the one who acts and the one who is acted upon. By this external criterion a subject and object, a perpetrator and a victim are distinguished. In sociological and psychological quality the situation may be completely different. It may happen that the two distinct categories merge. There are cases in which they are reversed and in the long chain of causative forces the victim assumes the role of a determinant.[14]

To understand violence it is necessary to focus on the chain of interactions between aggressor and victim, on the sequence that begins when two people encounter each other—and which ends when one harms, or even destroys, the other.

Violent acts, and violent interactions, do not make sense when viewed in isolation. The dilemmas people encounter are continuing, their personalities are constant, and their ways of relating to others reflect established habits and dispositions. Most violent conduct is no less lawful than other human conduct. If we examine different violent acts committed by the same person, we expect these acts to carry consistent meanings; we expect these acts to serve common needs; we expect them to result from pressures that operate persistently over time. We also expect that consistencies in a person's approach to others can produce situations in which violence always results—sometimes without the person being aware of the fact that he is the instigator of destructive (or self-destructive) games. And finally, some institutions in our society contain features that reliably encourage, provoke, or elicit violent conduct. These forces, also, contribute to shape the patterns of violence, and we must isolate and describe them.[15]

What are the data best studied if we wish to understand violence, and if we wish to prevent it? It seems of limited value to concentrate on accidentally or situationally produced violence, unless the circumstances involved are recurrent and

---

[14]H. Von Hentig, *The Criminal and His Victim* (New York: Anchor Books, 1967), pp. 382–83.

[15]For an insightful discussion of the issue of the consistency and specificity of violent acts, see A. Campbell and J. J. Gibbs (Eds.), *Violent Transactions: The Limits of Personality* (London: Basil Blackwell, 1986).

modifiable. It also seems of limited value to concentrate on once-in-a-lifetime violent persons, unless the sequences that lead to their violence are uniform and predictable. It seems most productive to study those people—almost all of them men—who become recurrently involved in acts of violence. These violence-prone men can be expected to tell us about the individual and social forces that produce violence. And these men account for the lion's share of our problem. For, statistically, few people in our society are embarked on consequential *careers* of violence.[16] The psychology of violence revolves around the identity and conduct of these select dedicated Violent Men.

Toward a Typology of Violence

What follows are some results of a research project conducted in California under a federal grant.[17] This project explored standard situations fraught with violence, delved into institutions plagued with threats of violence, and involved—as subjects—some of the most dangerous offenders in the state.

The study had its inception in an isolated meadow along an obscure dirt road, with the murder of a helplessly tied police officer by a pair of escaped felons. This incident, the second of its kind in a week, produced a memorandum from Governor Brown requesting a crash research program dealing with violence. Our project, which dates from this memorandum, was also shaped by subsequent demands. One of these originated in a concern with violence behind prison walls; the other was occasioned by an increase in assaults upon the police in two West Coast cities. These practical considerations dictated our areas of work and our areas of emphasis, and they did so because they coincided with our desire to study violence in settings in which it occurred frequently but took a restricted

---

[16]M. A. Peterson and H. Braiker (with S. M. Polich), *Who Commits Crime: A Survey of Prison Inmates* (Cambridge, MA: Oelgeschlager, Gunn & Hain, 1981).

[17]This research was carried out under a grant from the National Institute of Mental Health (Project MH-08970) to the Institute for the Study of Crime and Delinquency, Sacramento, California. J. Douglas Grant was Director of this study.

range of forms. We were thus able to concentrate on real-life circumstances without sacrificing the requirement for a systematic and restricted sample of test situations.

The Investigation

Our research effort was both pure and applied. Through our investigation we hoped to discover facts about the genesis of violent incidents that might help us to think of ways of preventing such incidents. We were also concerned with understanding violence as a form of human conduct: We hoped to contribute something to the ongoing knowledge of psychology (and more specifically of personology and social psychology) through our study of violence. Finally, we hoped to explore new avenues of field research; in this sense our study was partly intended as an exercise in methodology.

The Peer Interview

Probably the really unique feature of our study was the fact that our researchers also qualified as subjects: Convicted offenders produced and administered our prison interview schedule; paroled inmates negotiated with the parolees in our sample; police professionals conducted our police study. As a result, every one of our respondents was questioned by someone whom he could reliably identify as a peer.

The uniqueness of this procedure becomes obvious when we review transcriptions of interviews. The following excerpt is typical. It involves the aftermath of a prison gambling incident:

Interviewer: Was it the next day that you were going through the kitchen line and that he approached you and said he was coming down and wanted his stuff, and you better be there with it?

Subject: He said he was coming to get me, and I better be ready. The inference was—Was I going to be ready?

Interviewer: So you went back to the kitchen and got a shank and then went to your pad. Now this dude who was doing the talking to you now, this is the one who you were playing coon can with? The next morning one of the dudes approached you?

Subject: The next morning. The same dude. When I came out of my cell in the wing this guy approached me. He lived in the wing.

Interviewer: What is his message?

Subject: His message is just a play, and they were playing a pat hand. It wasn't anything different from the day before. I told him . . .

The questions being asked here derive from a prescribed system of inquiry, but the wording takes forms familiar to the respondent. Any listener would gain the impression that he is overhearing a snatch of conversation between two friends discussing a subject of mutual interest, using the most natural language possible. No constraints are introduced; the interviewee feels no need to translate or to explain; no information is lost; every nuance of the responses is understood and every detail explored.

In some instances, this sort of communication becomes almost private; it explores events familiar only to those who have lived in the world of the yard or in the jungle of the streets. The interview refers to actions that can be thus reviewed only by those who have experienced the pressures that produce them. The following inquiry into an incident in which a rumor has been spread conveys the flavor of this kind of communication:

Interviewer: So you were just tripping something about your knocking him. Do you know how this got back to the guy?

Subject: Yeah. A lot of guys knew him. He knew all the guys that I knew. It just happened that we knew one another. He was mad and he was bad, too . . . He whipped my ass. But I didn't mind that.

Interviewer: He said he could stand anything but to be called a trick, eh?

Subject:	Yeah. Being burnt is part of the game. "You been telling all my friends that I'm a trick." He was a prize fighter, really. The guy was an ex-pro. He was a heavyweight. We started arguing and I thought I better end this now, with a minimum amount of damage. There were a few blows thrown and I told him I was sorry. And I really was sorry that I had said that.
Interviewer:	Well, he sort of told you what his standards were, and you said, "let your conscience be your guide"?
Subject:	Yeah. He knocked the shit out of me. I wasn't expecting it, really.

Peer interviews contain evidence of their own reliability. Often they demonstrate the extent to which responses are understood by the interviewer, and bear witness to the degree to which understanding is acknowledged by the respondent. The feedback is instantaneous, and the subject can feel that there is no question of misinterpretation of his answer. The following conversation shows the interviewer clarifying (to himself and to the subject) some steps in a relatively complex sequence leading to an act of violence:

Interviewer:	You knew the assignment clerk, and so you went to him to get him to move them both in the same housing unit?
Subject:	Right.
Interviewer:	Now where does this other dude come in at?
Subject:	Well he liked the broad and wanted her for a cell partner after she moved into the ward.
Interviewer:	So actually there is three people involved. The old man, the broad and this dude who walks into the action?
Subject:	Right.
Interviewer:	Okay. So he said something to her and she said, "don't fuck with me. If you do, I'll get S"?
Subject:	Right.

Interviewer: So S came and talked to you, and you went to talk with the dude. He said, "this ain't none of your business. Get your stuff"?

Subject: Right.

Interviewer: So you got your stuff, thinking all the time that this dude means business.

Subject: He did mean business.

Nonprofessional research workers have been used in studies other than our own.[18] In our case, use of peer interviewers was quite intensive and systematic, because our objectives made such a procedure especially appropriate and necessary. We intended to interview people who had been reliably identified as participants in violent acts. This participation is in many circles defined as undesirable; our subjects would be especially aware of this fact, since we would have to locate them through institutions in which they had been (or were being) subjected to sanction. Thus, unless we somehow succeeded in convincing respondents that our research would not intensify their difficulties, our chances of securing cooperation were obviously slim. Interviewers would almost have to be persons known to be least likely to cast a critical eye on the data being generated.

Second, we felt it important that our interviews explore the meaning of violence for the person who had engaged in it. This emphasis on the phenomenology of violence presupposes that the interviewee feel free to discuss his feelings, attitudes, and perceptions in the most natural manner possible, using the language most appropriate to the subject matter and re-creating the frame of reference within which he operated at the time of the incidents. He would have to presuppose that

---

[18]J. Grant, "The Industry of Discovery: New Roles for the Nonprofessional," in A. Pearl and F. Riessman (Eds.), *New Careers for the Poor* (New York: Free Press of Glencoe, 1965), pp. 92–124; R. Schwitzgebel, *Streetcorner Research: An Experimental Approach to Juvenile Delinquency* (Cambridge, MA: Harvard University Press, 1954); L. N. Robins and N. W. Braroe, "The Lay Interviewer in Research," *Journal of Nervous and Mental Disease* (1964), 138: 70–78.

his interlocutor could share his assumptions and could understand his vocabulary sufficiently to make unfettered communication possible. He would have to presuppose, further, that his interviewer's interest focused on the "relevant" aspects of the situation as he himself saw them.

The use of peer interviews made it possible to gain access to information we could not otherwise obtain. Another aspect of the use of nonprofessional research aides relates to a less tangible and more general advantage. Most social researchers sense some difficulty in the initial approach to subject populations of vastly different backgrounds from their own. Some react at this juncture with an elaborate process of ingratiation or "gaining of rapport," in which the researcher, and the research, are presented in the (presumably) best light. This posturing is often transparently insincere and always wasteful. Worse, it usually achieves merely a wary and delicate stalemate, during which only a hit-and-run raid for data is possible before the subjects seem to discover what has happened to them.

During rare moments of honesty, we may admit that even when we induce subjects to cooperate, our dealings with them are seldom the exciting adventure we tell our students about. And the main problem here may not be one of communication and social distance at all—it may have nothing to do with habits of dress or the use of colloquial language. It may be that our subjects understand us only too well, knowing that what we ask is unreasonable and unfair. After all, we are supplicants and, at worst, invaders demanding booty of captive audiences. In return for vague promises or a modest remuneration we expect a person to bare his soul or to make controversial and potentially incriminating statements. The "communication" is one way: The researcher maintains his position as a recipient of nonreciprocated information.

We also make our informant aware that we are interested in him not as a person but as a "subject"—a representative of a type, or a case, or an item in a sample. He knows this because he knows who he is and who we are. He knows that he is being approached because he is the inhabitant of a ghetto or a prison, because he is a "consumer," or because he acts as an informer. And he knows that his aims are being subordinated to our own. How can he share our objectives, after all, if he cannot even see the results of the efforts in which he has participated?

The use of peer interviewers circumvents ethical problems in social science research, because it confronts research subjects with research workers who approach them as equals, and who can brief them in terms that make sense to them. For these briefings to occur honestly, the nonprofessional researcher must feel himself a partner of the enterprise. He can do this if he has been involved in the conceptualization and design of the research.

It is useful to have available the expertise of nonprofessionals at the design stage of a study. It is also helpful to gain the benefit of their perspective in the analysis of data. A well-chosen lay researcher can often be in a position to correct naive inferences by less experienced professionals. For example, one of our own research partners, Inmate Hallinan of San Quentin, once chided me (in writing) for drawing a hasty and incorrect conclusion from an interview we had conducted. The interviewee was an Indian leader, and I had made much of the presumed impact of his ethnic background. Luckily, my colleague Hallinan was there to point out that Indian heritage was unimportant, and that our man was impelled by the "need to establish a personal reputation as a prison tough guy." Hallinan's documentation of this interpretation follows:

> The first incident that the subject becomes involved in is the rat-packing of an Indian child molester in order to ostracize and punish the molester, and also to solidify his position among the low-riders. So, rather than being a leader of these Indians, he is using his Indian blood to further his own ends. He wants to be a tough con, someone to be feared and respected. "The new guys that come in, no one knows about them." "Once you get a reputation you have to protect it." The above statements, and others similar in nature, were made by the subject during the course of the interview. . . .
>
> How does the subject go about building a reputation? As he says, fighting for home boys, and interceding for other Indians? No. Of the ten incidents—actually nine, because No. 1 and No. 9 are the same—in No. 6 no violence occurred; No. 2 involved helping a friend, although the details

were vague; No. 7 was a fight of his own making; in No. 9 he was attacked; and No. 10 was the rat-packing incident. The remaining four involved custody. He was proudest of No. 8. In regards to this incident, the following dialogue occurred:

Interviewer: Do you think this incident helped your reputation?

Subject: It sure as hell did. I knocked down the Captain.

Interviewer: How did you feel just before you knocked him down?

Subject: Like a big man.

Interviewer: During?

Subject: I sure am doing it right this time . . .

> The word circulates that he has fought with the "bulls," implying that he will jump on a convict with little provocation. The facts are never pursued, but accepted prima facie, because those who pass on these rumors and exaggerations are the very ones who are most impressed by them. The rumor returns and the subject begins to believe his own yard reputation. . . .
>
> Our subject has completed the building of his reputation, petty though it is, and now he and his low-rider friends can observe and honor it. Not that the cons on the yard do, but the subject feels that they do, and this is all that really matters. If anything, he is tolerated, not respected and feared as he would like.

It is obvious that Inmate Hallinan is not only furnishing me with a lesson in perspective, but is also demonstrating that he can compete with professionals in his methodological acumen and his ability vividly to summarize and communicate research conclusions. And although this analysis is unusually literate, because Inmate Hallinan had invested lots of prison time in creative writing courses, much can be learned even from our most unlettered collaborators.

Sources of Data

Our information was obtained with the cooperation of officials and line staff in the California Department of Corrections and in two metropolitan police departments.

Samples of violent incidents were garnered from the central files of the Department of Corrections and from more detailed folders maintained in institutions and in county parole offices. They were also abstracted from arrest reports in the record units of the San Francisco and Oakland Police Departments. Our study of police records was confined to assaults on police officers, and our investigation of institutionalized offenders emphasized incidents of violence within prison walls.

The following groups of persons were individually interviewed: (a) 32 officers on the force of the Oakland Police Department who had suffered assaults—in most cases, on several occasions; (b) 19 men who had assaulted the police officers—in most instances, on several occasions (in all but one case, the assaulted officers were among those we interviewed); (c) 44 prison inmates (15 in the California Medical Facility of Vacaville, and 29 residents at San Quentin); (d) 33 parolees with violent records (12 from Sacramento County, and 21 living in Oakland).[19]

The policemen we interviewed were selected on the basis of their experience with assaults. Half of them (14) had been attacked by persons in our assaulter sample, but almost to a man the remainder of the officers were chosen because they had been attacked on at least three recent occasions and had

---

[19] Our police research was made possible through the cooperation of officials in the Oakland and San Francisco police departments. We are indebted in Oakland to Chief Gain, Chief Preston, Chief Toothman, Captains Guidici and Connelli of the Record Division, and Sergeant Lucas of the Bureau of Internal Affairs. We are grateful to Chief Cahill of the San Francisco Police Department for permitting access to records. Our inmate studies were made possible through assistance from Dr. Keating, former superintendent of the California Medical Facility, and Warden Wilson of San Quentin Prison. Our survey of parolees could not have been conducted without the help of various staff members of the Oakland and Sacramento County parole offices. The Department of Corrections of California issued directives providing cooperation and facilities at every level. Our study of institutional violence was initiated in consultation with a California Task Force created June 7, 1965. For the research recommendations of this group, see P. C. Mueller, H. Toch, and M. Molof, *Report to the Task Force to Study Violence in Prison* (Sacramento: California Department of Corrections, Research Division, Aug. 1965), mimeographed.

accumulated the most substantial records of such experiences in the memory of the department's Bureau of Internal Affairs.

Our police assaulter study concentrated on men with previous histories of assault. Although such a history was not a criterion for the selection of these men, it developed that most of them had assaulted more than one officer.

Our parolees were persons classified as chronic serious assaulters in a scale developed by the Research Division of the California Department of Corrections.[20] The sample is somewhat self-selected, in that the interviewees had to be located (which in some instances proved difficult) and had to volunteer for the interview. In each case, the man was approached with the cooperation of his parole agent and was compensated for the time he invested.

We chose the bulk of our inmate sample on the basis of the fact that the men (a) had been aggressors in some incident of prison violence within one calendar year of our study, and (b) had several violent encounters on their record. Several other inmates were added to this original sample because they were known to our inmate researchers as having a reputation for violence. Our inmate interviewees were also compensated, on the basis of pay scales authorized in the institution.[21]

The institutions we selected for our inmate survey were those most accessible to us. In the case of the California Medical Facility, we already had access to a group of prisoners being trained in research methodology; we created another such group (whose training was confined to the objectives of

---

[20] C. Spencer, *A Typology of Violent Offenders* (Sacramento: California Department of Corrections, Research Division: Research Report No. 23, Sept. 1966).

[21] It must be emphasized that although our interviewees were drawn from systematically selected pools, the samples themselves are not random. Police were interviewed as their shifts made them available; parolees and police assaulters had to make themselves available. Only prison samples are exhaustive, and they are confined to two institutions. Since each contains a special kind of population, this sample is even more biased than the others. Any possible unrepresentativeness of the sample is not critical, however, since the study aims at a qualitative typological analysis, rather than at extrapolations to special populations.

the study) at San Quentin Prison.[22] In both places, inmate interviewers operated in collaboration with professional personnel.

Continuity in staff from the prison to the parolee sample was assured because several of our interviewers were placed on parole during our study. In conjunction with the professional research staff, they conducted the parolee and police assaulter interviews.[23]

Our study of assaults on police officers was initiated at the invitation of the Oakland Police Department. We were happy to accept the invitation, because it made available to us a pool of violent incidents generated in a relatively homogeneous institutional context.

We secured authorization to analyze an equivalent incident sample in the San Francisco Police Department, to test the generalizability of our findings and to secure a large enough pool of incidents for more detailed analysis.

Our interviews with police officers took place in the Oakland Police Department. They were conducted by a professor of police administration and a graduate assistant, who both had been active members of metropolitan police departments and had intensive experience with research on police–community relations.[24]

Our interviews varied in length from somewhat less than an hour to several days. They were tape-recorded in their entirety. The same interview schedule was used for all interviews, although questions were added to secure supplementary information, as dictated by the characteristics of the sam-

---

[22] Our researchers in San Quentin worked under the guidance of Magoroh Maruyama. The group was composed of inmates R. Wilkerson, C. Smith, Fontes, Nacho, and Chaco. Our work at the California Medical Facility was conducted under the auspices of the New Careers Development Project, directed by J. Douglas Grant. The principal participants in our research were inmates Rodriguez, Lester, and C. Jackson.

[23] Rodriguez participated in our work as an inmate and parolee. Other parolees working with our project were J. Preston, K. Jackson, and W. Hunnicutt.

[24] The interviews were for the most part conducted by Prof. Raymond Galvin of the School of Police Administration of Michigan State University, assisted by Robert Wasserman.

ple and the context of the interview. In all instances, the same information about each incident was secured. In the case of inmate and parolee interviews, the analysis procedure was uniform in all essential respects.

The Interview Schedule

Our interviews were designed to provide a full picture of the violent encounters of our respondents. Each person was requested to list "incidents or fights" he had been involved in over the years. In relation to each such event, we inquired into the sequence of acts leading up to it, the contribution of various participants, and the feelings and attitudes of protagonists. We also tried to place each such encounter in the broader context of the person's relationship to others. All our questions were posed in as systematic a fashion as possible, without sacrificing the natural flow of informal communication.

The content of our interview was structured, with a standard series of queries directed at each incident mentioned by the respondent. Question-wording was left flexible, however, and interviewers were permitted to vary question order, as long as they maintained the step-by-step exploration of violence-prone sequences.

The introduction to the interview stressed its general information-gathering function. The interviewees were told that the purpose of our research was "to get some help with the problem of preventing fights or assaults." They were requested to provide "your side of the story of some of the fights you have experienced." Subjects in the police study were apprised of our concern with violence between police officers and civilians. All respondents were assured of complete anonymity, and were told that they could monitor the interview tape.

Each interview thus consisted of discrete examinations of individual incidents. Every respondent was asked to describe violent situations in his own words, including as much detail as he could. He was then taken through each incident again step by step. He was asked about his contact with the other party and about the beginning of the chain of events culminating in violence. He was asked to relate (or confirm) each successive step in the interaction. The interviewee was also called upon to describe his feelings before, during, and after each violent incident. Offhand, it might seem offensive to question experienced police officers or long-term convicts about "feelings." Surprisingly, however, we experienced no difficulty with this inquiry, which more often than not produced rich introspections and elaborate rationalizations of purpose. The following relatively short response (relating to a gang fight) is typical of the material we obtained:

Interviewer: How about during the incident: can you remember how you felt while you were fighting?

Subject: Yeah. Well, from the beginning of the fight, I felt low, got butterflies in my stomach, you know. But then you always feel that way, more or less, when you getting ready to fight. But after the first blow, you don't feel anything. Because you know either you going to win or you going to lose, and you're trying your best to win.

Interviewer: How about afterwards?

Subject: Afterwards? Well, I just felt, well, "I sure am small to whip that great big dude." This made me feel confidence in myself.

Interviewer: Kinda good?

Subject: Yeah. It makes you feel kinda good to know that you won. But actually it was senseless really. You know this.

Interviewer: Looking back on it now, how do you feel about it?

Subject: Well, looking back on it now, I feel that it was just one of those incidents while I was growing up. I feel that now maybe more or less if the situation would occur again I probably would, I'm not going to say that I would, walk away from it; it depends on how much he pushes, how much was said, and went on. But looking back on it, I don't think I would go through those chances again.

Another set of questions touched on the contribution of

persons other than the main contenders. We asked about outside efforts, if any, to encourage violence, or to try to prevent it. We inquired into the impact of spectators and friends, and into the role of community pressures. The following excerpt (relating to the same gang fight) exemplifies these questions and the sort of answers they obtained:

Interviewer: Did anybody else beside yourself encourage the fight?

Subject: Yes. This friend of mine, he told me, he say, "You know we with you, baby. Go ahead and dust him."

Interviewer: The guy that you jumped on, did he sort of challenge you? Did he encourage the fight too?

Subject: Yeah. Well, actually he encouraged it due to the fact that I hadn't said anything to him outside the party. So when he came out, he laughed, you know, he laughed. This righteously did make me angry cause he's more or less trying to floor show for the young ladies he's with. That is the whole thing.

Interviewer: During the fight, did anybody try to prevent it from going on?

Subject: No. Back towards this period of time, everybody was struggling for a reputation, recognition. You get a reputation, you go where you want, nobody messes with you, you get your understanding. This was more or less during that period of time; this was what it was for.

Interviewer: You think things would have been different if just you and him would have been by yourselves somewhere? Or do you think the fight would have come down anyway?

Subject: More or less. I think that if the situation had been different, it probably never would have transpired, due to the fact that I wouldn't have said anything to him, he wouldn't have said anything to me. But like I said, due to the fact that there were a lot of people around; this young man, his brother was supposed to have been semi-bad anyway and he felt that he had power. He was more or less going to whip me cause I was smaller than he was.

In relation to the violence itself, we inquired into the extent of the damage our subject had intended. We asked whether the harm corresponded to the intent, and we explored changes in the respondent's destructive objectives. In the case of fatal incidents, we asked whether the victim's death had been desired. In the following example, the answer is affirmative:

Interviewer: Now, when you were going down to get it on, did you have the intention of dusting him? Or get him off your back, or what?

Subject: Yeah, I was going to dust him, there's no doubt about that. Yeah, there was no doubt in my mind about dusting the dude. If he hadn't have come back there, then I would have assumed that the night before was just a play on his part to see how far he could push me; maybe he would not even have stabbed me. But when they pulled his bar, why, I was down at the end in a position that I could see along the tier, and instead of him coming on down the front stairs, and going like he should have with everybody else, he came out of his cell, kind of looked around a little bit, and walked toward the back stairs. Well, the moment he started heading toward the back stairs, I think in that moment, that was the time that I said, you know, "one of us has got to get dusted, man, and it's better him than me. So, let's not talk around or something when he comes down, let's get him. Let him say whatever he wants to say, and the first time he blinks his eyes for just a second, he's mine." On my part, the talking was done as soon as he started down the back stairs. I assumed then that he's serious. He's got his stuff, I've told him where I am, and he's coming directly to me. So as far as I was concerned it was the final thing, the moment he walked out of the door and started toward the back stairs.

Finally, each of our interviewees was asked to assume the role of his opponent and to review the incident from the other's point of view. Empathy was not notable in the responses to this question. Most frequently, our respondents regretted that the victims had not made a more timely inventory of their ways. This type of reply was not invariant, however. Some interviewees went to great pains to reconstruct their opponents' motives, as in the following example:

Interviewer: What was your reaction in the clothing room, when the guy said "move those shirts to another stack"?

Subject: I didn't leave him actually any out. From my point of view, the only out he had was to walk away and leave the shirts the way they were. I didn't give him any out. I believe that if I had given him an out—any kind of an out—that he may have taken it. I was just blunt and told him that this was what was going to happen. And it was a challenge more or less, you know.

Interviewer: But you would have moved the shirts had you been in his position?

Subject: I believe I would.

Interviewer: How about in the library?

Subject: Okay, as a matter of fact, I heard that some guy had just ripped off a book of his, a reference book, and had told him to go fuck himself. He was hot about that. He told me this later when I talked to him just before we went into the Lieutenant's office. He told me this. Some kind of a special book. He was the reference library clerk. You know where the reference section is? Well, that was his section. He was responsible for it. And someone had just taken a book and told him to fuck himself. He wasn't in a very good frame of mind when I walked in. And I was the next one in. I threatened his authority by denying this paper that he had sent me. I told him this isn't valid. In other words, "you are lying." He wouldn't even take the time to check it out. He didn't want to hear this. "It's not invalid, it's perfectly legal, and I did it and there is no question about it." This is the feeling that I got from him, you know. "There's no time for you. I sent you the thing. Now where is the material, and don't give me a lot of bullshit about it being in the filing cabinet because I don't have time." So one thing led to another. I made the mistake of walking behind the partition.

Interviewer: When you walked back there, looking at his point of view, do you think that you posed a threat?

Subject: Yes, I did. Probably I didn't have such a nice look on my face. I was very exasperated—if you will—put out.

At the conclusion of the regular interview, we subjected our respondents to several fairly general questions. We talked with them discursively about violence, and we delved briefly into their personal history. We also tried to involve them in an examination of their own data. We asked each whether he could discern any patterns or similarities in the incidents he had related to us. Some respondents rewarded us with insightful comments, but most of them produced material varying considerably in quality. We thus came to view our procedure of subject self-analysis as promising, but as too undeveloped at this stage to permit systematic use of the responses.

Analysis of the Interview Data

As previously indicated, the inmate and parolee interviews were subjected to a uniform analytic procedure. As a first step in this procedure, each incident was reduced directly from the tape recording to a diagrammatic form, in which the moves made by incident participants were graphically represented.[25] Relevant feelings and other observations pertaining to each incident were recorded with a checklist. These tasks were undertaken either by the interviewer or by a nonprofessional researcher belonging to his team.

The next step consisted of preparing a summary of the interpersonal pattern of the interviewee's violent involvements. In each case, this analysis was based on all the incidents obtained in the interview. This summary was prepared by a group comprising both professional and nonprofessional researchers. The procedure followed by these groups can be outlined as follows:

---

[25]We are indebted to Dr. Maruyama for the suggestion of this procedure, and for training personnel in its use.

1. Read aloud the diagrammed sequence for each incident.

2. Select out (through discussion) any formal similarities in the genesis of the incidents.

3. Select out (through discussion) any similarities in the approach of the interviewee to other participants in the incident.

4. Select out (through discussion) any possible inferences about the interviewee's social orientation, his approach to others, his special or general aims, as they contributed to specific incidents.

5. Check the resulting hypotheses against every incident in the interview to assess their applicability.

6. Review and revise as necessary.

The results of these group discussions were then dictated. (The subsequent analysis of the "study group" summaries will be discussed in a later chapter.)

To clarify our procedure, it may help to reproduce two segments from one of our interviews, and to trace their contribution to the analysis produced by the "study group." In this particular illustration, the cards are stacked by virtue of the fact that the incidents involved are almost replications of each other. In Chapter 5, which will explore the logic of "patterning" more intensively, several more complex illustrations will be developed.

The case of "Jack the Lady Killer"

Since Jack had recently served a long prison sentence for the murder of a close female friend, the discussion, in the initial stages of his interview, easily turned to this incident. In the free narrative portion, Jack related the circumstances of his crime as follows:

Interviewer: Tell us about the incident in which you finally killed her.

Subject: Well . . . She'd go to work every day and she'd come in at six or seven or eight o'clock at night, and never would bring no pay. So I told her, I ain't going to leave her anything. So we had a big argument. And I told her, I say, "Well, I'm leaving tomorrow. And I tried to do what was right, but I can see you don't want to accept." So we went and got—I went to the store and got two cans of beer. And set it down on the coffee table and she and I started drinking. So, I wasn't feeling bad when I came back. And I got cleaned up and went to bed. In the meantime, she was nagging—you know how a woman keep nagging and nagging—and I asked her, I said, "What's wrong with you, girl?" I said, "I'm telling you, I'm leaving tomorrow." And she said, "Yeah, tonight is your last night." I said, "Last night of what? What you talking about?" And so she said, "Well, you'll find out."

So I didn't pay her no mind, you know. And I'm sitting here sipping on a beer. And I started necking with her, and she had a butcher knife on the table. And I'm wrestling, trying to get the butcher knife away from her. And I takes the knife away from her. In the meantime, when I take the knife away from her, I throw it in the kitchen. She jumps up and she runs to the coffee table—we had a coffee table sitting on the end beside the bed. And I reached over there, and she had a little old penknife. I had one, and I gave her one about the same size. Oh, a real little small penknife. And I took the knife, I hit her right here. Hit her one time in the jugular vein or neck. After I'd hit her jugular vein, she kept coming after me with that other knife and I stuck her a few times in the stomach, you know.

There followed an exploration of the interviewee's quasi-marital relations with the victim, after which the interview reverted to the details of the final encounter:

Interviewer: I wonder if we could just go back to the rundown of that night? How were you feeling that day?

Subject: I wasn't drunk or nothing . . .

Interviewer: Was everything going along pretty good between you and her at the time?

Subject: Yeah.

Interviewer: And she came home that night. And what started the argument?

Subject: Money. The landlord come in behind her when she came in, about seven-thirty or eight o'clock. The land-lord come in behind her, and I had cooked her a good dinner and everything, and she walked in and kissed me on the cheek and tole me, she said, "Honey, I sure do thank you for cooking for me." She said, "Well, the landlord's here," and I said, "Well, my hands is dirty." Well, I had a apron on, you know. And I said, "Reach in my pocket and give him some money." And she said, "That's all right, I can give him some of mine." And the thing actually started over money. Because she had told me, well, he give her a receipt. And she had been working six days a week, you know, and if a person work six days a week, you know, and if a person don't come home with no money, some-thing wrong.

Interviewer: I don't understand that part. You say that she gave him the money and he gave her a receipt? Did she pay him some more money?

Subject: Yeah. She gave him ten dollars more. But she didn't have no money after the ten. She didn't have but five dollars and that was over a three or four week period. Well, she and I started arguing, and we ate and then I left and went to the store and bought me a half a pint and two cans of beer. And I came back to the house and she and I sat up and talked and talked, and I takes me a shower and I said, "I'm going to bed." But I had no idea that she was going to have a butcher knife under her pillow.

Interviewer: You said earlier that you said, "I'm leaving in the morn-ing," and she said, "This is your last night"?

Subject: Yeah, she mentioned that. I was laying there and said, "What?" And she said, "Well, you don't know." I had no idea that she had planned to hurt me or something. She had something and I didn't have nothing; I didn't even carry no knife, cause a penknife, it ain't even of no worth to you.

Interviewer: Well, how did you feel when you were going to bed? You were going to bed with her?

Subject: Yeah, see, we were together at the time.

Interviewer: And that was the last night?

Subject: Yeah, that's right.

Interviewer: How were you feeling at the time?

Subject: Well, I was disgusted. That's how I was feeling. I was depressed and disgusted. But I'd said over and over that I have tried everything in the world I can think of, and I couldn't make a go of it. So I decided I wanted to give it up.

Interviewer: She attack you with a butcher knife?

Subject: Yeah.

Interviewer: How did you feel then?

Subject: Well, I was scared actually, I was more scared than anything else.

Interviewer: Did you get angry?

Subject: Yeah, I got pretty mad.

Interviewer: Did you fight back?

Subject: No. The only fighting back I did was with my hand to protect myself from that knife. And she reached on the table and got that penknife.

Interviewer: Did she cut you?

Subject: No. I didn't get cut.

Interviewer: Was the penknife open?

Subject: No. Wait a minute, they said it was. I really don't know.

Interviewer: Things were happening pretty fast right then, huh?

Subject: Yeah. Things were pretty hot.

Interviewer: Then what happened?

Subject: Well, I got her in the jugular vein . . .

The interviewee was able to relate six other incidents of involvement in violence. In Incident 6, he returned to his problems with women. The free narrative of this unhappy situation runs as follows:

Subject: Let me see, that must have been in 1950—oh well, I
forgot what year. Anyway, I come home one evening
from work, and her boy friend was in my bed . . .

I started drinking some whiskey, I never will forget
it. She hadn't cooked. And I told her, I said "Girl," I
said, "I finally caught you at last! I'm asking you, do
you believe that you can fool around and me not know
about it?" I said, "Now, what you got to say for yourself?" So she said, "I don't have nothing to say." "I
gave you money so you could cook." She said, "I ain't
got no money." So I said, "Okay."

So I went down the street and bought myself a pint
of whiskey and came back, and I told the landlady, I
said, "I'm moving in the morning." And she said,
"Well, you going to pay me?" And I said, "I'm going
to pay you nothing," I said, "My rent's paid up till
tomorrow noon. I'll be out of here by noon."

And about ten o'clock at night, I took my clothes off
and went to bed. And she got up and started walking
the floor. I said, "Now, you got to go to bed, girl,
cause I'm moving in the morning." And she just kept
walking the floor and started cussing, and called me a
lot of bad names and things, and I told her, I said,
"You going to go to sleep, or I'm going to get up and
just beat your butt," you know, just like that. She kept
cussing me, and I said, "Well, okay, you just keep
walking the floor."

So, I don't know what got into her, but I was mad,
and the more she cussed the madder I would get, you
know. And I jumped up and went to the dresser, I
don't know why. I got there so quick, and I picked up
a mirror. When I picked up a mirror she saw the flash
from the light of the mirror and, you know, I didn't
even get the chance to touch her with it and she jumped
out of the upstairs window and hurt herself. And the
landlady called the police. And the police got there and
after I told them what happened they said, "Well, that
happened before to others," they said. "If we let you
go what would you do?" I said, "Let me get away,
man." I said, "Can I come back tomorrow and get my
clothes?" and he said, "Okay."

Interviewer: And that was the end of it?

| Subject: | Yeah, but that wasn't the end of it. He let me go. And we got out of the house, and he said, "Well, do you want to go?" And I said, "Yeah, but let me get my coat." And when I was reaching up in my clothes closet to get my coat she told him that I had a pistol. And when I reaches up there to get the pistol, I mean get my coat, he grabbed me. |

The detailed exploration of the incident follows:

Interviewer:	How were you feeling that day in general?
Subject:	Well, I just got in from work. You know how it is coming home from work. And I was happy, and it was payday, and I'd already planned to take her out that night. In other words, I was in high spirits till I got home.
Interviewer:	Then how were you feeling?
Subject:	Terrible. I started to get angry and everything. When I walked in there and seen them, it's no good feeling for no man to walk in and see his old lady in the rack with someone else.
Interviewer:	Oh, you saw them actually?
Subject:	Yeah. They was in the room; in my room, in my bed.
Interviewer:	Did she say anything then?
Subject:	Well, I tried to get in there, but they wouldn't open the door.
Interviewer:	How long had you known this girl?
Subject:	Oh, let's see, must have been about two years.
Interviewer:	Had you been living with her that long?
Subject:	No, I started living with her six months.
Interviewer:	Had you had any other hassles prior to that?
Subject:	No.
Interviewer:	So you were feeling pretty good that day, and then after you got home you started feeling terrible, angry at what was going on?

Subject: I was getting angrier and angrier. The more she would talk, the angrier I would get.

Interviewer: Just anger, is that all you felt?

Subject: Yeah.

Interviewer: How did you feel afterwards?

Subject: Well, after that happened, I said, "Well, it's hard to put your faith and hope in a person when they do you like that." And then I stopped thinking, what with people having things happening to them all the time . . .

Interviewer: You just felt philosophical about it?

Subject: Yeah.

The diagrammatic summary for the first incident is fairly long, because the sequence involves a relatively large number of steps. Incident 6, however, is a sequentially modest one, and we have reproduced the entire diagram in Figure 1. This

(1) X comes home, can't get into house because it is locked.	(2) Y has company Z (boyfriend). A (landlady) lets Z out back door. A then comes and lets X in the front door.
(3) X comes in, sees house in mess, also no food, says he is leaving tomorrow. Goes out and buys a pint of whiskey, comes back, drinks and goes to bed.	(4) Y is walking up and down the floor swearing at him (X).
(5) X tells Y to shut up.	(6) Y continues to swear at X.
(7) X decides to get even, gets up and grabs mirror, the mirror flashes on the ceiling.	(8) Y sees light against ceiling and jumps out the window thinking the mirror is a knife or something. Y calls the police. The police arrive and Y tells the police X is reaching for a gun. Police grab X and wrestle.
(9) X wrestles and knocks policeman on bed.	

Figure 1.1.   Diagram of Incident 6.

diagram serves to illustrate the type of data available to our "study group." The group also had access to the checklist, which in this particular incident notes, among other things, that the interviewee felt angry throughout the entire sequence.

In assessing the text of the "study group" summary, which follows below, we must recall that the group had seven summarized incidents available to it. The group's task was not easy, because the other five incidents were not simply replications of the two encounters we have reviewed. The contribution of our two involvements to the postulated pattern, however, does emerge in the group's report:

> OK-4 is a remarkable gentleman in several ways. For one, we have in him a situation in which there is almost a complete repetition of incidents, one in which even in minor details we have the same action occurring twice in the same way. For instance, we have a set of two situations which start with an announcement one evening to the effect "look woman, I'm going to leave you." Then there follows a feeling of annoyance because the woman to whom this announcement is made becomes angry and nags, disturbing our man's drinking and sleeping. Finally, there is a very violent act which is viewed as self-defense.
>
> We have two traffic situations in which our man thinks of himself as unprovokedly assaulted and where he reacts by pulling a large weapon and assaulting his apparent attacker. And in a few other incidents we find that he mobilizes a considerable amount of opposition. If this opposition is impressive enough he is not above whining, explaining, and trying to organize some kind of undignified retreat. But what seems to unify the entire set of incidents is that this man has a habit of placing other people into the most awkward situations without appearing to realize what he's doing—without anticipating the obvious reactions to his tactless opening moves. He isn't aware, for instance, that when you cohabit with a woman you just can't come in one evening and simply announce your imminent departure, and then expect to spend a congenial evening with her. Now, when the other person reacts—the person who is going to be abandoned or who has just been insulted— then we have a second stage in which our friend sees himself as attacked out of the clear blue sky. He can then be

quite brutal while viewing all of it blandly as an act of self-defense.

Afterwards, we have an indication, even in this scenario, of his real helplessness, as when he proceeds to give himself up to the police. So he has this pattern of provoking people in a rather selfish way, not seeing the consequences. There is a complete blindness to the other person's point of view. Then, if possible, fear and whining if aggression is not possible. And a kind of general demonstration of his weakness and his lack of ability to get along in the situations that he himself engineers.

The summary above may help to illustrate the role of the "study group" in our research. It should show that the group is a "pattern analysis" tool, in the sense that it functions to isolate common denominators in samples of encounters. It does so by focusing logic, social science analysis, and practical experience on a group of incidents in an effort to characterize the violent person's contribution to them as far as this may be possible without going beyond the information he has provided. The analytic process involved here is frequently intricate, since our incidents are often superficially heterogeneous and the inferences far from obvious at first reading. Despite this sophistication, however, the "study group" merely finds commonalities. It provides a bridge to the task of fitting patterns of conduct into more general categories, or assigning to them theoretical significance.

The final step in our self-assigned task consisted of evolving a typology of violence-proneness of precisely this kind. The object here was not simply that of grouping violent persons in terms of central themes governing their conduct, but of assessing the psychological import of these themes and of estimating their significance for programs of rehabilitation and prevention.

2

The Violent Incident as a Unit of Study: Motives for Police Assaults

The act of violence itself cannot serve as our unit of study, because its motives are never self-explanatory. We learn very little when we hear that a woman has been found strangled in her bed or that an inmate lies in the prison yard with a knife in his back. The least information we must have to make sense of violence includes the immediate antecedents of the violent act. We can start to speculate meaningfully when we discover that an acrimonious dispute has taken place in the woman's apartment and that our inmate has been threatened for failing to make good on a loan. The psychological unit of study implicit here is the "violent incident"—an interaction which begins when one person approaches another with some purpose in mind and ends in an act of aggression. Our investigation is concerned with what transpires between the two parties at the time, and with transactions that determine how the final step evolves out of the initial approach.[1]

Another way of talking about "incidents" is to talk of "games" or sequences of "moves." In this context, a violent incident would be a sequence beginning when two or more players make their opening move and ending when one player pro-

---

[1] A similar approach is taken to the analysis of violent incidents in sociological studies conducted subsequently to our research. See, for example, F. Luckenbill, "Criminal Homicide as a Situated Transaction," *Social Problems* (1977), 25: 176–186.

ceeds to hurt another. We are interested in such games because we wish to know why and how they are played—and ultimately, why some people have a propensity to play them.

There are several perspectives from which games can be studied. The one that is most cognitively oriented originates in "game theory."[2] In this type of approach, each move is seen as the rational response by one player to the play of another. The focus is on logical possibilities left open by preceding moves and on logical implications of each move for successive moves. These possibilities and implications can be conceptualized and quantified. But in this type of approach the players can be abstractions. A given game, for instance, could be played on a chess board, in the stock market, or on the battlefield; it could be played by computers or spy networks; it could end with a bankruptcy hearing or the destruction of one nation by another. And the "players" in such games are always guided by rational, calculated self-interest.

By contrast, our focus must be on the perceptions and motives and needs of real players in concrete settings.[3] We must study the psychological results of their moves, in the sense of finding out how one person's action affects the other person's feelings and perceptions, and how this second person acts as a result. When we can thus describe sequences of actions and

---

[2]M. Shubik, *Game Theory and Related Approaches to Social Behavior* (New York: Wiley, 1964); T. C. Schelling, *The Strategy of Conflict* (Cambridge, MA: Harvard University Press, 1963); A. Rapoport, *Fights, Games and Debates* (Ann Arbor: University of Michigan Press, 1960).

[3]The definition of "games" we are using here is closely analogous to that offered by Eric Berne in *Games People Play* (New York: Grove Press, 1964). Berne's analysis—like ours—focuses on the roles played by people in recurrent interpersonal transactions; Berne sees "games" as standardized sequences of moves, just as we do. Where Berne differs with us is in his assumption that game sequences are predetermined and pre-designed. For Berne, games lead to "well-defined, predictable outcomes": they have "concealed motivation"; they involve "a snare or 'gimmick.'"(p. 48) In our view, games spring from personal orientations that produce characteristic opening moves. Therefore, sequences are *cumulatively* determined, in the form of actions and reactions by the players. In violence-prone encounters, we find violence emerging rather than intended. As we see it, the successive moves of game participants carry increased probabilities of destructive consequences: They carry decreased probabilities of constructive solutions.

reactions that end in violence, we can sensibly proceed to the question of why people permit themselves to participate in such games, or why they feel compelled to do so.

The dissection of violent incidents into types of moves is a difficult one. The task is facilitated if the incidents take place in a relatively uniform setting, and it is made even easier if they are described in relatively standardized fashion. It is for this reason that we began our study of violent incidents by analyzing samples of arrest reports that charged citizens with assault on police officers.

Assault (or battery) committed on police officers had become at the time of our study an increasingly popular violent "game." The Los Angeles Police Department, for instance, reported that it had experienced an almost 400 percent increase in attacks on its members between 1952 and 1965[4]; other law enforcement agencies had issued similar statistics. The Oakland Police Department saw a 55 percent increase in this type of encounter in the year preceding our study.[5]

Police assaults are far from chance encounters. The typical assault on a police officer takes place on a slum precinct street, and it is perpetrated by a young Black man who has had previous brushes with the law. Who the police officer may be is also important; in an internal memorandum, the Crime Analysis Section of the Oakland Police Department pointed out that younger, less experienced officers tended to get disproportionately assaulted. The Oakland analysts also noted that there are some officers (irrespective of age or experience) who appeared to be especially assault-prone.[6] This fact is an important one because the officer who uses force against a citizen can charge the citizen with assault by way of justification. This type of charge is known as a "cover charge" in the trade.

Our own concern is somewhat independent of who gets

---

[4] Los Angeles Police Department, Administrative Research Unit, Planning and Research Division, *Attacks on Los Angeles Police Officers* (Mimeographed report, dated April 18, 1966), p. 9.

[5] Oakland Police Department Crime Analysis Section, memorandum related to "Survey of 148–243 P.C. Offenses Against Oakland Police Officers," undated manuscript.

[6] Ibid., appended table (not numbered).

assaulted and who does the assaulting, although it ultimately returns to this question. Our problem, first, is how the *typical* police assault usually evolves from the initial contact between a police officer and a civilian. What kinds of actions set off the sequence toward violence? How is the initial occasion for conflict reinforced or compounded? What stimulates the physical part of the conflict? What sorts of feelings are involved? How does one party perceive the other, and what constitutes the basis of their impression? In sum, how do routine interactions degenerate and how do tensions escalate in the type of game represented by police–civilian contacts?

As a first step in our analysis, we constructed a code for the categorization of the reactions of police assaulters—of persons involved in incidents in which they assaulted police officers. This code (together with instructions for its use) is included in this book as an appendix.

The instrument was designed on the basis of incident descriptions relating to assaults on officers, obtained from the Arrest Report files of the Oakland Police Department. The code was then applied to a more systematically drawn sample of Oakland reports—an exhaustive review of the 100 most recent incidents available. The Code was later used, both as a simple classification scheme and in the form of a more sophisticated "sequential" analysis, with a set of 344 incidents obtained from the San Francisco Police Department. The bulk of this chapter reports the results of these investigations, together with illustrations covering the salient findings.

Our Police Assaulter Code divides the motives displayed in our incidents into five general categories, each comprising several more specific ones. These categories were applied in two ways: (1) every move present in the incident was recorded and coded; (2) the move leading most directly and immediately to the assault on the officer was separated out as a "primary" cause, and all other moves were relegated to the status of "secondary" causes. The coding was done by a trained graduate student; the operation included a reliability study, which insured identical results in independent codings of subsamples.[7]

---

[7] I am indebted to S. Sherman for his assistance in this part of the study.

Table 2.1 provides information in terms of the general categories into which we classified causes of assaults in our code. We see that violence against police officers comes about in parallel fashion in the two communities we surveyed. If we examine the last columns first, for instance, we note that the two categories that are more important than others in accounting for assaults in both Oakland and San Francisco are (1) reactions against some perceived tampering with the person in the shape of physical or verbal contact by the officer, and (2) reactions following some indication of hostility directed at the officer, such as threats or expressions of contempt. Such threats or warnings diminish somewhat in importance when we consider immediate or primary causes only, as summarized in the first two columns of the table. Here we note that in both Oakland and San Francisco, the second-most-important immediate motivation to assault an officer is the desire to rescue or defend a person receiving the officer's attention. This cause appears almost exclusively at the end of causal sequences leading to assault. Another immediate cause of violence ap-

Table 2.1

Gross Categories of Interpersonal Causes of Violence Against Police Officers in Oakland (N = 100) and San Francisco (N = 344)

In rank order of frequency (as per Oakland sample)	As primary causes		As contributory causes		Total	
	Oak-land	San Francisco	Oak-land	San Francisco	Oak-land	San Francisco
Assault in defense of personal autonomy (touching, orders, etc.)	24	108	32	214	56	322
Assault as expression of contempt (retaliation, etc.)	14	56	39	191	53	247
Assault in effort to escape	19	72	22	68	41	140
Assault to prevent being moved	13	55	21	50	34	105
Assault to protest captivity	14	43	20	46	34	89
Assault as extension of other violence	13	17	19	75	32	92
Assault in defense of others	23	91	5	12	28	103

pears to be the desire to escape from the officer. This desire, however, may also appear at earlier stages of the proceedings.

The two main differences between Oakland and San Francisco are the greater predominance of rescue efforts in Oakland and the relative frequency of efforts to escape arrest in San Francisco. These differences may be related to the ethnic composition of Oakland and the arrest procedure in San Francisco, respectively. The latter is a risky assumption, but we can conjecture that the lesser use of paddy wagons in San Francisco makes of the arrest more a one-stage process, whereas in Oakland some of the tension following arrest is reserved for the arrival of the wagon officers.

The information we have presented so far is of somewhat limited interest. It does not enable us to visualize how the typical officer finds himself typically assaulted, because we have extracted slices out of live sequences. It is now incumbent on us to show how these items generally group themselves in real life. To achieve this aim, we return to the incident descriptions and record *in series* the steps leading to each assault. We then group these series. In doing this, we start with the opening move and take all the sequences in which the same first move leads to a similar second move; we then combine all two-move series that are followed by the same third move, and so forth.

For instance, we may start with all the episodes in which, to begin with, a suspect objects to being arrested; some of the episodes will end right here, with the officer being subjected to violence because of the suspect's bitterness at being detained; in other instances, the subject may next try to escape, and we then have a two-step series, "objection to arrest, followed by struggle to get away." If violence does not result at this juncture, it might occur when the suspect is recaptured and an effort is made to transport him to jail. This would give us "objection to arrest followed by struggle to escape, followed by refusal to be transported, resulting in violence." We continue grouping in this fashion until we have no cases left over.

Such sequences are lists of the "moves" in the "games" that produce assaults. They represent preliminary or preparatory reactions by the assaulter to the approaches and actions of the officer. As such, they are steps or junctures at which violence becomes increasingly probable and less avoidable.

The method of analysis outlined here was applied to 344 arrest reports secured from the files of the San Francisco Police Department. The incidents were recorded in three blocks of several months each between 1962 and 1965. (Each of these samples was complete, and we have no reason to assume a systematic bias relating to the missing months.)[8]

In the remainder of this chapter, we shall review the principal chains of action and reaction that precede the assaults on the officers. There are two main sequences, and together they account for over two thirds (255 out of 344) of the incidents. We shall present one sequence in a schematic frequency table and then illustrate, with excerpts from some of the police reports, all the major types of interactions involved.

Pressing the Police Button

Figure 2.1 traces the main set of sequences, which starts with a suspect's reaction to a verbal approach by an officer. This group covers fully half our sample. It is the type of sequence where, in the first step, the officer starts an interaction with a civilian by means of an order, a demand, a suggestion, a question, a request, or some other communication. Usually, no serious offense has been committed by the civilian (where there is a formal infraction, the most common is a traffic violation) and the contact is classifiable either as preventive police work or as an effort to cope with a nuisance act. A group of boys is "told to move" or "questioned as to what they are doing"; an errant driver is "told to stop" or "notified" of his violation; a person who is engaged in an altercation is queried as to "what the problem was" or is "instructed to be quiet" or "told to go home." A request for name, address, or identification may also provide the opening spark of the sequence.

The violence may occur as early as immediately after the initial approach but more often does not materialize until one

---

[8]The reports used covered every month of 1962; September, November, and December of 1963; and January through September of 1964.

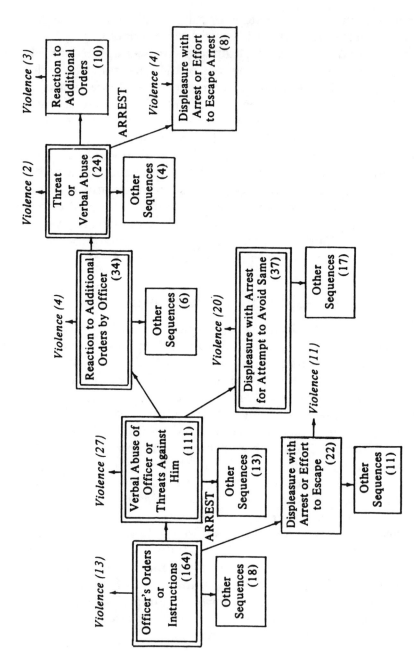

Figure 2.1. Most frequent sequence leading to police assaults (San Francisco incidents, $N = 344$).

or two further exchanges have taken place. Most typically, the civilian first fails to cooperate with the officer. In three fifths of all the episodes we studied, the person somewhat manifests his displeasure with the officer's approach, and he attacks the officer after the officer has made additional moves. An arrest is often the final precipitant of the attack.

Situations in which violence occurs as soon as the officer has made his opening move provide the fewest clues concerning the motives involved. We know that the civilian is reacting to some highly charged, nonroutine interpretation of the officer's act, but we usually do not know precisely what he is reacting to. The officer, who tends to view his own action as harmless, plausible, and routine, tends to make the assumption that some "irrational" disposition of the attacker might be causing him to react precipitantly in the face of no real provocation and discouraging odds.[9] This assumption— and the basis for it—are illustrated in the following incident:

> While on routine patrol, Reporting Officers observed the below suspect standing at the above location for a lengthy period of time. [The officers] questioned suspect and asked for identification. The suspect stated he did not possess any. Suspect's mannerisms and actions were such that [the officers] felt suspect possibly could be under the influence of a drug. Officer G., who was driving, got out of the driver's side of the Radio Car, and [his partner] Officer C., opened the passenger's side of the car to get out; without provocation, suspect struck Officer C. twice in the face, opening a gash over his right eye.

Since we do not know what "mannerisms and action" are being referred to here, it is hard to evaluate the diagnosis. It does appear that when the officers resolved to suddenly descend on the presumed addict, he rather badly panicked. This lends credence to the postulation of a special state of mind—

---

[9]Quinsey and Varney have noted the same perspective among mental hospital staff who were assaulted by patients. V. L. Quinsey and G. W. Varney, "Characteristics of Assaults and Assaulters in a Maximum Security Psychiatric Unit," *Crime and/et Justice* (1977a), 5: 212–220.

as does the nature of the violence, which started with two slaps administered to one officer and ended with the biting of the other officer's leg.

Much more usual in cases of "one-step" games is police attention to a transparently intoxicated individual, as in the following report:

> While on foot patrol this date, an unknown citizen stated to me that there was a woman in the vicinity of E and T Sts. standing in the street shouting and drinking liquor. At approximately 10:40 P.M., I observed the defendant walking in the middle of E St. drinking from a pint bottle of gin, and shouting lewd language to citizens between swallows. At this time she had bloodshot eyes, strong AB [alcoholic breath], slurred speech, and staggering walk. When I attempted to talk to the defendant she threw the bottle at me and started to kick me. At this time two other officers arrived and it took force to subdue the defendant and place her under arrest. In the ensuing struggle she kicked the reporting officer on the shinbone of the right leg. The defendant has a long record of drunk arrests in this city.

Here the state of mind of the person, which enhances the probability of violence, is clearly manifest in her actions prior to the arrival of the officer. In this connection it is worth noting that the role of alcohol in assaults on police officers—the incidence is extremely high—no doubt varies from one situation to another. It is probably safe to assume that being drunk serves to sharpen whatever psychological reactions occur and that these can take many forms. If a drunk challenges an officer to a duel, for instance, he may be displaying an "I'll fight anyone in the house, regardless of uniform" attitude, a sharpened contempt for sources of sanctions, a relatively casual assessment of possible consequences, a "devil may care" mood, or one of many other violence-prone frames of mind. Moreover, alcohol obviously also becomes a factor in less direct ways, such as causing the individual to violate the law and therefore making him subject to arrest; making the person more conspicuous (as he winds his way through traffic or along the pavement), or producing greater vulnerability if drinking is habitual. The actual impact may therefore be a complex of such factors, as in the individual who is driving in an alcoholic stupor with a license suspended (as a result of similar prior activity), who is apprehended speeding the wrong way on a one way street, and who strikes the officer in the face because he knows that his ticket may have serious consequences, or because his judgment is impaired by alcohol, or because he is suffused with the joy of direct action.

Where there is no chemical reason for the hypothetical irrationality of the "short game" police assaulter, we can sometimes draw an analogous inference from the self-selected status of such persons. We assume that some type of special motive is advertised by the fact that the person charges in where others fear to tread—or where others see no cause for action. The police assaulter's response, after all, is a nonroutine or unconventional reaction to a situation where acquiescence is the rule. It is easy to illustrate this by examining incidents in which one person out of a group makes a stand. Such occurs, for instance, after a waitress identifies several unwelcome customers to two officers called to a restaurant:

> She pointed out several of the patrons and when I asked them to leave all left but one. I asked him to leave several times and when he refused I ordered him to leave and he turned, striking me in the right eye.

In a second incident, inhabitants of the City Prison Misdemeanor Tank are escorted back to their cell by an officer:

> On the above-mentioned date at 1:15 P.M. while moving the 2:00 P.M. court return prisoners to Toper Tank #2 for their noon meal I instructed the prisoners to enter the cell; all did except the above-mentioned suspect. I instructed him to enter the cell like the other prisoners but he refused and told me, "Don't tell me what to do." He began to curse. I told him I would place him in isolation if he didn't enter the cell. At this time he swung with his fists at me hitting me on the left arm and inflicting scratches on the Reporting Officer's left arm. He was very belligerent. I then placed the suspect in isolation cell #4 with the assistance of several

officers. He stated that he would "make a big case out of this."

In both instances, the officers have been served notice that they are dealing with an individual who is not amenable to a standard approach. In such instances, it seems as if police routine calls for the invocation of additional power. The officer escalates verbally from a request to an order or from an order to a threat. No doubt such show of authority or use of fear often motivates compliance. In the case of very resentful individuals, however, it can initiate the transition from truculence to violence.

This sequence—a change from passive to violent in the face of a standard sequence of police approaches—sometimes occurs with more extended interactions. The following incident, for instance, represents a three-step version of such an encounter:

> Officer M. investigated and found that there was no reason for D. to be stopping autos, and told him to go to the sidewalk, and D. refused to go to the sidewalk. Officer M. asked the Suspect D. to show some identification and D. refused, and started to leave the area. Officer M. called to D. to come back and to show some identification, and he again refused, and he then struck Officer M. about the face and body.

Here the person's strategy of not responding, and finally of physically withdrawing from the scene, faces the officer with a situation where he must almost embarrassingly chase him. In turn, the suppressed resentment revealed by the person's refusal to respond bursts forth as he feels himself increasingly "crowded" and helpless in the face of orders and injunctions. The following incident, involving a pedestrian and an officer directing downtown traffic, reveals this sequence more dramatically:

> The subject was told to stop at the island and wait for the vehicular traffic to clear the intersection. The subject continued across the street and as she passed the officer, pushed

his outstretched arm down and then proceeded North on P. Officer Z. overtook the subject and tapped her on the shoulder to gain her attention in order to reprimand her. The subject turned around and struck the officer in the face; he then attempted to detain her, but she began struggling and trying to get away, and the above officer found it necessary to place the subject in handcuffs.

This example is of special interest, not only because it provides a fairly clear picture of the officer's dilemma, but also because it contains evidence of the fact that the last steps of the sequence cannot be interpreted unless they are viewed in the context of the preceding steps. The report notes the following:

> Numerous persons were present at the scene who felt that the above officer had mishandled the situation; a Mr. M. L. was the only subject who wished to give us his name as a witness. He, as well as most of the other parties present, admitted that they had only witnessed the officer placing the subject in handcuffs.

The following is a somewhat different version of the same sequence. It features a civilian who retains control of the situation and of himself, and who tries to stay "cool" even at the juncture of physical contact. The civilian warns the officer of the fact that he intends to resist if the action is escalated. The officer must face the showdown, however, because his only perceived alternative would be to admit defeat:

> As auto boosting is a constant problem in the park, I approached suspect, identified myself and asked him what he was doing around auto. He said that he was looking at it. Suspect was carrying motorcycle-type helmet and I asked him if motorcycle parked nearby was his ('63 Yamaha registered to suspect). He replied that it was. I then asked suspect for some identification and he stated that he would show me nothing. He then walked over to the motorcycle and removed a knapsack from it and walked away. I followed suspect and again showed my identification; he said that he understood that I was a policeman but would refuse

to talk to me. As suspect was walking rapidly away, I attempted to block his line of departure. Suspect then pushed me aside and stated, "If you touch me, I'll hurt you." I attempted to physically restrain suspect and we both fell to the ground. Suspect continued his threats of bodily harm and upon arising attempted to pull me to the ground. I then persuaded suspect to peacefully accompany me to the police stables.

Warnings and challenges are often issued by persons who view their encounters with police officers as "man-to-man" confrontations, a premise which officers find it impossible to grant by virtue of their role as representatives of law and authority. The challenging individual may finally resort to violence as a last-ditch effort to establish his premise of inviolability in the face of a conclusive demonstration of its invalidity:

Stopping to investigate, these officers made identification and asked subject to do likewise, and then asked what he was attempting to do. Subject refused to make any identification, or to answer questions as to his intentions, but replied to the initial question, "Who gives a fuck who you are." He then continued to use profanity, directing his statements to these officers, still refusing to answer any questions. Upon being searched for weapons, just after placing subject under arrest, he stated, "You better not give me a chance, because if you do, I'll drop both of you." . . . He repeated this threat two other times, stating he was going to strike these officers whenever he had the opportunity. The patrol wagon had been summoned and before its arrival the subject turned quickly and struck out at these officers with his closed fists, and kicked Officer H. in the left leg.

Another type of incident begins with an officer subjecting an individual to a sanction that the latter wishes to avoid. When the man indicates his unwillingness to comply, the officer ignores his protests, and thereby converts the situation (as the person sees it) into a confrontation between two hostile parties. The officer responds by placing the individual under arrest, thereby demonstrating his own authority and power. The person now feels his powerlessness and thus reacts by requesting that the officer encounter him on a "man-to-man" basis. This type of incident is an almost inevitable consequence of the exercise of police authority in a context where its legitimacy is not granted:

> Reporting Officer on routine patrol this date at 4:25 P.M. was in the process of writing a traffic citation for a Viol. 22514— fire hydrant CVC [Civic Vehicle Code] to an auto, when a NMA [Negro Male] came running out and jumped into the car. I asked him to wait until I finished the citation. He said, "You ain't giving me a tag," started his auto, and moved it to another spot. I finished the citation and tried to hand it to him as he came back [and] he stated, "I ain't takin' no tag." Reporting Officer walked over to his auto, placed the citation on his windshield. He ran over, grabbed the citation from the windshield and stated to me, "You white mother f_____." I asked him to repeat what he said. He replied, "S_____ you, you Mother F_____." I told him he was under arrest. He then placed his hands on my shoulder attempting to shove me out of his way, using profanities all the time. At this time, Reporting Officer pinned him to his car. He was struggling to get away, when another NMA came over and asked what was going on. The suspect at that time stated to me, "Take off your badge and gun and fight." I wrestled the suspect to my bike in an attempt to get assistance. The suspect broke away and ran. Reporting Officer pursued him and was attempting to bring him back . . . when the suspect repeated his statement about taking my gun and badge off and fighting him.

In the following variant the person establishes at the outset that he views the officer's interest in him as illegitimate, but he collaborates to the extent of permitting himself to be arrested and booked. When the officer, however, takes one step further (by asking him to move), the man apparently decides he must take a stand. In an incident such as this, we seem to see three factors intersect. First, there is the assumption that police are acting unfairly. Second, the person concludes that police unfairness has reached a point where it cannot be further tolerated, or where the officer, in a manner of speaking, has divested himself of his badge by going too far. Third, the person must feel a sufficient sense of potency (or disregard of consequence) to initiate violence. In the following report, the last sentence illustrates the operation of this premise:

> The suspect was staggering and stepped into a doorway. When I asked him what he was doing, he replied, "None of your business, Daddy." The suspect had a heavy alcoholic breath and was staggering. The speech was slurred and he dropped his wallet on the sidewalk. I placed him under arrest for violation of 647F PC and transported him to Co. "I" via "I-4." After the suspect was booked, I placed him in the #3 cell at Co. "I." The lock on the cell door would not work so I asked the suspect to move to Cell #1. The suspect replied, "You move me, Mother." When I entered the cell, the suspect struck me in the stomach with his right hand and attempted to knee me in the groin. I was forced to use my night stick in an effort to subdue the suspect. During the struggle, the suspect attempted to pull my service revolver from my holster. The suspect was subdued and placed in Cell #1. . . . At the hospital the suspect stated to reporting officer that he has killed before and won't rest until he has killed five policemen.

"Tackling" a police officer is an act that can serve a variety of purposes. Some of these relate to the perceived role of the police, while others are somewhat more general, having to do with the person's self-image and with his appraisal of his social role. Among police-related incentives is the assumption (prevalent in the late sixties) that law enforcement is a tool or symbol of oppression. The following incident is one that on the surface does not appear to fall into this group. On first impression, it represents an explosive reaction by an intoxicated individual to what he sees as an act of personal harassment:

> The driver was approached by the Reporting Officers and asked why his auto was in such a position. He replied "What the Hell is the difference—this is a drive-in." He was then asked for his driver's license. He replied, "What the hell are you bastards bothering me for—leave me alone." The subject was observed to have a strong odor of alcohol on

his breath and appeared to be in a state of excitement. The subject was placed under arrest and the officers attempted to escort him to the police vehicle. At this time the subject turned and struck the reporting officer in the face. He was thrown to the ground by the reporting officer and an attempt was made to handcuff him.

The incident, however, acquires different connotations as we continue to review the report:

During the struggle with the subject approximately fifteen Negroes from the drive-in and occupants of the subject's vehicle gathered about the reporting officers threatening violence towards the police. A statement was yelled at the officers, "This isn't Mississippi, you bastards. We are sick of the police bothering the black people." There were several agitators who consistently shouted jeers and abusive statements towards the police. The reporting officers had been forced to call for assistance over the police radio due to the immediate situation which closely resembled a near riot. After the subject had been transferred to the station for booking the reporting officer questioned the subject's wife as to the possible reason for his actions. She stated that "he had been drinking and that he was angry because he was unable to find a job, etc., and that he was generally angry at all white people, because of this."

Here the police are perceived as an illegitimate and hostile "outside" force, and (in at least the case of the main contender) conflict with the police is welcomed as a form of social protest.

A related motive stems from the assumption that police act as invading forces when they transact business on one's turf, neighborhood, city block or vicinity, and that any officer is an aggressing enemy if he engages in a conflict with one's neighbor. The following incident shows the operation of these assumptions in a degenerating encounter following a questionable arrest:

While on patrol, Reporting Officers stopped to cite an auto for parking on the sidewalk. Below Suspect #1 stated, "keep movin', you got no business here." Reporting Officers advised Suspect 1 that his auto was parked on the sidewalk and if it wasn't moved, it would be cited. Suspect 1 at this time became very loud and profane stating, "You f_____ cops can't tell me what do." Reporting Officers began writing a citation for the suspect. He continued his loud and profane harangue. . . . Reporting Officers advised him to cease using that type of language on the street and in the presence of others and suspect stated, "Just write the ticket and get your ass out of here." At this point Reporting Officers stated to suspect that he was under arrest, whereupon suspect ran through the doorway and up the stairs with the Reporting Officers in pursuit. Our entrance to the doorway was blocked by Suspects 2, 3, 4 and two or three unknowns. Reporting Officers forced their way past these persons and entered the flat and cornered Suspect 1 in the bathroom, where he continued to resist our efforts to place handcuffs on him. As Reporting Officers were attempting to restrain him, Suspects 2, 3, 4 set upon Reporting Officers, grabbing Officer D. by the throat, coat lapel and necktie and Suspect 2 stating, "You're not going to take him out of here." It became necessary for Off. D. to use force in an effort to get Suspects 2, 3, and 4 to relinquish their holds. Off. W. while attempting to restrain Suspect 1 was kneed in the leg several times by Suspect 1. Off. W. then ran downstairs to the patrol car in an effort to get assistance and suspects tried to stop him from going down the stairs. Suspect 4 stated, "Let's get him, he's going for help." Suspect 1 then ran out the rear door and as officer attempted to pursue Suspect 1, Suspects 2, 3, and 4 continued grabbing Officer D. and pulled his tie from his collar. By the time Off. D. freed himself from 2, 3, and 4, Suspect 1 escaped over a fence from the rear.

In another type of incident similar factors operate, except that the officer flagrantly invites connotations assigned to him. In this example, the officer initiates the encounter by making a relatively petty demand of one person and by arbitrarily requesting identification of another. The officer thus becomes an involuntary participant in a somewhat lighthearted game, which he ultimately puts an end to by physically restraining one of the players on a transparently flimsy pretense—thus revealing a complete loss of self-control. The only citizen who intervenes on behalf of the officer in this incident is later identified as an off-duty fireman:

> While on patrol at approx. 6:20 P.M., this date, Reporting Officer observed Suspect #2 standing in front of _____, throw a magazine on the street. When asked to pick same up he did so after some argument. (Aforementioned location has been a problem area in this district for several months, i.e., juveniles congregating and abusing merchants and pedestrians verbally and physically). I then asked Suspect #1, who was sitting on a motorcycle at the same location, for ID and registration, and when he produced his driver's license, he had no registration for the mtr/cycle. He took a card, business card type or something similar, and threw it on the street. After telling him to pick same up, he did and then proceeded to tear the card into small pieces and threw same on the street. When I told him to pick up the pieces, he replied, I'M SICK AND TIRED OF YOU F_____G COPS TELLING ME WHAT TO DO." I then took Suspect #1 by the arms, telling him he was under arrest for littering, and started to take him to the radio car. Suspect #1 pulled away and told me I was taking him nowhere and a scuffle ensued, during which I suffered a sprained right thumb and several superficial scratches on the right hand. At one point during the scuffle a private citizen, name unknown, attempted to help me, but was knocked to the ground by Suspect #2, and according to reportee, was also kicked by Suspect #2 while he was on the ground. While I was attempting to subdue Suspect #1 further, Suspect #3, who had been standing by while the scuffle was occurring, approached the private citizen and stated that he had better stay out of the fight if he knew what was good for him, threatening him with bodily harm.

Undoubtedly, a disproportionate number of attacks on police officers originate with men whose self-image includes being a champion or a defender, taking on overwhelming forces, or demonstrating toughness in pitched battles with lawmen. The following incident, for example, has a distinctly "Wild West" flavor, with the gunman advising womenfolk to leave the scene as he prepares to charge into devastating opposition with his bare fists:

While on patrol this date, reporting officers observed the below described suspect accompanied by the below arrested juvenile parked on the crest of B Heights in a pick-up truck.

Upon questioning both subjects the suspect pushed the juvenile and told her to run and proceeded to attack both officers. Off. S. suffered a possible fractured finger during the scuffle. Upon subduing the suspect, Off. S. went in pursuit of the juvenile, while reporting officer stayed with suspect.

Suspect then attacked this officer, pushing me off a small cliff after a brief struggle in which this officer suffered a laceration of the neck and sprained middle finger and hand.

The young man in this incident makes his escape and is arrested at home ten days later. The next afternoon, in the corridors of the city prison, another officer becomes the proving ground for his self-perceived toughness and manhood:

At approx. 3:20 P.M. on this date, the below described prisoner was observed walking in the corridor of the Misdemeanor Wing, City Prison, by reporting officer. Due to his unusual demeanor, I questioned subject as to why he was wandering about, and at this juncture, he said "You _____ cops, are all the same, etc., I'm going to get you." Subject then lunged at me in a vicious manner in a vain try to commit violence upon me. Reporting officer was then forced to use reasonable restraint measures in order to contain said subject.

Police officers sometimes unwittingly cooperate with self-defined champions by letting them play their role and crowding them into a duel. In the following incident, for instance, an arrest is made (as it very often is) for uncooperativeness and refusal to comply. This type of act confirms and reinforces the individual's role as a defender of principle and a champion of his kind. He can then in good conscience fight the officers on behalf of his role:

In response to a call, Reporting Officers observed a very large group of juveniles in the playground. They were standing in a circle, within which a fight was in progress. As we tried to disperse the crowd and break up the fight, the below arrested juvenile refused to move. After telling him twice, he finally moved with a large group of WMJ's [white male juveniles] and NMJ's of which he appeared to be the leader. At the corner the gang stopped and refused to move. Reporting Officers again told the arrested to move on and he refused. At this time he was told that he was under arrest, whereupon he called the Reporting Officers "Mother _____" several times. As we tried to place him in the radio car, he started fighting, striking Officer R. with his fist and kicking Officer L. in the chest.

Even a relatively innocent inquiry by a polite officer can prompt a violent response from a person who views his manhood as challenged or his reputation as at stake. An individual contacted in public, for instance, may use the occasion to give a "benefit performance" to his potential admirers:

This date while Reporting Officer was on routine patrol, I observed the below arrested suspect walking. Reporting Officer had not seen the below arrested in some time and rolled the window of the radio car down and said to suspect, "May I talk to you for a minute Mr. S." With this the below arrested suspect with a large number of people around said in a very loud voice, "Kiss my a_____ you mother f_____." Reporting Officer got out of the radio car and told the suspect he was under arrest; at this point suspect repeated the above phrase twice in a loud shouting voice as to attract a large number of people. At this point Reporting Officer grabbed suspect by the arm and told him he had been placed under arrest and attempted to get him to the radio car, so as to radio for patrol wagon. At this point suspect raised his right hand and struck Reporting Officer in the right shoulder, and had to be physically restrained.

Subsequently in this incident, the person's challenge to the police and its relationship to his self-image are made explicit in conversation with the officers:

Suspect stated at this point and also at a later point in the Patrol Wagon to Reporting Officer that "I am too smart and foxy to be caught by you police. I've made thousands of dollars on 6th Street rolling drunks and you haven't caught me yet. You never will." Reporting Officer asked suspect if he always managed to be released and he stated, "Yes. I had a jury trial once and got off because of a hung jury, I'm too smart to be caught. I even bragged about it to an inspector in the Robbery Detail and told him I had committed strong arms in the Southern District, but that I always picked on drunks and people who could not identify me or who refused to get involved at a later point." Suspect was then asked if he always got rid of incriminating evidence and he stated, "Sure, I'm not stupid. I'm too foxy to be caught."

None of the above is intended to imply that police tend to function as passive stimuli to assaults on themselves. Our premise is that an assault grows out of an interpersonal sequence in which both parties participate to some measure. We assume that each assault is the product of a unique transaction between the assaulter and the victim and that it could not occur in the same way if either party acted differently in his or her relation to the other. We would further assume that even where the assaulter contributes most of the motivation (as in the last of the above incidents) the officer somehow makes the nature of the contribution possible. He does so, at minimum, by acting in accord with the assaulter's expectations; more seriously, he may unknowingly play an assigned role in the other person's "game."

Interestingly enough, even in an analysis of police records one finds incidents which seem to result primarily from actions by the officer (with the other person's motives playing a subsidiary role). The assault described below, for instance, seems to arise out of the officer's effort to cope with his hurt self-esteem:

While on duty this date the arresting officer saw Suspect #2 throw a bottle at a passing auto, barely missing the window. When told to pick the bottle up from the street he became belligerent and refused to comply. At this time the #1 Suspect intervened, saying, "Go pick the m____ f____ bottle up. You don't want to go to jail. That m____ f____ caused me to get in trouble when I had just come out of the pen." I asked him if he were aware that it was a violation of the Police Code to use profanity in public, but he ignored me and continued to make obscene remarks. When it became evident that he had no intention of stopping I told him that he was under arrest, but he continued to walk away. I grabbed his arm, but he jerked away so I grasped his coat lapels and tried to talk to him but he began struggling to free himself. The #2 Suspect grabbed my arm and attempted to break my hold upon B's coat, saying, "That's my brother. You're not going to take him to jail." I told him to take his hands off me and stop interfering or he would go to jail also. While I was attempting to cuff B, M (#2 Suspect) removed his coat and grabbed me from behind. I released B., threw M against an auto, and used my club on him, and when B. advanced on me from behind I struck him also. He ran from the scene and I caught him a block away with the assistance of a Special Officer who came to my assistance. Several other Specials from the dance also stood by because of the menacing crowd until the wagon and a park radio car arrived.

Here the officer seems to go out of his way to assert his authority and attempt to control citizens. He translates refusals to comply with his wishes into law violations and ends up attacking a person who technically is making his job easier. The officer is also resorting to considerable force, so that a sequence which starts with a petty provocation ends with a lacerated skull. There is also some indication that the officer has almost succeeded in promoting a riot.

In another incident, an officer undertakes fairly insistent questioning of a drunk whom he finds waiting for a cab.

While on foot patrol, Reporting Officer observed defendant R. L. standing in the S. Corner of C. street. F. was leaning against a pole. I approached him, asked why and what his business was at this hour in this vicinity. He stated that he was waiting for a cab. Asked where he made the phone call, he stated that it was made from the R. Bar and that he was told by the operator to wait on the corner. Subject was very uncooperative in answering questions, such as, "Where

> do you live? What is your address? How long have you
> been waiting here?" F. would not give his home address.
> When he refused to answer any questions, I placed him
> under arrest for 152 MPC. When told that he was under
> arrest F. remarked "F_____ you, cop." When I placed him
> against the side of a building to search him, he began to
> move about and began to move his arms and hands, push-
> ing me aside, using his arms and hands in a swing manner.
> I had to strike the defendant once in the abdomen to restrain
> him from becoming violent and until the radio car arrived
> to transport him to the Richmond Station. The defendant
> used the four letter word several times.

The officer arrests the man because he cannot extricate himself from the dilemma of having arbitrary questions inade-
quately answered. Moreover, it is the officer who commits the
violent act in this situation, and attacks a person who is virtually defenseless. Here, again, one infers excessive irritability
in the officer from his use of serious force against an individual
who seems neither disposed nor able to present real problems.
And the notation "the defendant used the four letter word
several times," which is offered in justification, seems more
of a reflection of the officer's sensitivity than a logical explanation.

When one indicates, as we did at the outset, that most
assaults on police officers start with an officer verbally ap-
proaching a civilian, one leaves open the question of what
kind of officer approaches what sort of civilian, how he approaches him, and under what circumstances. Our illustrations
suggest that violence does not result from just any police approach selected at random. Rather, the degeneration of an
interaction can usually be traced to psychological dispositions
and motives that pre-date the incident. These motives endow
an otherwise innocuous opening move with explosive connotations, which either may be revealed at once or may emerge
cumulatively as the interaction between the parties unfolds.

The Extension of Violence

The second most frequent group of sequences leading to police
assaults, covering some 100 incidents, is of a somewhat dif-

ferent order, in that violence exists to begin with. Half of these sequences tend to be relatively short, ending in an assault within two steps of their inception. Here the officer intervenes in a conflict among civilians, and his purpose is to identify the aggressor (if any) and to deal with him. The assault generally takes place in response to the officer's effort to cope with the suspected aggressor.

The reason why civilian violence transfers to the police, and the manner in which it does so, vary from one incident to another. The common denominator in most incidents is (1) that violence is already accepted as a means to cope with problems, and (2) that the officer may be perceived as a new problem.

The only type of situation to which this analysis does not apply is one in which the violence has no interpersonal connotations at all. We occasionally encounter an individual blindly bent on a rampage of destruction, and to him a police officer can be merely another object to be indiscriminately destroyed:

> At approximately 4:10 A.M. this date Sgt. A. and me were called by the above complainants, who stated to us that the below arrested person came into the hot dog stand, picked up the push broom and struck the counter causing considerable damage to said counter. The below arrested then ran into W. Do-Nut Shop and deliberately pushed over a large tray of doughnuts. Upon seeing reporting officers enter, he ran to the extreme rear of the premises, whereupon he picked up a ladder and attempted to strike officers, and he then threw ladder at Sgt. A.'s head. Considerable force was necessary in properly restraining him and during which time both officers were repeatedly kicked and struck with fists. In removing him from this rear room he deliberately kicked over a large rack containing snails and doughnuts. He then kicked over a metal container with approximately ½ gallon of jelly. Upon taking him to the sidewalk area he attempted to kick the plate glass window of the adjoining premises and during which time both officers were kicked again.

A different type of incident is one in which the aggressor is a person who habitually reacts to disappointment and discomfort with rage and destruction. Such a person may attack several police officers after smashing his furniture or his children, but he will not do so simply because the officers are present and available. The police, rather, are subject to attack because they act as another source of frustration. To the person, the connotation of the police becomes comparable to that of the divorcing wife or incriminating witness or crying child who precede the officer as victims:

> Victim stated that at approximately 1:35 A.M. this date, he heard a loud noise, whereupon he looked out his front apartment door and observed that the adjoining apartment belonging to the reportee had its front door torn from its hinges and lying on the ground, and that loud noises were being emitted from the apartment. The reportee and her cousin P. came running out of their apartment and took refuge in the victim's apartment, stating that the suspect had kicked down the front door, entered the apartment, torn the reportee's Immigration Registration Card, threatened her life, and was now overturning the furniture. Victim's wife summoned the police whereupon the suspect fled the building, only to immediately return and re-enter the victim's apartment and strike at him with a beer can opener, missing the victim with the can opener, but striking him on the nose with his knuckles, causing victim to defend himself. Victim displayed a slight swelling of the nose, but declined medical treatment. Reportee stated that her divorce from the suspect became final in December, and she displayed a restraining order. When responding officers attempted to place the suspect under arrest, he resisted by striking and kicking out at the officers, compelling them to use force necessary to effect the arrest. A Bureau of Identification check revealed that the suspect has a past record of 148 PC (corporeal injury to wife and children).

There are various ways in which an officer who intervenes in a conflict situation can be perceived by participants as a source of annoyance or as an objectionable development. In some incidents, for example, the officer is defined as illegitimately interfering in what the person views as his private affairs:

Reportee stated that her husband, the suspect, had arrived home shortly before, and had broken the window next to the door, entering the premises. The suspect was asked by the Reporting Officers what had occurred, and he stated he had broken the window and did not like our presence in his apartment. When told we were requested to come up by his wife, he became very belligerent and stated that we'd never come through his doors without a warrant. He was advised that we were merely attempting to ascertain what had occurred in the interests of preserving the peace and in the interests of his wife's safety in that she was emotionally distraught and literally shaking in what was assumed to be fear. The suspect became very bellicose, and ordered us from the "f_____g house." At this time he took a swing at Officer N. In the course of the next few minutes it took considerable effort to restrain his onslaught of fists and feet, Officer N. incurring a severe laceration of the index finger of his left hand. Once handcuffed, the suspect attempted to further carry on with his violence to the point that it was necessary to handcuff his ankles together.

Sometimes the frustration experienced by the aggressor is a by-product of the officer's routine. For instance, it is accepted police procedure in cases of domestic dispute for investigators to interview the victim, and then to listen to the aggressor's side of the story. Although this procedure is fair, it is also risky. An angry and excited man may be instructed to be silent and may be forced to listen to unfriendly characterizations of himself. Not infrequently, he uses the time to work himself up into another rage. When he begins to give vent to this anger, the next step usually involves ordering him to be calm, which may serve to annoy him further. When as a result he explodes, and has to be physically immobilized, his impotence and humiliation become a source of extreme frustration to him. It is probably partly because of such procedures that violence generated by violence does not easily abate over time:

Reporting Officers attempted to arbitrate and abate the disturbance; however, the below arrested person continued arguing and shouting in a loud voice, waving his arms about, and it was necessary to leave him in one room while

Reporting Officers conversed with the other two subjects in an adjoining room. The subject was advised to refrain from interrupting the conversation several times and in spite of Reporting Officers' admonitions continued to shout and finally entered the room where Reporting Officers were attempting to converse with the reportee, and when asked to leave again, turned to Officer H. and swung with his right hand, striking the officer on the shoulder; Officer H. stepped back out of the room, the defendant followed him and grappled with him, attempting to throw him over the railing into the stairwell. The stairwell is approximately 20 to 25 feet in depth, this being a third floor flat. The defendant was subdued by Reporting Officers and handcuffed. However, he did continue to struggle and it was necessary to physically carry him down the stairwell where he was transported to Co. D. At Co. D, in removing the handcuffs from the suspect he again attempted to attack Reporting Officers and again was physically restrained.

The following incident shows the sequence from initial resentment through frustration, cumulating over the interviewing process:

The suspect, who was obviously the aggressor, started yelling at this citizen and attempted to strike him for no apparent reason. Reporting Officers decided to investigate further and entered the apartment house. As we came into the hallway, we heard screams for help and we ran up to the second floor in time to observe the suspect hitting at a woman who we learned was suspect's wife. The suspect ran into the apartment and closed the door. Reporting Officers entered the apartment and found the suspect sitting in the living room, and upon our asking what the trouble was the suspect belligerently demanded that we get out of the house before he put us out. Reporting Officers calmed the suspect momentarily and interviewed his wife, who stated that her husband, the suspect, "Was trying to throw me down the stairs." Witnesses to the suspect trying to throw the victim down the stairs were the victim's parents. . . . During the interview of the victim the suspect became more excited and belligerent and, upon the arrival of additional officers, H., R., and S., the suspect grabbed Officer

S. and attempted to forcibly eject him from the apartment. After a struggle the suspect was subdued and Officer S. broke the upper plate in his mouth when he bumped his chin on the suspect's elbow.

It is easy for an officer trying to curb aggression to be seen by the aggressor as a partisan, a contender, or an enemy siding with the other party. Violence directed at the police can be viewed as another phase of a continuing battle. It may be assumed, moreover, that while the fight with the other civilian was fair (even if the other civilian was a frail woman in the process of being choked or beaten to death), the officer's intervention represents an illegitimate, unfair intrusion by an obvious bully. Ironically enough, this view may be shared by the losing contender, even after the latter has been rescued through police action. We thus often witness the strange spectacle of the officer being clawed by the victim while trying to subdue the assailant. The following scene (in which the officer is ultimately reduced to despair and almost pulls his gun on a group of women) depicts this kind of sequence:

We were met by the reportee who ran up to the radio car with torn shirt in his hand and stated the below named suspect was beating up some people at a party, and he asked Reporting Officer's assistance. We went into the house with him and suspect had a woman by the throat against the wall in a bedroom of the house. I told him to release her but he refused to answer. I told him a second time and took hold of his wrist to remove his hand from the area of the woman's throat. I pulled his hand away and told him to come with us. He then swore at me and swung at me. I knocked him down on the bed, and he came up with both fists, kicking. In the ensuing struggle a large number of females who had come from different rooms in the house attacked my partner and I as we were struggling with the suspect. There were at least 15 women fighting and clawing and striking at us while we were attempting to subdue the suspect. We were finally able to place handcuffs on the suspect, and my partner held him down while I went to call for assistance. Two of the women who had started the fight and had refused to back up when I told them to, struck both Reporting Officers several times and were arrested with suspect. My partner, Officer F., incurred a laceration of the hand by one of the suspects. It is unknown which one. His wristwatch disappeared completely and his tie was torn from his shirt. Officer Q. sustained the loss of the button from the front of his shirt and also damage to his hat during the struggle. At least one of the women who was striking me was holding a baby in her arms, and it was very difficult to subdue her without injuring the child. I finally threatened in a loud voice to pull my gun if they (the women) didn't back up. At this time they backed up but continued to yell and scream and harass the officers and antagonize the male suspect.

An officer dealing with a gang-related conflict is apt to be viewed as a contending party by participants who feel a need to demonstrate their toughness or manhood. The following incident is one which seems to combine both of these motives:

While on routine patrol, Reporting Officers observed a number of juveniles involved in a fight at the above location. When Reporting Officers attempted to stop the fight, Suspect #1 swung his fist at Officer H. in an effort to strike him. Officer S. and Sgt. L. then tried to grab Suspect #1 but were struck about the face by him. Suspect #1 broke away and ran through the service station to a corner where there were large containers of garden rakes and hoes. Suspect #1 removed a rake from the container and swung it at the pursuing officers, narrowly missing same. Suspect #1 was forced to drop the rake, at gun point, but considerable force was necessary to arrest and handcuff Suspect #1. . . . Suspect #1 was taken to the [hospital] for treatment, where he shouted obscene verbal abuse toward all persons he came in contact with . . . , and stated that "some white man would pay for what had been done to him." Suspect verbally repeated all the badge numbers of the policemen around him, and stated he would remember these when he got a gun. . . . Suspect #1 also stated that he was a member of a boxing group being coached by Officer S., and that the only reason he was participating in the activity was to get the opportunity to beat some policeman.

Some persons see the appearance of police in a conflict as always a partisan act because of strong feelings about the police or about their own role vis-à-vis the police. In other instances, violence may be extended to police officers simply because of the excitement or amusement this expanded activity might seem to promise. This sort of game is played in a fairly light-hearted fashion by its originators, but it tends to be taken very seriously by some officers involuntarily involved in it:

> This date at approximately 2:00 A.M. Reporting Officers observed the below suspects come out of the S. Club. Once the suspects were on the street we further observed Suspect H. jump on the back of Suspect T. and begin lewd physical gestures (humping). After this act both parties fell to the street and on regaining their stance both parties began swinging at each other. Reporting Officers got out of the radio car and when we attempted to separate the parties, they turned on us and began striking officers with their closed fists and attempted to kick officers. A reasonable amount of force was used to subdue the parties and they were handcuffed. On arrival of the park wagon, and as Suspect T. was entering into the wagon, he again attempted to kick officers in the area of the groin.

Finally, there are occasions in which officers appear to attach sinister connotations to minor physical involvement, or seem to make insufficient allowance for the agitated condition of persons encountered in post-conflict situations. Such incidents lie on the border between the need to protect police integrity and the requiring of unreasonably rigid standards of conduct:

> Reporting Officer approached the below arrested and asked what the trouble was. Suspect stated to officer that he was just in a fight with one J.R. The suspect was highly excited and was dramatizing his story by repeatedly poking Reporting Officer in the chest with his finger. Officer advised the suspect to cease poking him with his finger. The suspect disregarded this advice and at this point placed his hand on officer's arm in an offensive manner. At this point officer pushed the suspect away and placed him under arrest on the below charges.

Here we see the other side of the coin. It is the officer in this case who plays the more violence-prone role; it is he who reacts angrily to the excited gestures of the other; and it is he whose motives thus shape the unscheduled outcome of the incident.

From Incident, to Person, and Back

If we can summarize our course of action in the analysis of police assaulter incidents, it has been a process of finding general categories such that the unique incident acquires more depth. We have proceeded from simple classifications to chronological accounts in order to locate feelings and perceptions that enter into these short-term-motivated moves. We have found that once we reduce incidents to standard game form, it becomes possible to inquire into the various ways in which different participants play these games. Our main benefit here is not simply the achieving of order, but the fact that when we come to view grouped incidents as similar games differently played, we become more aware of the unique personal contributions of players. And we have seen that these personal contributions occur in the shape of violence-prone premises and their behavioral consequences.

To be sure, we have thus far accomplished little. The picture we have presented is confusing and chaotic. It comprises a large number—and an imposing variety—of discrete incidents. And our observations about these incidents are admittedly impressionistic and disjointed. But we have taken a necessary first step in the achievement of psychological ordering. We can next inquire into the place of the incident in the person's life and into the role the same incident plays in the lives of others.

Once we have come to understand the incident as an interpersonal product, we shall focus on our main concern, which is that of trying to achieve some understanding of the protagonists of violent games, and of their central motives.

3

The Violent Incident in its Personal Context

Our analysis of police assaults, as summarized above, has suggested that incidents such as those we have described are largely precipitated by the feelings of one or another of the parties involved. In the case studies that follow, we shall examine this relationship in some depth. We shall try to show that the various occasions of violence in the life of a person can be symptoms or manifestations of his personality. We shall draw on three interviews: one with a chronic police assaulter, one with an officer who has been often assaulted, and one with a troublesome prison inmate. In each case, we shall record incidents of violence, trace the motives behind them, and examine these motives.

We shall confine ourselves in this chapter to the involvement of one person (our subject) in each incident. The next chapter will deal with the relative contribution of two violence-prone people involved in the same incident.

Jimmy, the Precarious Teaser

We interviewed Jimmy in prison, where he had recently been returned on a charge of statutory rape. Jimmy was 23 years old, with a work record consisting of a successful career as a minor league pimp. Jimmy's "rap sheet" included many and diverse offenses, such as forcible rape, crime against children, kidnapping, intoxication, grand theft, petty theft, and disturbing the peace. Most revealing, there were several instances of battery and assaults with deadly weapons, and two attacks on police officers. The police incident that Jimmy chose to discuss with us is not included on this record because it took place while he was in his pre-teens.

As the scene opens, Jimmy is being turned away from a school dance by a police officer who is aware of Jimmy's record of delinquent involvements and who apparently wishes to preserve peace and decorum in the ballroom. Jimmy is smarting at the rejection, and is embued with resentment against the police in general and against the officer in particular. He therefore reacts by throwing a can at the officer's feet and by making a disparaging remark. A lengthy sequence follows, and it can probably be best captured by reproducing the interview excerpt relating to it:

Interviewer: So you wanted to show him that you didn't like him; so you put this can down. And is that when you started singing?

Subject: Yes.

Interviewer: Can you give us a little demonstration of how you were singing?

Subject: Well, it wasn't nothing, you know, that I could . . . I remember all the words, you know . . . but I was . . .

Interviewer: What were the lines about?

Subject: No . . . I'll tell it . . . you know, this song about his son, you know. A song . . . "f_____" and all that, you know. "Got jumped on . . . his daddy's a police," you know. "His daddy's a punk," all that, you know. But he couldn't hear . . . he could hear me singing, but he couldn't hear the words.

Interviewer: Could he hear it now and then, like "son" and "police" and "punk" and key words like that?

Subject: He could probably hear something like "police" possibly . . . I say it out loud. "Police are sissies."

Interviewer: So he did have some indication that this song you were singing might have something to do with him, huh?

Yeah. He might have, you know. It was . . . it was against the police department, you know. So, well, I guess since he's a part of the police department, he gotta you know . . . so I told him, "It ain't nothing, anyhow."

Interviewer: But so far, you think this is all pretty amusing?

Subject: Yeah. I knew it was irritating him. That's why . . . that was my purpose of doing it.

Interviewer: How did he show that he was irritated?

Subject: Well, when he hit me, you know, it showed me that he was irritated, I hadn't provoked him to hit me by . . . I mean, I didn't swing at him, and I didn't say nothing to him directly that would provoke him like that, but you know . . . What I was saying, I guess, that could have provoked him, when I kept on singing and "shining" him on, knowing that he was walking aside of me, and he kept on telling me to shut up and I wouldn't shut up, cause I was off the school grounds. He had no . . . I mean freedom of speech, you know.

Interviewer: Let's get this game a little bit in detail. You start singing and he was showing that he doesn't like this singing?

Subject: Yeah.

Interviewer: And he's showing this by what? By telling you to stop?

Subject: Yeah.

Interviewer: In a tone of voice that kinda gave you the feeling that . . .

Subject: He didn't like it.

Interviewer: Did your volume increase or decrease?

Subject: Increase as soon as I'd passed those gates.

Interviewer: Your volume increased as soon as you'd passed through the gates, and he kept on telling you to stop? Then what? He didn't hit you right away . . . he told you not to walk?

Subject: He told me to shut up.

Interviewer: He told you to shut up . . . and certainly you weren't doing that?

Subject: No, I wouldn't shut up.

Interviewer: So then, what was his next move?

Subject: He said, "Come here," and I said, "Man, well, I'm going home." You know, like that. And he said, "What are . . . ?" He said something funny, he said, "Well, this'll teach you to shut up." Or something like that. And that's when he hit me, you know. It just glanced off and you know, and tears started coming down my eyes.

This sequence is highly revealing, because it suggests a pattern of deliberate teasing, with intention to irritate. Jimmy appears to be gaining satisfaction from the fact that he is producing considerable irritation to the officer, while he himself is retaining both equanimity and control over the transaction. The officer's pain and annoyance grows, however, to the point where he feels that it is necessary to resort to violence, and at this juncture the entire situation changes for Jimmy. He now loses his "cool," and feels terribly hurt. He concludes that retaliation is in order and proceeds to secure his shotgun:

Interviewer: What was on your mind when you went to get the shotgun?

Subject: Shooting him if I can . . . you know, . . . I wanted . . . I wanted to hurt him, you know.

Interviewer: You wanted to hurt him. So you must have been awfully mad?

Subject: Yeah, I was pretty mad. You know, that was the first time, you know, I was ever hit in my face at all, you know. In my face, and left a scar on my body, first time any blood was ever drawn on my face.

His feeling, at this juncture, is that the officer has committed an unjust act. He views his own actions as relatively harmless, and, although he recognizes their provocative character, he sees the reaction as out of proportion. In other words, although the game has the inevitable consequence of producing a violent reaction, its aims are short-term and therefore the result is seen as arbitrary, capricious, and unjust. Jimmy now perceives himself faced with an act of unprovoked brutality:

Subject: And, see, I hadn't did nothing for him to hit me for, you know.

Interviewer: You knew you had been annoying him. But you thought . . .

Subject: In my own way, I was annoying him, but it wasn't enough to provoke him to use his billy club on me.

Interviewer: I got you. So it was at the point where he hit you with this billy club that things stopped being funny and started . . .

Subject: Getting stiff.

Jimmy is next apprehended and is immobilized by being handcuffed to a pole in the vicinity of the school, pending transportation to the police station. This is a terribly hurtful and humiliating experience for Jimmy because it is potentially damaging to his prized self-image and his reputation. He feels that the tables are turned and that the officer is now in control and showing him contempt—a situation he finds utterly intolerable:

Interviewer: You mentioned that he had taken you over there to show you off?

Subject: Yeah. You know, parade me like I was some kind of a freak or a clown or something.

Interviewer: This is how you felt? At the time they are taking you, you are awfully mad? Now you are standing out there, handcuffed to the door of the school. Now the feeling on top of your mind is that of being mad at this guy and being awfully upset about the fact that here you're being exposed as a kind of show?

Subject: Yeah. I was kinda feeling embarrassed by being exposed like I was a freak.

Interviewer: That was on top of your mind now?

Subject: Yeah. That was on top, but you know, it is being moved out, you know, 'cause all my animosity was building up toward J., you know. He was my prime subject at the moment.

Interviewer: So every once in awhile this anger that you felt towards this man was still peeking through?

Subject: Yeah. Every time I see his face, you know. He would leave me and go into the dance. Like, well, "this punk ain't going nowhere." You know, something like that. Well, he knowed I couldn't go nowhere, so . . .

Interviewer: So you felt that he was showing you contempt by not watching you even?

Subject: Yeah.

Although Jimmy is reluctant to discuss other incidents in which he has been involved in physical conflict with police officers, he is fairly voluble about verbal conflicts he claims to have engaged in with various officers:

Interviewer: Have you had a lot of arguments with them?

Subject: The police? I cussed them out practically every time they arrest me.

Interviewer: About how many times is that? That you can remember.

Subject: About a thousand.

Interviewer: Really, you have been arrested a thousand times?

Subject: I don't know, I . . . I . . . just off and on, you know. They pick me up for something like . . . they don't actually put me in jail, but they stop me. I say, "Punk, why the hell don't you leave me alone? Don't know what the hell you do but fuck with me all day long, anyhow."

Interviewer: Just about every time you get stopped or arrested, or they have any communication with you?

Subject: Yeah. Any time I have communications with the police, I . . . I get violent.

Interviewer: And that has happened quite often?

Subject: Quite often.

In exploring the details of such conflicts as Jimmy sees them, the following account is obtained:

Interviewer: Yeah. Now I'm wondering about one thing here: Here are the officers coming up to you, and then they get all this stuff back, and yet, you know, somehow, you don't go to jail. You don't get hit over the head with a nightstick. You don't have to hit anybody. How do you get out of this? You know, what happens that makes it possible for you . . . one of you to go one way and the other, the other way?

Subject: I don't know.

Interviewer: Well, what happens usually? Here I am, and I'm an officer, and I come up to you and I say, "Look fellow, may I see your I.D.?" And you say, "Naw, I don't have to show you nothing. I didn't do nothing. Look here punk," and all that. Then what? What's the next step?

Subject: Well, you says, "Get in the car." and I say, "I'm not getting in the car or nothing like that," you know.

Interviewer: Yeah. Then what?

Subject: "Well, we just want to find out who you are," you know. "If you got any warrants." "Well, I ain't got any warrants out for me. You can take my word for it." You know, like that.

Interviewer: Yeah.

Subject: Then I walks away. That's when he usually grabs me and . . .

Interviewer: He usually grabs you, and then you go to the police station?

Subject: Sometimes they don't even take you down there when they call in. 'Cause he can't arrest me for nothing, you know.

Interviewer: You mean he can grab you and put you in the car and you won't hit him?

Subject: Uh huh.

Interviewer: So you are just sitting . . .

Subject: I won't . . . I won't . . . I won't be the one to provoke anything. If he hits me first, I might hit him. I'm not for sure.

Interviewer: But isn't this usually what happens? So they put you in the car and you just sit there, and they call the police station and they let you go, telling you, "don't do it again," or something like that?

Subject: Yeah. He says, "You'd better . . . "

Interviewer: Change your attitude. Is that usually how it ends? They tell you to change your attitude, then you go away and . . .

Subject: And I tell 'em, "Well, my attitude is better than yours, sucker!" You know, I just walk on.

Interviewer: Oh, and that's it? That usually ends it?

Subject: As far as my conversation with the police.

Interviewer: Do you usually have the last word or do you find something said as you walk away?

Subject: Most of the time I have the last word, but quite a few times I be so far away that they can't do nothing about it, you see.

Interviewer: Well, how do you feel about these sorts of conversations? You know, now that you're sitting there looking back at it, what do you think of it, if anything?

Subject: I mean, it's still a joke to me.

According to this characterization, Jimmy successfully defies hundreds of police officers and leaves them irritated and impotent while he walks away unscathed. He views himself as coolly manipulating the feelings of the officers, with no consequences to himself. Unfortunately, the situation as he described it does not accurately summarize all his encounters. A 1965 police arrest report, for instance, described the terminal sequence of one of Jimmy's less successful interactions with the police:

> We approached suspect to assume custody. Complainants took suspect by the arm to escort suspect to our vehicle and suspect refused to go. Complainant and Witness 1 each took one of suspect's arms and began walking him back to the car. Complainant and Witness 1 were able to get handcuffs on suspect, who continued to resist violently, and refused to get in the patrol car. Officers forced suspect into the car and suspect let off a continuous stream of insults toward officers from S. Avenue to the jail. As Reporting Officers pulled into the jail entrance suspect leaned back on seat, raised his feet and kicked at the divider between the seats. When Witness 1 was able to stop suspect [he] made a lunge at Witness through the left door which Witness 1 had opened to take suspect from vehicle. Suspect at this time fell from the vehicle to the ground. Complainant and Witness 1 picked suspect up and carried him from car to the jail. En route, suspect kicked Witness 1 and Complainant several times. Once in the jail, Reporting Officers were attempting to re-move handcuffs when suspect kicked Officer D. in the groin. Jailers were finally able to remove handcuffs and suspect during the interim spit directly into Officer D.'s face, saliva also hit Officer M. Suspect was finally put into a padded cell at City Jail.

Again, the picture we obtain is that of an effort to generate irritation in others, which boomerangs because it succeeds. When pawns become the controlling parties because they react forcefully, our man loses his "cool" completely and lashes out frantically and helplessly. He also becomes aware, at this juncture, of the fantasy world in which his aggressive games have taken place:

Subject: Well, you know, when I'm actually under arrest, you know, it's a serious matter, you know. It's something . . . it's something . . . I gotta face reality then.

Interviewer: When you only have arguments with them, how do you see it?

Subject: It's nothing, you know.

Interviewer: A joke?

Subject: Yeah.

Interviewer: So that's more like this same thing then?

Subject: Oh, yeah, you know. That's the attitude I always have taken, you know. That seems like the only thing I can irritate them with, you know.

Jimmy's involvement with police officers fits into a pattern that manifests itself in relation to various other persons in his life. For instance, Jimmy tells us about a form of entertainment practiced by a social group to which he belonged as a boy, which consisted of contacting a rival gang, with a view to provoking them into a fight:

Subject: We know something is going to happen every time a club is there.

Interviewer: Oh you do? Did you say you let 'em in to take stock, until you are able to fight?

Subject: Usually, you know. That's what it all is, a gladiator school.

Interviewer: But they don't have to do a thing. When you guys get ready . . .

Subject: They'll know about it.

Interviewer: Yeah. Then they don't have to do anything?

Subject: Yeah. But they go on . . . they will provoke the fight. Won't provoke, but we will make 'em fight, you know. We'll say certain things, you know. One of 'em goin' get mad, you know, and soon as he gets mad, all of 'em have to go into it, you know, 'cause if they don't, they're fools.

Jimmy himself, when questioned, sees the similarity between this game and the incident with the police officer at the school dance:

Interviewer: Seems like you were sort of egging (the police officer) on. Do you see yourself doing the same thing when one of these gangs, . . . when you get ready to pick a fight?

Subject: Oh, yeah.

Interviewer: So this usually is there . . . that you know that they are getting more and more annoyed, and that sooner or later they will give you the opportunity to attack?

Subject: Yeah.

Interviewer: Do you see the same thing when you don't fight the police? You know, sort of a fun game, like when you fight these guys?

Subject: Part of the game.

Jimmy then elaborates on the nature of the game, stressing the pride he feels in the fact that he can retain his equanimity while manipulating the feelings of others. His "coolness" is obviously equated with status and with "reputation" achieved by demonstrating one's superiority over persons who reveal their vulnerability:

Subject: This is what I do. You see, I . . . I can take things that other persons can't take, and I can accept things that another person can't accept. You know, I can know how far I have to go before I really will get mad, you know. I can see . . . a person can stand here and slap me all day, you know. I won't show a thing. He can talk about anything, you know, and I can accept all this. But I can take another person, and I can say one word and get him mad.

One final—and major—area in which Jimmy plays his violence-producing game is in relation to the women in his life. Jimmy admits to hitting women. He attaches little importance to this activity and even proclaims that the evidence indicates that women like to be beaten. The evidence he adduces is that women will keep saying things to him that are predictably productive of violence. The things they say, it appears, are in the nature of "love-talk" and of hints about marriage. Here it becomes clear that Jimmy himself has led various girls on with promises and hints, and that he then precipitates conflict by proclaiming that he has every intention of retaining his independence:

Interviewer: Did you do anything to provoke her into picking up the phone?

Subject: I told her I wasn't going to marry her, yeah.

Interviewer: Could you have told her in such a way that she wouldn't have wanted to pick up the phone?

Subject: I could have, you know, but it didn't cross my mind. I wanted to make her mad, but I didn't want her to pick up the telephone.

Interviewer: Was the same thing happening then . . . that you were trying to provoke her?

Subject: I wanted to provoke her into saying that she was sorry, and didn't mean it the way it sounded. She knowed she was going to get hit.

Interviewer: Because she was pushing you? And you were being pushed.

Subject: Yeah. I am being threatened with my freedom.

Interviewer: Your freedom?

Subject: The last act.

Jimmy, in other words, provokes violence with police, with rival gang members, and with women in his "stable" by deliberately teasing them until they are forced to react. The purpose of this game may have relatively little to do with the victim as such. Rather, it serves the purpose of permitting Jimmy to test his stance as a man of steel and as a person capable of controlling not only his own destiny but also the feelings and reactions of his fellows. Unfortunately, he often fails both of these tests.

Officer Jones: The Power of Persuasion

Officer Jones, who has been assaulted more frequently than almost any of his fellow officers, sees himself as a practitioner of applied psychology. In dealing with people, he advises and claims the need for patience, flexibility, and diplomacy wherever possible. He puts the matter this way:

Subject: Well, I would like to think that I'm a student of people. I've been dealing with people for a good part of my life in the sense that I've spent, you know, almost ten years on the police force. This is a long time. If I told you that you just seemed to know, it might not make sense to you, but it's just maybe 'cause I . . . the guys kid me around here and say that I got the, you know, the old bullshit, but you'd be surprised how this will go. I think if it was a car stop, by the attitude of the driver, the immediate attitude of the driver; how he takes his license out, if he does—what he says to you. The man who says, "What are you stopping me for? What's going on?" Well, he is not going to . . . you can be nice to him, you can kill him with kindness, or you can be rather abrupt and you can treat him, talk to him the same way. I think you should look at the person and you just decide. I've spent so many years working around whores, narcotics addicts; I had an incident yesterday where this prostitute tried to cash a stolen payroll check. And by being nice to her (I bought her a pack of cigarettes), we talked; the other officer I was with wanted to make a lot of noise. He wouldn't have got to first base. She admitted being a hype; she gave me her kit and some narcotics she had on her person. She also told me where the check came from, and the fact that it involved more than one person. So, you see, again, by being nice and by saying that, you know, "If I can help you, I will; I'll try my damndest to get you to the hospital." 'Cause she was starting to go through withdrawals. This is one way to handle a person.

But Officer Jones also prides himself on his reputation for a consistent willingness to take physical action where appropriate. His " rep," in other words, depends (as he sees it) on his known readiness to back up his commands and threats with action:

Subject: . . . Well, now, there's another reason too, and perhaps, you will understand it and other people wouldn't. When you walk a beat and you've been walking it for a long time, it's a little different than a car beat. You know people, and there's a certain reputation that an officer gets, and an officer gets a reputation of being a good cop, what they call a square cop. They call me a square cop. Even guys I have arrested say, "Well, Officer Jones will give you a fair shake, provided you treat him right. But if you're wrong you're going to go to jail." And I'm not adverse to telling them that if I have trouble I will give them lumps if that's what they want, and I'm not afraid of them. So, again, it's a matter of, well, it's not really a false sense of pride, but it's pride in the fact that you know that you can handle your beat, that you can keep it clean, and that you're big enough and man enough to be able to take care of whatever happens to come down the line.

Officer Jones forms quick judgments about civilians, classifying them as candidates for either persuasion or intimidation. In some cases he feels the need to use a direct and aggressive approach consisting of "no-nonsense" injunctions and of physical threats. In the case of one "mean" individual, for instance, Officer Jones reports:

Subject: I have had occasion over a period of years to have to fight with this man. The last time I had trouble with him . . . now, this again, as long as we're not talking for the courts, this is not what you would call regular police procedure. However, again, I will run my beat the way I see I have to. I told J. he had been involved in a beating of a man and his wallet being taken. The man refused to make a complaint because he's afraid of J. On __th Street, just on the other side of T's Bar, I got hold of J., got him up against the wall, I drew

> my service revolver and stuck the barrel of my gun up
> to the cylinder in his mouth, and I told J. that if he
> pulled any more capers on my beat, that there would
> be two witnesses to his murder, he and I, and he'd be
> dead. Now, this is the only type, this is the only thing
> this man would understand. This man spent time in
> the Leavenworth army stockade for almost beating his
> commanding officer to death during the Second World
> War. This is the type of man you're dealing with.

The officer's approach to this particular individual is in the
nature of a physical confrontation, a display of power, a challenge, a bluff, an announcement of his readiness to fight if
necessary. Officer Jones conveys to the man that "I will use
the slightest excuse to engage in a duel with you, and I know
I can lick you." He does this in a man-to-man encounter,
without invoking the law or calling upon his brother officers.
In one incident, for instance, he has a summons to serve on
the same problem person. He proceeds at once to the pool
hall where he knows this man to hang out. "He was a pretty
tough man," the officer explains, "But then, this is going back
a few years; perhaps I was in a bit better shape and wasn't
too worried about being able to take him." And as Officer
Jones approaches his confrontation with the suspect, he does
so feeling that he will "take him." He tells us:

Subject: I had the feeling, knowing him, that it's either going
            to be a Mexican standoff or a fight. Either he is going
            to go along with me, only because he's afraid that I'm
            either going to shoot him or beat him, or he's going
            to figure that he's got nothing to lose and he's probably
            got more help than I do, 'cause I'm by myself.

In other words, Officer Jones knows that he is walking into
a room full of enemies, but he also knows that he will get his
man. He knows this because he had confidence in himself, in
his fists, and in his gun. He therefore proceeds to the pool-
room, bursts through the door, and the following scene unfolds:

Subject: I walk in, I said, "J., I got a warrant for your arrest," and I had it in my left hand. And I said, "You're going to jail with me." And he looked at me, and he knew my name, and he said, "Well, Officer," he said, "I'm not going to go to jail." And I said, "Well, you're going to go to jail." I said "There's only two ways to go; you're either going to walk out of here with me, or you're going to get dragged out." Now, again, I know the man, I've had dealings with him before, and this is the only way that you're going to get across to him. There's no other possible way to do it. So, at this point he picks up a pool ball and throws it at me, which I ducked. He grabs the pool cue and he swings, and I head for him. Now I don't have my gun out, but I go after him and I got hit across the arm, I got my arm fractured, but I didn't know that at the time. Well, we fought and we grappled from the rear of the pool hall where this occurred. Now, this is about four tables back (you know the size of a pool table) so this is about, we'll say, 50 feet from the front. And all these other people in here. Now, up to now nobody's said anything. They're just backed away. Well, the fight ensues. We go all the way to the front of the pool hall, where I knock him through the front of the plate glass window, and I go out after him onto the middle of the street. Finally I get him down and with my hand and my stick, I beat him into a semi-stupor, and at this time, I look up and I see a very, very unhappy crowd of people.

Now, we carry two-way radios now; at this time we didn't. We had to go to the call box. The nearest call box was a block and a half away. At this time someone in the crowd said, "Let's get him," and I drew my service revolver and I said, "The first person that comes close is going to be shot." I said, "This man's in custody; I have a warrant for his arrest, and I'm warning anyone in the crowd, if they come and try to take this prisoner, I'm going to shoot." Well, he starts coming to, and he starts hollering, you know, "Help me, help me," you know, "Don't let them take me away."

Well, a man comes out of a restaurant, and I said to him, "Call the police." And he just shook his head and didn't do anything; he just turned around and walked away. So I know I'm not going to get any help from the crowd. I've got to get to this call box. I'm hoping that a car, a police car, will come by, but none does. So, I walk this prisoner, walk and drag him, and he's fighting; he's not going to go that easy. With my gun drawn, and I have literally to threaten the crowd that I'm going to shoot and I have to walk a block and a half to the call box. I get to the call box, and this guy starts to run away from me and I have to chase him again. I grab him; I bring him back to the call box, and then I phone in and ask for help, right away. Well, as soon as that call went out, I got help right there. But during this time there must have been 150 people surrounding me again. They'd followed me up the street to the call box. And I had to continually turn around with my gun drawn in order to . . . and I had to keep saying, "The first one that gets within six feet of me is going to be shot, and I'm not fooling." And I had pulled the hammer back on the gun, which is usually a sign, if you do this, that you're going to, you're definitely going to do something. So then, again, as I say, we got the wagon there and, well, first a police car came and he was put in the back of the wagon, and he was transported to the hospital, and then from the hospital back to the jail. And then I went up for treatment.

It is obvious that Officer Jones has placed himself, at least by the time the incident ends, into an extremely dangerous and explosive situation. At each juncture of the sequence, he has seen no alternative to a show of force, to an ultimatum, to a demand for complete surrender. Officer Jones is a man who uses last resorts as first steps. Obviously, in at least this instance, he has narrowly escaped the consequences of desperate bluffs.

Officer Jones views himself as a Man, and it is important to him to preserve his self-image of invulnerability and omnipotence. Even in the face of highly probable danger, he favors a frontal approach. In one incident, for instance, there is a problem with a large, intoxicated sailor who has been disturbing patrons in a tavern. As Officer Jones enters, the sailor is quietly sitting on a bar stool:

Subject: . . . I tell him, "Get off the stool and come outside."
He just sat there, and I told him, I says, "Did you hear
what I said? Get off the stool." He just looked at me
and very slowly and very, very calculatedly, I mean,
this is done for my benefit . . . he's all the time looking
at me, and then in order to get behind him, an officer
in front of him and me behind him, I took my hand
and I put it in the small of his back, so I could move
around him. And he told me, "Get your hands off
me." And I said, "Just never mind—outside!" And
that was the extent of having touched him at this time.

Interviewer: Alright, now you get outside. He does come slowly,
calculatedly.

Subject: Yes, very slowly . . .

Interviewer: You don't consider him to be drunk at this time?

Subject: No. There's a definite odor of alcohol. You know that
the man has been drinking, but he's not drunk. At
least he has none of the usual symptoms of a drunk.

Interviewer: What do you think about this guy at this time?

Subject: Well, I think that we're going to have trouble with
him. He's giving me one of these hard looks. He's a
big kid and he's got a lot of cuts on his face. He's got
a lot of scars, he's . . . after being on the police force
for ten years, sometimes you can just tell. And he looks
like he's going to be trouble.

Interviewer: So you think he's going to be trouble?

Subject: Right.

Again, we note that Officer Jones knows he is facing a duel,
but he is not really concerned about evading it. He evaluates
his opponent and waits calmly for the encounter. Several minutes later it comes, and the sailor requires 25 blows with the
baton to put him out of action. In the first round, oddly enough,
Officer Jones' main concern appears to be the fact that the
fight may appear unfair to spectators:

Subject: . . . But our primary thing too is we don't want . . .
the image is bad enough. The image is worse when

there's three policemen and one guy fighting, although people may not realize that the older you get you're not as swift as you were. Now, here's a twenty-one-year-old sailor in the pink of condition, and he's big, and he's tough. And you're dealing with guys in their thirties and, sure, we're a little bit soft, and maybe not just as quick, and so, consequently, we've got our work cut out for us. And the idea here is too that we know that the three of us can put the guy down. We can do it without risking hurting him. But if it's one to one, somebody's going to get hurt.

Interviewer: So, you're grappling with him . . .

Subject: Right.

Interviewer: . . . and he's cussing and fighting, and you're just trying to get him down.

Subject: . . . down. And then my partner, and then this other officer comes up, and between the two of us, we finally, well, I get a nice shot at his jaw with my right hand, and it stunned him, and we got the wagon door open, down so that we jackknifed him, both arms up, so that we can throw the cuffs on him, and get him in that wagon, and then we said, "Well, let's get out of here, and down to the jail."

Interviewer: Is he still cussing?

Subject: Right, and he's still fighting. So then he starts kicking again, he kicks out, he keeps kicking out, and he gets hit one more time and he's unconscious.

Officer Jones' recounting of the two incidents we have quoted contains several indications of the pleasure he derives from physical conquest. The officer appears to enjoy dealing with a worthy opponent and conquering him after a good fight. His conception of himself is that of a man who dares to take risks and who emerges vindicated; a man who achieves the respect of his enemies, because he faces them squarely, and a man who finds it unnecessary to yield or to compromise. His incidents of violence are thus demonstrations of his manliness, and they arise, at least in part, because he welcomes the opportunity of putting his masculinity to the test.

We have so far provided two contrasting illustrations to show that violent incidents can reflect pervasive personal needs. We have in each case traced a psychological theme—sometimes distinguished by different orchestrations—running through the person's career. This theme appears as a recurrent pattern amid variations occasioned by time, place, and social context.

Themes of violence are not manifest in a person's conduct as ritualistic sets of repeat performances. The life of a violent person, like that of any other, is a flowing, sequential stream, and patterns take shape, evolve, and die over time. To fully understand the consistency amid change, we must review a violent career longitudinally, and trace its evolution through stages. For this sort of picture, we turn to our third interviewee, an inmate with a reputation as an influential problem prisoner.

Sam, the Giant-Killer: Mobilizing Violent Predispositions

In tracing his violence, Sam assigns a strong catalytic role to fear. He tells us that his prison problems stemmed from dark expectations, which were shaped by lurid images traced for him by veteran inmates. He refers to a conversation in county jail, where he was awaiting transfer to his first state institution:

> And they talked this shit, you know, "You got to do this, and you got to do this," and man, you think it's just like the movies, I mean you go in there and chug, chug, and you know, beat on you all the time and all—at least this is the impression I got from all these people because they fed me a lot of shit. And by the time I did get to the prison, you know how Vacaville is, with all them doors going like that, man you're just like this, and I was pushed to the point of panic that I possibly would have killed.

Sam tells us how his irrational apprehension caused him to get into several fights shortly after arrival in prison. The first one, he relates, was

Subject: . . . over nothing. . . . We was watching TV. Well, you know, you're all in your whites and you're fish, and all that. And this dude kept walking back and forth, hitting my leg. He hit it about four times.

Interviewer: Was he in whites also?

Subject: No, he was a con who was there, he had a little skull cap on, you know, and he was really one of Those. And I didn't pay any attention to him until about the third time it happened. And then I knew something's going on here because he had plenty of room to get by me. The fourth time he come by, he kicked my foot and he had his spit-shine Romeos on, you know. And then I noticed his partners around me. He had his partners standing there and everything. I seen what he was going to do, so I fired on him before he could do anything and split. That was all there was to that. But it was out of panic, because I was scared to death after I leapt up and seen what was happening to me.

The next fight occurred on the first day of Sam's arrival at his next step on the prison ladder. Sam described himself as feeling "pretty good" because of his reception at this prison:

Subject: We got there and they let us go eat and everything, and you know, here they are out in the open and, more or less, the feeling of fear left me. And I went on and ate and everything, and later they assigned us to cells. They put me in with one of the penitentiary troublemakers. He was back in medium security doing thirty days for messing up. You just never could get to the guy. He was one of Those that wouldn't conform to anything. I might add he eventually became my best partner after this. He was a big dude; he was about 6'2", and everything, and he was one of Those. I wasn't in the cell 10 minutes.

Interviewer: He was a bully?

Subject: Yeah. I had my stuff laying on his bed. He wasn't there at the time, he was taking a shower. He come back and he threw my things on the floor. I just thought, "Here I go, man, I know, I'm not supposed to let him do this." And he damn near annihilated me. He whipped me down once and I got up then and jumped on his back, again. We fought around there about three different times in one night. I had to get him, you know. And finally it was all right. I couldn't whip the sucker, man, and he knew it. But he was tired of getting bruises too. So then we just let it go and become real partners after that.

Interviewer: How did you feel just before the incident? Did you have any of the same feeling? I think you stated that when he threw your stuff on the floor, you thought, "Well, I got to do something."

Subject: Well, what I think I was feeling was like at Vacaville. I was getting one of these sissy complexes because I look young, anyway, and they tend to come around me, you know. And I was getting one of these complexes about it and this is what dawned on me, is that the fact that I was scared, I was afraid of him personally, but I didn't have the same kind of fear complex that I did with this other thing. I was more afraid of the other guys than I was of him. And this is one of the reasons if he dumps me, man, still he's going to know.

Sam's comments reflect the admixture of fear, awe, and admiration in which he holds "Those," as he calls the prison power figures. Sam feels that the encounter he describes is a test case, and that he must fight in order not to be classified as vulnerable to sexual advances and to exploitation. He reports feeling wonderful after the fight, because he had passed his test: "I felt like now, well, I was putting myself on." He feels accepted not only by the man whom he has tackled, but "by this one fight, I completely lost this complex I was getting." In the next breath, Sam admits that his apprehensions may not have been based on real danger; he ventures the guess that "I was putting it on myself."

Next, we discover that Sam and his imposing cell partner have become best friends, a fact of which Sam is immensely proud, particularly because this places him in a position of reflected power and prestige: "He was 'The Man' there, at

Chino, when I was there. He had all the action . . . and me and him were tight, and so this put me right in with him, and I felt that this is the only way I'm going to make it in here."

On the other hand, Sam soon develops the feeling that he might not be sufficiently earning his keep: "I felt I had to do something, 'cause I wasn't doing nothing but going for a big free ride." The 'something' he chose to do is to assault a debtor who had been slow in repaying a loan. The intervention is an unsolicited one:

Interviewer: Had your partner given you any indication that you had to do something?

Subject: No.

Interviewer: You were doing it because you thought this is the way it's supposed to be played?

Subject: Yeah.

Interviewer: Did you talk this over with your partner at all, that you were going to do this?

Subject: I just said, "If he don't have the stuff, man, let's just bust him up." Only, I hit him before he did; he would have hit him too.

Interviewer: Was he hurt?

Subject: No. I just put a knot on his head.

This proffered act of violence gives Sam more confidence in his ability to survive on his own terms: "After I had done this, I really started relaxing," he says, "because I knew, myself: 'Well, I can handle this in here.'" Sam adds somewhat nostalgically, "things kind of tapered off for me after that." And Sam feels that he no longer needed "the feeling of protection and easiness" he derived from his powerful partner: "Like I say, after this happened, then I felt I could cope with it by myself—I didn't need anyone."

Despite this talk of independence and of self-assurance Sam's next battle finds him once again embroiled shoulder to shoulder with his powerful friend, and it results in a further feeling of consolidated power. Again, his opponent is one of "Those,"

"Those" who have to be defeated in order to demonstrate one's worth. The scene opens with a cozy evening by the institutional fireside:

Subject: Well, they got barracks there like camps. We're living in the barracks at the time, and were all jacked up on beans, and were watching this card game.

Interviewer: You were loaded on Benzedrine pills?

Subject: Yeah, and we were watching these cats play cards, and we were standing behind this colored dude. He was one of these big iron-lifters, you know. About ninety feet wide, you know, he was one of Those. And he turned around and told us, "W., man, don't stand behind me, punk, when I'm playing," you know. And I just looked at my partner and he looked at me, you know, and didn't say nothing, just stood there. 'Cause we were running the barracks anyway. We felt we did.

Interviewer: Who was W.?

Subject: He was my partner. I just looked at him for his reaction, and he looked at me for mine. I just smiled and he smiled and we stood there. We felt like, you know, more or less, what I said was, "Do what you want, I'm with you." And he looked at me like, you know, "You there?" You know, because he wasn't about to whip that big sucker. And he turned around again, and he said, you know, "I told you not to stand behind me." And he said, you know, "Fuck you, man." And the dude got up and we were both on him, man. And we beat him to a pulp. Fixed him up bad, man. And nobody jumped in, you know. Course, we had about six or seven partners in the barracks and at the time there was only about four colored dudes in there. And they didn't get into it; you know how they are, man, about half of them got to have tin with them. So they didn't get in it. So we just, once we got going we just wasted the dude. And that was that. Sent him on down to the hospital. And after that I felt like a king, man. I felt like, you know, "I'm the man. You're not going to mess with me."

Again, Sam feels that he passed the test of reacting to defiance by a prison bully, that he has redeemed himself by loyally supporting his friend, and, above all, that he has solidified his empire further. He gets almost ecstatic in describing his feelings of enhanced worth: "I felt like I could handle the whole bit, you know. I felt like, 'The Man,' you know. I felt like everybody looking up to me, and. . . ."

Sam informs us that his victim had recently arrived in prison, and had been loudly boasting of his sexual prowess and his wealth on the street. Sam thought he had demonstrated to the man "what a phony he was," and had incidentally shown everyone else "that this guy is a nothing. He's a loud-mouthed punk."

Sam is not proud of his next fight, nor did he like it at the time. The reason for his reservations has to do with the identity of his opponent, who is relatively small in size.

Subject: . . . And we were playing handball; we played quite a bit, and we were playing two guys for stuff and we were beating them and I was playing up front, cause I was shorter and this little Mexican dude was playing up there with me and I was beating him bad up in front. And he started loud-talking me and I was letting it go and letting it go, 'cause he was nothing, you know, I mean it was just ridiculous, somebody you just don't hit.

Interviewer: He posed no threat while he was doing this loud-talking?

Subject: No. I'd be loud-talking him back, you know, and something like that and laughing at him and all that, telling him, "Well, you can't play, you don't belong on the court," and all that. And so we were battling it out there, man, I guess we had about five or six strokes going right into each other and boom! he missed, and he blew it, man, and I wasn't even looking and he hit me, you know. And he didn't even hit me hard enough to hardly turn my head, and I just grabbed the dude and I said, "Man, hey, you know what; come to yourself," and pushed him back. And, well, he come at me again, you know, swinging like that, so I pushed. . . ."

Sam tells us that his restraint in this conflict was in itself somewhat of a demonstration of worth; "I think I was trying to show the people that I wasn't trying to hurt him; I didn't feel I had to prove anything to them."

The next battle occurred in the gymnasium and involved another one of "Those"—a powerfully built Black person who failed to respect Sam's integrity by questioning his jurisdiction over a set of weights. This fight took place in the ring at the request of the coach, which proved convenient to Sam, " 'cause I wanted to see what I could do in the ring." The fight ended in a draw and was followed (like Sam's other prison fights) by a relationship of mutual respect and cordiality.

The next fight involves an effort to teach a lesson to a delinquent narcotics peddler. Once again, the object is to demonstrate "that he couldn't do this to me," rather than to rectify injustice in the world generally:

Subject: . . . I bought some stuff from this dude and it was a burn. I don't know what it was, some kind of garbage, man. Went up there and plucked it off a spoon and it was, anyway, it wasn't what it was supposed to be. And I come back down and hit on the dude. I was living in the honor unit then. Told him I wanted my stuff back now, man, that this ain't what's happening, you know. "Think I'm some kind of punk or something?" And he tried to give me a big story, man, "I don't want to hear anything about it, I want my stuff now, man." And he told me he ain't got it, man, so I just fired on him. Punched him out, man. Got my stuff back the next day.

Interviewer: How long had you known this guy?

Subject: Oh, I knew him for about two years. Had dealings with him. I didn't, I never did particularly like the guy, 'cause he'd burned some other people before, you know. And this was the first time. He used to score for me all the time and shit like that. It's the first time I ever got anything from him that was a burn. I guess it, more or less, goes back to the old prestige thing. I just dumped it in a spoon and I seen it wasn't stuff and picked it up and put it back in the paper and took it back over.

Interviewer: What were you feeling when all this was going on?

Subject: I thought, "Boy, this sucker's out of sight, man. He can't do this to me." And, threw it back on him.

We encounter Sam next as a civilian, but the change from prison blues to tailored suits does not appear to be accompanied by a striking psychological transformation. The first conflict Sam narrates not only is a replication of his prison encounters, but starts, as Sam sees it, because his opponent reminds him of the type of inmate who used to annoy him in the institution. His enemy is "one of Those"—operationally defined as a large-sized, loud Black person who thinks he can pick on Sam. Sam's companion represents power Sam is buying into (his boss's son); the fight itself is intended as a dramatic demonstration of Sam's immunity to harassment:

Subject: . . . I was down there in the Tulip Room . . . And I was with my boss's son and we'd been out drinking wine and hitting all the bars and drinking whiskey too. Pretty juiced. We're in there, you know, and it was packed, and these impressions again, you know. Typical loud-mouthed type. For some reason there, I just can't communicate with them at all. I have no patience with them. And he walked by me and poked me out of the way, walked right up front and I thought, "That's the way it goes," you know. I was mad, and we stood there for about, I guess, about ten minutes or something, and we were going to leave and he was coming back and he poked my boss's son out of the way, and was coming like he was going to do it to me, and I just fired on him and decked him. And that was it. And everybody jumped on us, you know, and I split . . .

Interviewer: You were drinking wine?

Subject: Yeah. Wine's the only thing that'll do that to me. And I think what it was is he pushed me back to what was going on in the penitentiary, you know. This kind of disgusted me.

Interviewer: The guy was a bully?

Subject: Well, that's what he was doing, you know. Pushing
              people out of the way, growing a little goatee and all
              that, you know, and looking like something else.

Interviewer: Was he pushing other people around?

Subject: Yeah. He was bumping into everybody, man, you know.
              And he wasn't loud-talking or nothing, you know, but
              he—I could see it in him. And I think it flashed me
              back to the penitentiary, which was an unpleasant thing.
              And this brought my anger on more and then, when
              I seen that he was going to bump into me, I just blew
              it completely and tried to smash what I seen.

Interviewer: You wanted to hurt him?

Subject: Yeah. I would have really wasted him, but I got jumped
              on.

Sam's next civilian encounter also involves a large-sized Black
opponent, and takes place in front of a bowling alley. In this
instance, Sam is interceding on behalf of his teen-age brother,
who he feels is being bullied. The object of the intervention,
as Sam sees it, is to teach the large bully about Sam's ability
to protect his brother: "I felt like I needed to let him know
that this guy [Sam's brother] had something—some protection
for him."

Sam tells us next about an earlier encounter, which he thinks
may be in large part responsible for his prejudice against Negroes, and against Black bullies in particular:

Subject: . . . Yeah. This was back when I was about sixteen,
              you know, had a hole down there, and we used to go
              down there and play pool all the time, me and this
              dude. And we were in the pool hall, that nigger in
              there, you know, and the dude was shooting next to
              me and he hit me with his cue, you know, not too
              accidentally, but, "get out of the way." And I was shoot-
              ing at the time, you know, and I took the cue, man,
              and jerked it out of his hand, and threw it on the floor,
              and we went at it. And, man, they broke it up and
              made us go outside and so we went out in the alley
              and I started punching him, man, I started wasting

him. And he pulled a blade on me and . . . , I still didn't feel any fear of him cause I was dumping him pretty good. So I jumped back, you know, man, and he got me, got my arm with a knife and then I got around there in back of him and we were wrassling around there and he got loose again and I went at him again, man, and he got me across the head through my hair up here and I panicked and ran. You know, I figured, "You win." That's all there was to it.

Interviewer: You were sixteen then, and how old are you now?

Subject: Twenty-six.

Interviewer: How well can you remember how you felt before? What were you doing that day?

Subject: We were just smoking a little weed and shooting pool, you know, jiving with the rest of them.

Interviewer: You were generally feeling good?

Subject: Yeah.

Interviewer: And then, this guy pushed it? Did you feel he was a bully or was he trying to roll over you, or how did you feel?

Subject: Yeah, and I felt it as a, more or less, Black–White thing. I felt that I belonged in there because I knew people in there and we got along real tight, you know.

Interviewer: Oh, you were saying it was a colored or a Negro pool hall and he was making as if you didn't belong in there? Any words exchanged?

Subject: Oh, I guess so, I can't remember, though.

Interviewer: Was there anything said before the time you went to shoot and he went to shoot too? Did he look at you, were you looking at him?

Subject: I don't think so, I can't remember. No, it was just one of these things, he was poking me, and, "Watch it, jitterbug." That kind of thing, you know, and I'm already bent over, set to shoot, you know.

Interviewer: He said, "Watch it, jitterbug?"

Subject: Yeah, something like that.

We see that even in this early fight, the incident starts with someone questioning Sam's right to consider himself "one of Them," and with a slighting, deprecatory allusion. Sam prides himself on the privilege of moving in relatively exclusive circles, and he finds this privilege abruptly challenged. To make matters worse, Sam discovers that he cannot successfully demonstrate his worth and that he must leave the battle scene badly defeated. (He returns later with a knife, but a friend convinces him to forego revenge.) The inability to meet the test of this conflict, and the necessity imposed on him to evacuate an arena in which he had felt accepted, easily lends credibility to his hypothesis that his racist sentiment could have originated in this fight. The incident, since it was unsuccessful, was undoubtedly traumatic.

Our interviewer tries to take Sam further back in time, and Sam recalls the first encounter that he views as memorable.

Subject: Yeah. The first fight that you could call it, that had
              any impression on me, was when I was thirteen in
              junior high school. And I was going to Kit Carson. You
              know that park they got by there? I always seemed to
              run with older people than me, for some reason, I don't
              know why. And I was running with these guys and
              they had some kind of open house over there at night
              time or something and everybody, you know, "Meet
              at the park, man," and we were drinking beer and all
              that shit. And these dudes from high school were over
              there with us, and I knew one of them, he lived a
              couple of doors from me and he was with his partner
              and they were bullying everybody and all that shit.
              And he was messing with this one dude, and this other
              guy that was with him told me to get down behind
              him, you know, and he was going to push him over,
              you know. So I got down behind him and he pushed
              the cat over me. And that was it, you know. The dude
              wanted to fight but the other dude said, "Leave them
              alone," you know, and all that. But the next day in
              school the sucker got me and we used the park at noon
              and all this, man, and I was panicked, you know, and

> so I was going to go regardless, you know, got to keep
> up with things. And I went over there at noon, man,
> and we fought, and he beat the f_____ out of me.
> And that was it, though, you know.

Interviewer: What sort of person was he?

Subject: Well, he was the typical sort of a guy like me, I guess,
except older, and trying to be a hoodlum, you know.

Here, again, Sam is associating with powerful persons who
might transfer some of their status to him. Again, Sam seeks
to behave like a Man, and as a result feels he must pass a test;
and he does not feel that his defeat was completely ignomi-
nious, because he thinks the test consisted of his willingness
to face discouraging odds, rather than of his victory over
them. A parallel with later incidents is the definition of the
opponent as a harassing bully, despite the fact that the precipitating action makes the definition dubious.

Sam is asked why he had to go to the park and face inevitable
defeat, and his response is revealing: "I'd come up from San
Francisco," he says, "and I wanted to be accepted by everybody." Our interviewer prods him with regard to this point:

Interviewer: Does that ring a bell? When you got to Vacaville and
when you got to Chino, is that the same thing?

Subject: Yeah, same thing. Acceptance. I felt I needed this acceptance.

Sam claims that the incident in the park also left a strong
impression on him and that it contributed to shaping his subsequent violent encounters. For one, he continues to be afraid
of his opponent and "was probably mad at myself for being
afraid." Second, he felt that the incident had turned him "into
a hoodlum":

Subject: . . . I was determined not to ever let that happen again.
I felt shame and all that, you kmow—all the girls
watching.

Interviewer: And that changed your life, more or less?

Subject: Yeah. I think right there that told me I had to prove something to people. I got to let them know that they can't walk on me. That I'm as good as they are, if not better. I know this was the changing point of my whole life, because I was a real studious person before this, and after this happened I started running with the more wilder crowds. The wilder the better, you know. And that's when my trouble started.

The incident in the park also has a sequel thirteen years later—partly, Sam tells us, as a result of the grudge carefully nurtured throughout the interval. At the time of this second incident, Sam is a member of a "tough" clique that at one time has included his opponent. He describes himself as a key figure.

Interviewer: What was your status with the clique? Were you one of the toughest dudes?

Subject: Well, if there was trouble someone would have to come and get me too, you know. They know I'd go with them.

Interviewer: Usually in a clique there are some dudes that are tougher than others, and if there's a beef, they're going to get him because this dude is a good fighter.[1]

Subject: I put up a pretty good front with those people I used to know; there was quite a few of them that I knew could take me, but I always had it there. They had doubt. I never fought them. All my friends, we used to run around with, we never fought. I would put this doubt on them all the time, protecting myself.

Interviewer: There are two things going. You were using the clique action to mask over the fear, and then you were also bluffing, would you say?

Subject: Right.

---

[1]This statement is an explanation addressed by one interviewer to the other.

Interviewer: Even amongst the clique itself, you were one of the toughest dudes?

Subject: Right.

Interviewer: Did this put any demands on you?

Subject: Yeah, because when the fight started, I was always the first one in it. And things like that. I would get to a point where a friend of mine would start a hassle and I would get in there with him and hit the guy before he could. Stuff like that, you know. Sure got some broken bones that way.

The return engagement Sam had been looking forward to takes the same, familiar form as his previous and subsequent conflicts. Sam is attached to people of some status; Sam is challenged by a person he can define as a "bully"; Sam redeems himself, consolidates his status in the group, and disposes of his opponent, whom he both fears and hates:

Subject: He got out of the service, and he was an insulting person. And I treated him nice, I talked to him nice. We'd run around and get drunk, you know, stuff like that, he was one of the clique again. But I never liked him because I knew he beat me and made me look bad when I was young. And one day we were sitting in there in the bar drinking, and he started it with me and threw a drink on me and I jumped on him then and beat the shit out of him. And everybody let me do it, nobody broke it up. And I felt pretty good after that, you know, an old debt paid.

Interviewer: What comments led up to his throwing a drink at you?

Subject: Oh, "Fuck you," and all that, you know. You'd try to talk to him, or something—I was trying to get him to settle down. He was talking that kind of language loud and there was people in the bar and everything. And this was a bar where most everyone knew me, and liked me, and I was really accepted here. Here was a group I was accepted in and wanted to belong to, not for a mask, but I felt I had friends there. Not just somebody to protect me or run with or hide with. And

> I felt I really had friends here, because if I had a prob-
> lem I could go in there and talk to them, and all that,
> and they'd tell me their problems.

Interviewer: This guy was insulting a home, then?

Subject: Right. He was insulting a home, he was insulting me
because he was breaking down everything I had built
up in here. As far as I was concerned, he was getting
out of hand. And I never actually really accepted him
since he'd come back, 'cause I never forgot.

The last incident in Sam's interview again involves a "bully,"
and the scene is a nightclub in which Sam is on intimate terms
with the owner. The bully in this incident is "drunk, loud-
mouthing and everything," and is being escorted out of the
establishment by Sam's patron. The man attacks Sam's influential friend, and Sam intervenes. The bully then turns on Sam
and attacks him with a broken pitcher. Sam stabs the bully
and leaves the scene.

As Sam reviews his incidents of violence, he sees them as
an effort to handle fear by displaying a "mask" of toughness.
He sees himself as going out of his way to arrange for tests
or demonstrations of his worth and his prowess.

Subject: . . . It was a way I could prove myself and give myself
confidence. Now, I think I would avoid any kind of
situation like that. And before, if I seen trouble, I would
get near it, not, more or less, into it, but near it, in
case it wanted to come my way. Because I felt I could
go over here. Test, you know.

Interviewer: You would say, now, that that was a similarity in your
pattern, that you would set yourself up so you could
fight in order to test yourself?

Subject: Right. I wouldn't go to the point of just getting myself
right into it, but I would be close enough, to where if
it did come to me, I would be right there.

Interviewer: You put yourself in a vulnerable position?

Subject: Vulnerable positions. Testing myself.

As we examine Sam's incidents of violence, we see that they

relate to each in several different but interlocking ways. First, there is a replication of precipitating stimuli: In almost every instance, Sam sees the other person as someone whose defeat can help achieve or consolidate his status and prestige. There are several sorts of people who can acquire this meaning for Sam. Among others, there are powerful people whose victory over Sam could convert Sam into a satellite or exploitee; there are smaller-status persons whose actions imply that Sam could be taken advantage of in small but symbolically significant ways; there are persons who directly challenge Sam's status, and individuals who claim recognition that could cut into Sam's empire; and there are people who stand in the way of Sam's powerful friends, who are viewed as opportunities to consolidate Sam's standing as a Loyal Supporter.

Every one of these potential enemies must take some action (or must appear to take some action) that Sam can define as an illegitimate claim. People who do not play this role are immune to Sam's violence: Powerful persons who permit Sam to be a minor partner, or powerless persons who are willing to remain passive have nothing to fear from Sam. It is only the person who makes a move toward Sam that Sam can define as challenging or encroaching who become stimuli to his violence. And they do so because they can be converted into proving grounds for the consolidation of Sam's worth, which is ratified by acceptance. In this fashion, almost every opponent can be substituted for every other opponent, and Sam's incidents of violence are repeat performances, with different actors playing essentially the same roles.

Sam's incidents are also, however, related to each other somewhat in the fashion in which rehearsals are related to subsequent performances. In every setting in which Sam demonstrates his worth through violence, he reinforces the premise that the road to self-esteem must be paved with defeated challengers. Curiously enough, this premise is strengthened by both success and failure; success indicates that violence works; failure signifies the need for further violence to achieve redemption; both assumptions are based on (and feed back into) the more fundamental premise that violence commands respect and that respect is the measure of personal worth.

Although fundamental assumptions such as these have their

origin in subcultural norms and in personal childhood experiences, they acquire shape through implementation. In the case of Sam, two unhappy first encounters focused his suspicion and dislike on specific people and categories of people as sources of possible humiliation and challengers of his worth. On the other hand, it is clear that Sam is mistaken in attributing his violent involvements to such experiences, in view of the fact that all the elements associated with Sam's later incidents are already present in his very first ones.

The relationship among incidents within a violence-prone pattern is thus one in which premises are shared, and in which the documentation is gradually accumulated. The premises relate to the role of other people as impediments or aids to the achievement of one's objectives, and to the way in which these aids and impediments should be handled. The documentation has it that violence does the job.

4

The Intersection of Perspectives of Violence

Every conflict between two parties is in reality two conflicts: one, the contest which is seen by the aggressor, and the other, the situation perceived by the victim. These different perspectives often represent systematic divergencies in the way the world in general is viewed and approached. They tell us as much about the person as they do about the events being described. And in the case of violence, they can often reveal who contributed what to bringing the conflict to culmination.

Games That Go Sour in the Night

As a first illustration, we shall examine an incident that begins with a disgruntled policeman who has been ordered to investigate reports of firecracker explosions. The time is dusk, and the sequence is initiated near a school building, where the officer sees what appears to be "the figure of a man" sitting on a bench in the playground. The officer decides to investigate, stops his car, and begins to approach the sitting shadow. The latter happens to be a Black teenager, of solid middle-class family. The boy relates what happens next:

> So he said, "What are you doing here?"
> I said, "I was just sitting here."
> So he says, "Come around here."
> So the set-up was that there was a long fence, and I was

sitting right in the middle of it. . . . So he said, "Come all the way around," and I said, "I was on my way toward home."

So he said he wanted to talk to me. So I said, "Well, I haven't done anything wrong. I'll tell you my name if you tell me what I did wrong."

So he goes to the car and says something about a youth or a man into the radio—such-and-such a street what we were on. And then he comes back, and he says, "Look, I don't want any trouble from you." And I said, "Look, I don't want any trouble either."

So he walked to one end, to the opposite side of the fence; so I started walking in the other direction, up to the end of the bench about ten or fifteen feet. So, he walks up that way and I walk back the other way. So he says, "Listen here, I don't want any trouble from you." I said, "I don't want any trouble either. Just tell me what I did wrong and we can talk. I haven't done anything wrong."

So he gets into his car and he drives up to one end of the fence. And all of a sudden, I'm thinking to myself, you know, "this is a dumb cop" . . . So I started running to the other end of the playground and I yelled to him, "You'll never catch me this way."

It is obvious that the policeman is perceived as arbitrary in his demands, and that he mobilizes a stubborn, resentful response in the young man. The youth brings into play a pattern of aggressive playfulness designed to produce an evening's amusement out of the incident. How does the officer respond to this game? We must turn to the officer's version of the encounter for an answer to this question. The officer tells us,

He gets up off the bench and he turns around, and at this point I think he's either under the influence of alcohol or dope or something, 'cause he's got a goofy, dreamy look about him, and he gives me a little cynical laugh, and backs up on his feet facing me, with the fence between us, and he says, "Come on in and get me." Well, at this point I was ready to go in and get him.

There's two gates. It's a block long, and one's at the west end of the school, and the other at the east end of the school. I'd walk west, he would walk east; I'd walk east, he'd walk west; and we played this little game for about three or four minutes. And I finally walked over to my car with my one eye on him, and I grabbed the horn, and told them that I needed another unit there, I had somebody in the school yard who refused to identify himself or to come out. So I heard them dispatch a unit out there, and I turned to put the mike back, and I saw him walking fast away from me, which would be north across the school yard.

So I get in the car and I blast up to the west end of the yard. I ran through the gate; he saw me and changed his course and he ran out east, through the gate, and slammed it as he was running down the road, and he was laughing like crazy, you know. And I hear him yell something about, "You're going to die," or some stupid thing. Well, I'm out the gate, and he's gone, you know, it's very obvious to me that I'm never going to apprehend him, he was running like a deer.

So, now, my vehicle is a block away, so I run back to my vehicle, get on the radio and I told them that there was a possible 50–50 loose, which is from the Welfare and Institution Code, referring to a person that is mentally unbalanced. He had yelled something that in my opinion was a possible threat to my life, and I think that we should get somebody up there and flush him out before he hurts somebody.

We note that the officer feels that he must persevere after having made his opening move. He copes with the boy's playful response by convincing himself that he is faced with a raving, dangerous lunatic. He also concludes that his opponent must be speedily curbed. This fact has consequences in the next scene of drama. Here the young man—who could have easily made his escape—instead decides to return to renew his interaction with the officer, which he regards as entertaining. The officer, unfortunately, does not. The following description of his second encounter with the boy reveals the grimness of his view:

. . . I'm walking at him like this, you know, talking to him because I honestly believe at this point that the guy is a nut. . . . But, anyway, I told him, "Look, kid, now, I don't want to chase you. Come back." I estimated his age at this time at about 19 years old. He was 16. He says, "Look, man, what do you want me for? I didn't do anything." Well, I says, "Look, if I have to chase you, there's going to be a real problem. You might as well come over here." And he's still backing away, only now he's taking a few bigger steps. And I guess I'm about as close as from here to the cabinet, five or six feet. So, then I come out with, "Now look, I don't want to shoot you." Which was the classic statement. I didn't have my revolver out, and I would never have taken it out 'cause naturally a misdemeanor (refusal to identify, 647E of the Penal Code) is certainly no grounds. But it did shock him enough, so that he stopped and said, "What do you mean, shoot me?" And when he stopped I grabbed him by the right arm. I got sort of a half-nelson on him, and I'm walking him back to the car, and I says, "Look, you get in the car." And then the beef starts. He comes out with, "Get your hands off me, you [obscenity], I'm not getting in no police car." And the beef's on. The kid was big, and I don't mind telling you, he gave me one hell of a hassle; we were all over the street.

We see that the officer has parlayed himself into a state of concern such that he loses his equanimity, and even offers to shoot the boy. He then attempts to physically control the dangerous monster he has mentally created, all the while continuing to exaggerate the magnitude of the opposition. This new development presents the boy with a somewhat different type of playmate from the "Dumb Cop" whom he had originally tackled. The dawning of this discovery is traced for us in the boy's version of the return engagement:

. . . Here he comes flying down the hill; he almost hits me; he stops the car; he jumps out, and I back away. He says, "Now, listen here, you nut," or something like that, and he says, "If you run or try to get away again, I'm going to shoot you." Well, I have a fairly good knowledge of the law, and I know that you have to have done a felony or he can't shoot you. And I hadn't done a felony or anything. And he says, "Come get into the car and we'll talk." So, I knew right then and there that that was a lie, right there. First of all, he wants to talk, now he wants to get me into the car. I said, "No, I'm not going to get into the car unless you tell me what I did wrong." Then he keeps trying to ask me my name. I wasn't going to tell him my name or anything, unless I could get some understanding why he wants me.

So he starts coming toward me, and I can't run 'cause he'll shoot me, so I just stood there. So he comes up, runs up to me, and he jumps on me. You know, he doesn't have—you know, he just overpowers me and gets me into a full-nelson. Well, right then and there I knew it was hopeless to run or try to get away; so, you know, naturally your body's going to tense up when somebody grabs you. So I told him, "Let me go. I'm going to go over to the car and let's talk." In the meantime he's really struggling with me and I'm trying to tell him to let me go, I'm willing to talk. All of a sudden he gets this attitude that I'm strong. "Strong as a horse" his exact words. He said, "He's strong as an ox (or horse)."

The tables have turned, and it is now the boy who perceives the officer as irrational. In fact, later in the interview he refers to the point of his return engagement as an experience of discovery. He tells us,

> . . . I was feeling pretty good right then cause I figured, "This cop, he's dumb. I haven't done anything wrong, I should give him trouble; he was giving me trouble, I should give me trouble." But, then, after he grabbed me, I says, "Oh, no. This can't be, it's all over now. We're through playing games, I have to talk to him, now. He means business."

At this juncture, both participants are suffused with panic, and as a result have become unable to transact business with each other. Whereas the boy feels ready to throw in the sponge, the officer conceives of himself as engaged in a desperate fight to subdue him. The lines of communication, such as they were, are now nonexistent. We turn to the officer's description of the final debacle:

> . . . So, then I really start putting the heat on him. And he starts bucking a little bit. All you can hear out of him,

"You're choking me." See, but he's starting to slow down a little bit. So I figure, well this is it. Boy, I'm getting tired, I'm either going to have to do him in now, or forget about it. So, I gave it all I had and finally put the kid on the ground. . . . As I recall, I had exerted so much strength that my left arm, I couldn't even unfold my hand the muscles were so cramped up. . . . And this is what it took to get the kid down. And he's put into the car.

So far, we have seen how two persons' perspectives may intersect to produce violence, but we have not yet shown that these persons may have reacted typically. In order to illustrate this point, consider the following incident involving the same officer, at a time when the latter was custodian of a police paddy wagon. The officer has recalled an incident involving a prisoner who had been arrested for prowling:

He didn't give the reporting officer, the arresting officer, any trouble whatsoever, completely cooperative. Quiet, hard-working man, type-thing over-all. Obviously from his hands, you know, the man worked. I opened the door of the patrol car; we got to the wagon, and I says, "All right, step out of the car," I said, "Put your hands up on the back of the wagon." "What for?" "I want to search you." "I haven't got anything on me," and he starts to go into the wagon. I've got one side open and I pulled him back, and I said, "You're going to be searched." Naturally, anybody that gets in my car, now, is searched, and I don't care if he has been searched fifty thousand times, you know, exaggerating a bit. If he's getting in my car, when I'm inside with him, he's going to be searched. This is a common good safety practice. That's it.

He refuses to put his hands up on the back of the wagon. So I grabbed his big right paw and I slap it up on the back of the wagon, and my partner's got the other one, and we searched him. He's not struggling. He's jerking a little bit, but it's all for the crowd, which is about 30 strong now. You know, shucking and jiving individuals, teenagers. I said, "All right, get in the wagon and sit up front." He turns around and he has one step on the wagon. He steps up on it, and he says "What?" "Get in the wagon and sit down up front," you know. If we have to stop fast and somebody's in the back, it's kind of painful, you know. He turns around and he says, "You make me get in." This is typical. . . . Anyway, he turns around facing me up on this one step and I say, "All right, now, get in." I'm going to push him back and close the door. The man is immense, and I don't particularly want to fight him. At this point, he grabbed me by my badge and my shirt, and yanks me, and I went right over the top step and right into the wagon. We're both inside now. In fact, both my shins were skinned, in that I didn't step on the step, I went right over the top of it. And the beef's on. All I want to do is get out of that wagon. . . . I'm like one of those rubber balls on the end of a paddle, because he's throwing me around like nothing, you know. . . . So, finally, I gave a big yank, like this, and he comes in on top of me, and I whack my head on the lock up on the front of the wagon, and I can feel the blood trickling down my neck. So I figured, "Fellow, the hell with you." I was mad—angry, I don't think I was mad. My head was split open. I put the wood on him as much as I could.

It would appear that the officer is again persevering in the face of danger signals; that his relative inflexibility and tendency to push people again produce a confrontational situation; that he sees himself again as a giant-killer, and that he again resorts to extreme force in a moment of panic. To complete the parallel, consider the brief after-play which occurred several minutes later, while the wagon was under way.

. . . So we're going in, and he says, "White fella, someday you're going to be alone on that street, and I'm going to kill you." And I tell him, "Mr. Smith, I'm going to put one right through the middle of your head." Not ashamed to admit it. Cold, hard facts. Mr. Smith can break my arms off and serve them to his family for dinner if he wants to, and I won't fight him again; I'll kill him first.

The other of our two contenders, the boy who had assaulted this officer, has been expelled from several schools, in every case for fights involving serious damage to other children. Typically these fights started with persistent harassment of an opponent, in a cumulatively degenerating game.

Concerning the incident with the officer, the boy expresses the view that the responsibility for this conflict would have to be shared. On the one hand, he describes the officer as a "pretty tense guy." At the station "he got us in this room together, and he was writing everything up; and he comes in, and he gets his cup of coffee. He's kind of shaky, and you could see his neck muscles were all tense and everything, and he says, 'If you'd just told me your name and everything, this never would have happened!' The boy remarks that the officer is "still trying to get something out of me. He's stubborn; he's going to have to change." At the same time, the boy admits, "I guess I wasn't flexible either, and that's the main thing that happened."

The boy summarizes at least part of the pattern of his own violent involvements as follows:

Subject: They're always the same. Like the one I got into with the policeman was a matter of communication. He accused me of doing something wrong. I wanted to know what I did wrong, and he wanted to know my name. Both stubborn, we—neither of us wanted to give in.

And curiously enough, if the officer could describe his own pattern of violence, he would probably provide the same type of characterization. Our incident thus represents a collision between two organisms of very similar construction.

Out of the Bushes and Into the Frying Pan

Late one night, a call goes out over the police radio summoning several units to the scene of a noisy party. The celebration is taking place in a recessed valley, surrounded by parking lots and heavily trafficked roads. Officer Rains is the first to respond to the call. He relates,

Upon arriving on the scene I take the high road, turning off the lights on the police car and got out, turned down my radio, and got out of the car and looked down into this little valley and there was approximately, oh, to the best of my recollection, about twelve to eighteen juveniles there, in their late teens—eighteen, nineteen, and in their twenties. And they had, they had these big gallons of Gallo wine jugs and they were drinking and playing on the bongos. It was a group of male Negroes, male Indians, male Mexicans, and male Whites. And there was both female and male. And the girls were scantily dressed, like they were having a pretty good orgy going on down there. And I get back on the radio and call for cover. So they block off the other side of the park so that we can make, shall we say, an adequate raid on the group.

Having assessed the situation, Officer Rains embarks on a one-man operation, which brings him into contact with young Gomer Smith, who is leaving the scene of the festivities:

Well, I get out of the police car after I call for cover and I head towards a stairway coming up from this little valley. And I'm behind a bush and I see a subject coming up the hill, staggering, and it looks to me like the subject is very intoxicated and I just waited and remained silent till the subject got, you know, got approximately ten, fifteen feet away from me, and I put the flashlight on him and tell him to stop and I've got him in a state of fright. And I put the flashlight on myself so he knows who it is, that it's a police officer, and the first thing that comes out is, "What the fuck do you want, cop?" And I tell him he's under arrest for 647E, for being drunk and also disturbing the peace.

Officer Rains, at this point, has a prisoner on his hands, and he is worried about protecting the secrecy of the impending raid. He is also concerned about the possibility of a riot. Meanwhile the prisoner is giving every indication of wanting to escape, and of being willing to override the objection of his captor. Officer Rains is, therefore, keeping one eye on the crowd, and another on his charge:

. . . And at this time, I get a glance out of my eye where he's standing up and he's coming towards me and he takes a swing at me. And as he takes a swing, using his weight, I grab his arm, and I flip him right down on his back and

> I pile on top of him. And I've got my hand underneath his chin like a semi, oh, throttle to keep his mouth shut so the group won't come up there. And I've got a hammerlock on him and I put the handcuffs on him, and all of a sudden, "What the fuck are you doing? Don't hurt me, I quit, I give, I give."

Officer Rains has met his prisoner's effort to escape with substantial force, and as a result has him securely in custody. Unfortunately, the scuffle has alarmed the celebrants in the valley, and most of them have scattered to safety.

The officer's prisoner, in the interim, feels that he has been subjected to a sudden, unprovoked, arbitrary, and brutal attack. He describes his own reaction as an instinctive response to a physical assault, as well as an expression of his desire to be elsewhere:

Interviewer: You were just walking through the park minding your own business, you say?

Subject: That's right.

Interviewer: Did [the officer] say anything? He didn't say one word?

Subject: He just came out.

Interviewer: What was the first thing he said?

Subject: Jumped out and tried to grab me, so I tried to run, myself. Started kicking me when he had the handcuffs on me.

Interviewer: You were trying to get away, you say?

Subject: Yeah, I wasn't going to stay there.

Interviewer: Was he a uniformed officer?

Subject: Yeah. Blue uniform. I didn't know who in the hell it was first.

Interviewer: So first, you didn't know he was an officer?

Subject: First I didn't, no.

Interviewer: But it became quickly obvious that he was an officer, cause he had this uniform and badge?

Subject: Yeah.

Interviewer: At what stage do you think you may have hit him?

Subject: I don't know, my reflexes, you know. . . . When some-
             one jumps on you, you know. Before some guys tried
             to jump out and scare me, I just reflex. Natural reflexes.
             You just jump up and start hitting them. I don't know.
             It happened so quick.

On the surface, this relatively mild encounter would appear
to contain its own adequate explanation for the conflict. A
young man is taken by surprise and he panics; an officer feels
compelled to use force to retain a prisoner in custody. Of
course, we are not precisely sure why the officer decided to
endanger a major raid in order to take an innocuous-looking
prisoner, and it is not entirely clear why the young man did
not resign himself to his fate. But we can chalk up these details
to human error and to impulse.

In order to arrive at a less situation-bound explanation of
the interaction, we can draw on the past records of our contenders, which contain incidents of a similar nature. In the
case of the officer, for instance, we discover that he has been
repeatedly assaulted, and that the precipitating events have
invariably been relatively minor. The following incident, for
example, is one such case. The officer is sitting in his parked
car, and

> . . . I'm taking a statement from a victim of a vicious armed
> robbery. He was hog-tied and stabbed. Bleeding. And I had
> a complainant or a witness who I was taking a statement
> from. We transported the victim to the hospital via the
> ambulance and I was, or the witness was, in the back seat
> of the patrol car, and I was gathering the information about
> the incident. I had one friendly witness at the scene who
> would talk, nobody else would talk or tell me a thing that
> happened about the incident.
>
> And I was taking a statement from this gentleman and a
> group of approximately six male Negroes went by several
> times, yelling obscenities toward me or towards a police
> officer in general, like, "Look at that fucking cop; hey, dude,
> let's get that dude; hey, look at that motherfucker over there

talking to that fink." And this went on for several minutes after four or five passes. And I decided about this time that some action should be taken.

So, I called what I thought was the ring leader, or the one instigating all this over to the patrol car, with negative results. So I got out of the patrol car and went over to this one subject, whose name I believe was J_____ G_____. Well, right away I get a bunch of static from him like, "Fuck you, cop; what do you want, cop," and all this noise, as I'm trying to get some information out of him . . . the name, whereabouts. . . . So I take him along with two other male Negroes because three of them split the scene right away; they ran. I made them kneel down beside the patrol car.

I tested to get on the radio, and the witness in the back seat of the patrol car was a little anxious and excited about other people being around, and I just ignored him. I was more concerned about these three subjects who I placed under arrest before I brought them to the police car for profanity and disturbing the peace.

Again, a major operation is in process, in the sense that the officer is securing information from an important witness about an important crime. His attention shifts to a group of teenagers who (he feels) are casting aspersions on the police force, and he decides that "some action" should be taken. The action he takes is drastic, but not overly effective. Two of his three prisoners escape, his important witness is no longer interested in testifying, and Officer Rains becomes obsessed with the need to retain his one remaining charge:

Subject: . . . He was about ready to make his exit, and I latched on to him.

Interviewer: He started to run and you grabbed him?

Subject: He started up to run.

Interviewer: How did you grab him?

Subject: I grabbed him. . . . I just grabbed him, I don't know how.

Interviewer: On the shoulder or around . . . ?

Subject: I think it was the neck. I don't know if I had him by his clothes, but a struggle started to ensue and finally I got a hammer lock on the subject and I dragged him back to the police car. . . .

Again, the officer has felt compelled to do something physically extreme to retain what little is left of the self-defeating and embarrassing situation he has created. This sequence becomes more obvious as the situation creates additional pressure and embarrassment. Now, the officer's reaction becomes almost bizarre:

Subject: . . . And then the crowd started gathering. Maybe twelve male Negroes were in the crowd, and there were people looking out of the windows, and there was a shouting match going on back and forth and J., the one I had the arm lock on, started saying, "Let's get this dude, get this cop." Well, I started to get a little more scared or afraid and I started to put a little more pressure on the boy's arm and he started yelling for a little more assistance and his brother came up and attempted to grab J. away from me. And I was backed completely into the back seat of the patrol car, with J. right in front of me. So I put out my foot and I give a thrust out, and I kicked, I think it was J.'s brother, right in the chest, knocking him back approximately, oh, halfway across the street. And I told him if he came anymore, I'd break his brother's arm.

Officer Rains, it seems, is prone to take precipitous action in the face of short-term provocations, at the expense of more serious business. He also acts in pursuit of evanescent goals, and he resorts to violence in awkward efforts to extricate himself from impossible situations of his own making. A third illustration may make the pattern even clearer: Officer Rains is on patrol, and he encounters a group of teenagers who excite his curiosity. He recognizes one member of the group, and he therefore feels that it would be easy to ask a few routine questions. He asks them, and a girl belonging to the group objects:

Interviewer: So, really, you wanted to stop and talk to them because there was at least one guy you knew and you wanted to talk to him about the situation?

Subject: Right.

Interviewer: The girl immediately starts to say some profanity about you?

Subject: Right. I asked her, I said, "Hold on a minute, I want to talk to you." And she says, "Fuck you, cop," and this was the straw that broke the camel's back.

Interviewer: Well, what do you think about when somebody says that?

Subject: You can't take it personally. This is something that— you know, I'm called so many names out there, and your own vocabulary is, turns into . . . you're a garbage mouth really because you're with it, you talk their language, and so, this doesn't bother me. But this was something—well, this was a personal affront to general law enforcement authority. I knew this girl before. No respect for her parents, a pure incorrigible, and so this is the straw that broke the camel's back. She was going. . . .

Interviewer: So at this time you get out of the car and you say, "You're under arrest."

Subject: Right.

Again, there is a relatively minor provocation (profanity directed at the police force, as Officer Rains sees it), and his response is to proceed to an immediate arrest. The problem is that the girl he has arrested takes one look at the police car and decides that she does not want to go to jail:

Interviewer: Now when she gets to the car, she decides that she isn't going in?

Subject: Right.

Interviewer: And is she saying anything at this time?

Subject: She's just saying she's not going in. She's not going to go downtown.

Interviewer: Are you saying anything to her?

Subject: I can't recall, but I think I was saying, "Yes, you are." And I mean, it was just a . . .

Interviewer: Sort of a Mexican standoff?

Subject: Yeah.

Interviewer: So you're trying to push her in various ways to try to trip her up so she'll go in, and these don't seem to work out so well.

Subject: I'm trying to play it as cool as possible, mainly because of the crowd that had already gathered.

Interviewer: What would you have done if there wasn't a crowd there?

Subject: I wouldn't have played around. She would have gone. I would have put her in the way I did the last time, no and's, if's or but's about it. If you have a crowd, you have to play with the crowd and public opinion.

The officer again feels compelled to use force in order to follow through on the difficult situation he has concocted, but the force is comparatively mild because of the presence of witnesses. The girl is finally convinced—not by the officer, but by her friends—to get into the squad car. But as she sits watching the officer write his report, the arbitrariness and seriousness of the predicament, as she sees it, make her extremely angry. She reacts by leaning over the front seat of the car and tearing out the microphone. The officer becomes aware of the fact that the situation is now out of his control, and he becomes alarmed:

Subject: . . . I get ahold of the mike, and the mike's laying on the front floor of the car and she's got the box (my report box) and has got ahold of that, and I'm trying to keep that down . . . she's throwing everything out of the box, the penal code, all my reports, there was maybe 400 pieces of paper and assignment cards, ticket book, everything went out of the car piece by piece. And she started to swear at this time, "I'm not going," and I was a great distance away from the car . . .

Interviewer: You said she was getting mad here; she's not insane, she's mad?

Subject: She been had.

Finally, he subdues the girl, but not before he himself has sustained serious injury, and not before considerable reinforcements have had to arrive to aid him. Again, his role in the promotion of violence has been to take sudden action against a person emotionally unprepared for this type of contingency. And again, he resorts to violence when he is faced with the helpless rage of his victim.

But what of our friend Gomer Smith, Officer Rains' opponent in the first incident we described? Smith, we may recall, had tried to make a precipitous exit when he saw Officer Rains emerge from the bushes. When the officer moved to detain him, Smith lashed out at the officer, claiming that his "reflexes" had gained the upper hand. Smith has had several violent encounters in his career. He recalls one, for instance, which took place one evening while he was walking home with his fiancée:

Subject: . . . We were walking down 14th Avenue and these guys drove by and started calling my broad a whore, and so I picked up a coke bottle and threw it at 'em and they stopped. And they jumped out and just, you know, starting firing on me, so I started fighting back. And I knocked one down and two jumped back, and I picked up a paper rack and broke it over their heads.

Interviewer: Over their heads, or one of them?

Subject: Yeah. I started hitting them with the rack and then they split. The guy lay there and I just walked away and left him there.

As in the incident with the police officer, Smith here sees himself the subject of an unprovoked assault by superior forces. This aspect of the situation, he maintains, makes him especially angry:

Interviewer: You must have been pretty mad when you picked up the paper rack.

Subject: Well, I . . . one against three.

The same theme of battling against unprovoked aggression by "bullies" runs through a fight Gomer Smith had in a prison yard one afternoon:

Subject: We's standing by the barracks. Wait a minute. This colored guy, you know. ... . He's been cutting in line on me at lunch and stuff, you know.

Interviewer: Always in front of you?

Subject: Yeah, I didn't give . . . I didn't care, you know. But this one time he come in, right in the door and he try to smart off to somebody, you know. Like he was a big tough one, you know. So he just runs up to me and called me "fat boy" or some shit, you know. So I just hauled off and hit him. Some of his partners were there.

Interviewer: Did he say anything else?

Subject: No.

Interviewer: Had he said anything before to you?

Subject: Naw.

Interviewer: But he had bothered you? He had cut in?

Subject: Yeah.

Interviewer: Now, at the time that he said "fat boy" . . . were there a lot of people standing around?

Subject: Yeah.

Interviewer: How did you feel them?

Subject: Just got pissed off, you know. I don't like people to push me around, that's all.

Here Smith is quite explicit about the fact that the main precipitant of violence for him is an effort by anyone, especially a person who conceives of himself as having status, to use him unfairly. Smith sees this kind of thing in the episode with Officer Rains, as well as in other incidents:

Interviewer: . . . You say you don't like people pushing you around or that you hit this guy because he was pushing you around. You feel the same way about officers?

Subject: Yeah.

Interviewer: Did you feel the same way about these three guys that came along and hollered at you while you were walking with your girl?

Subject: Yeah. I felt the same.

Interviewer: Have you felt the same way in the other fights you've had? That people were pushing you around and you got in a fight with them because you want to stop them pushing you?

Subject: Yeah.

In our interview, we asked Smith whether he could recall having had any fights in his life that were not due to someone "pushing him around." He responded that he had been involved in some acts of violence in efforts to help his friends, and he cited the following illustration:

Subject: Like see, one time up in the park, these three guys walked through the park, you know, four of them. . . . And they were drunk, you know, and they stuck one of my friends' little brother's face in the water, you know. And so my two friends, the two brothers, you know, this little kid, they were walking through the park looking for him. I was sitting up on the hill with my girl friend, you know, and I saw them fighting, so I just went down and helped them.

Again, we note, the opponent is a person who can be defined as abusive and the object of the game is to try to counter unwarranted abuse.

The interaction between Officer Rains and Gomer Smith is thus a familiar situation for both contenders. Officer Rains, whose contribution to the incident is probably the major one, reacted to Smith as he routinely reacts to people whom he views as irritants. Smith, on the other hand, categorized the officer's action in a class (which generally provokes him to violence) of unfair harassment by an arbitrary aggressor. The incident, therefore, represents the collision of two violence-prone modes of response to violence-prone modes of provocation—each characteristic of the man involved.

A Question of Manhood and Honor

Sometimes the response of two parties to each other is such that it inevitably produces reciprocal misconceptions. Each person comes to see the other as representing what he views as hateful or threatening or humiliating or fear-inspiring. As a result, he reacts negatively, and the other person reciprocates, which reinforces the original preconception. The confrontation that finally takes place is between two symbols rather than between two real people. The following arrest report described an episode which represents an encounter of this type.

> Arresting Officers responded to a call of a family fight. Upon arrival, suspect was in front of his home. Arresting Officers attempted to talk with suspect to find the cause of the disturbance. Suspect was very belligerent and obnoxious. Suspect had hands in the coat pocket of a long overcoat. Arresting Officers were exercising courtesy and patience. Suspect would not even tell Arresting Officer his name, age, or anything. Arresting Officers asked suspect to remove his hands from the pockets. Suspect told Arresting Officers, "I don't have to tell you shit and I don't have to take my hands out of my pockets." Suspect was ordered to take his hands from his pockets and show what he had in his pockets. Because of the attitude of the suspect and the nature of the call, Arresting Officers felt it was imperative that suspect remove his hands and so suspect was again ordered to remove his hands. Suspect restated, "I don't have to do shit." Arresting Officers were forced to force the suspect to remove his hands. In doing so suspect struggled and resisted and had to be forced into police vehicle. Suspect willfully delayed and obstructed Arresting Officers while

attempting to discharge their duties by refusing to remove his hands and refusing to give name or any identification. After being placed in police vehicle, Suspect screamed, "You white m_____f_____s, etc." Suspect was ordered to cease the screaming and he only screamed that much louder. Suspect would not quiet down and Arresting Officers had to get in the back seat with the suspect when he further resisted and again force had to be used. Suspect then stopped screaming and yelling profane language such as "m_____ f_____ etc., etc., etc." And only talked, did not scream. Suspect still refused and resisted by not giving name, birthdate, etc., and would only reply with more abusive language, stating he "Did not have to give you shit." Threatened to urinate on the seat if he were not allowed to get out of the patrol car. During the entire time the suspect kept threatening Arresting Officers by saying, "Me and my Black Brothers will get you. If I go to jail for anything, Oakland will burn just like Watts. We have plans for Oakland, Richmond, Marin City, and all those. Me and my Muslin Brothers will get you, Whitey."

Two officers were present in the incident, but only one became involved in physical conflict. The report was written by this person, and as a result it is as much of a subjective history as it is an objective account. The officer covered the same episode informally in our interview, and here again he stressed the extent to which he preclassified his opponent as soon as he found him sitting in the front seat of his car:

Subject: . . . He said, "I'm on private property, you can't do anything to me." And I asked him if he'd step out of the car, we just wanted to talk to him, see if we could find some answers to this. And so he got out of the car and he had on a long trench coat, rain coat, and he stuck his hands in the pockets of this trench coat. And he constantly kept saying, "You can't do anything to me, I'm on private property." And his attitude bothered me a little bit, so I asked him if he'd take his hands out of his pockets.

Interviewer: In what way did it bother you?

Subject: Well, it bothered me in the way that I thought he would become more irritable, and I wanted to see his hands. I felt that his hands in his pockets were a threat to me.

Interviewer: You felt he possibly had a weapon?

Subject: Yes. I had no idea what he had in his pockets and his attitude was such that I figured that he might be carrying a weapon. So I said, "Would you take your hands out of your pockets, please." And he says, "Why, you think I have a gun or a knife?" I says, "Well, you take your hands out of your pockets, there's no question about it, don't even have to bother with it." He says, "I'm not going to take them out." And I said, "Take your hands out of your pockets, 'cause I want to see your hands." He told me he wasn't going to take them out and he kept his hands in his pockets and he moved them towards me and so I told him one more time, I said, "Take your hands out of your pockets." And he said something like, "Make me, you can't make me, I'm on private property, you can't do anything to me." So I felt that with his attitude this way, I felt that it was imperative that I take the man's hands out of his pockets. So I grabbed one arm and my partner grabbed the other arm and we pulled his hands out of his pockets and he started to fight. So we wrestled him and I got him in an arm lock and we took him across and put him in the back seat of the patrol car. At this time we decided that we were going to arrest him for interfering with an officer, not resisting, but interfering, because he was obstructing us in doing our duties. We felt that we had to see his hands. So we put him in the back seat of the patrol car and he went wild. He was sliding back and forth across the seat and kicked the glass and beat on it with his hands and screamed.

Interviewer: Was he screaming when you took his hands out of his pockets?

Subject: He just kept saying that we couldn't do it, he was on private property.

Interviewer: But you did do it. Was he abusive at all at this time?

Subject: Well, he became abusive as we took hold of him.

In this description, we see that the officer becomes irritated by what he views as unforgivable defiance of his authority ("his attitude bothered me") and on this basis classifies the man as a troublemaker.[1] This category implies the type of person who is likely to become more troublesome, and who therefore must be neutralized ("I thought he would become more irritable. . . . I felt that his hands in his pockets were a threat to me"). The officer becomes stern and inflexible ("You take your hands out of your pockets, there is no question about it"), and when this produces no results, his stereotype of the man becomes reinforced. He also seems to feel that at this stage he must assert police authority at all cost ("I felt that it was imperative that I take the man's hands out of his pockets"), and must use physical force. It is at this juncture—and only at this juncture—that the civilian becomes violent.

When the civilian's violent reaction occurs, the officer sees it as directed, not at himself, but at the police force, and at the institution of law and order; he also sees himself as the target of a one-man Black nationalist riot. This conception emerges in a description of the prisoner's behavior after he was transferred into the wagon:

Subject: He screamed all the time and it was all vile, vulgar language and it was all directed at the White mother-fucking police. And how come we were all so stupid, and didn't any of us have any education. That policemen in Berkeley were much better policemen because they had two years of college and that he was going to get his Black brothers and they were going to burn Oakland and . . .

Interviewer: He just had all sorts of general suggestions?

---

[1] This initial premise has been identified as the prototypical motive for police assaults of civilians. See W. A. Westley, *Violence and the Police* (Cambridge, MA: MIT Press, 1970); P. Chevigny, *Police Power* (New York: Pantheon, 1969); A. J. Reiss, Jr., *The Police and the Public* (New Haven, CT: Yale University Press, 1971).

Subject: Social reforms.

Interviewer: All right, now, you just think that he's trying to cause trouble. At any time along the line are you worried about this developing, besides the immediate problem of handling him? You don't see any problems?

Subject: No indication from the crowd in the street, but I don't doubt for a minute that he's going to do it. He mentioned several times that he was a Black Muslim and that he was going to get his Black brothers and that I would be the first one that they got. His abuse was more directed at me than at my partner and he said that he'd find out where I lived and he'd burn my place and he'd get me.

This same conception of the issue, as one of a physical contest involving status, honor, and the social role of the police, becomes explicit in more general discussion of civilian–police confrontations:

Subject: I feel that it couldn't be personal. The guy doesn't know me. Chances are very slim that I've ever seen him before. I probably don't know him from Adam, so I can't possibly feel that it's personal to me. It's directed at law and order, at . . . not justice. . . . Things, today, are growing so that the trend is, rather than correct a man when he's done something wrong, is to tell him that he's done something wrong, don't do it again. I can remember when I was a kid, if you talked to a police officer like I've been talked to, you would either wind up in the hospital or your folks would have you down at the jail and find out why. Now, I'm not saying that you should got out and beat up all the citizens, but I'm saying only that the respect for law enforcement is gone, not diminishing, it's gone. There is no respect for law enforcement at all.

The officer feels that the ideal solution for police–community problems is a physical fitness training program during which officers would learn to inspire physical respect among the civilians they encounter:

Subject: The goals of this kind of program would be, like I say, physical fitness and mental fitness, which would give a guy confidence. This is one thing that makes people aggressive. They lack the confidence; they don't feel that they can handle a situation. They feel inadequate to handle a situation when a guy fights with them. Some of the guys come on like they've never had a fight. They don't know how to handle themselves. Where it's knock the guy down or you'll get knocked down, it's not necessarily size that counts, or muscle. We have a lot of guys that are health fanatics, who lift weights; don't do anything else. And I think if a person checks, he'll find out that weight-lifters wind up on the injured list possibly more than anybody else because their muscles are not tooled for running, stretching, wrestling, or anything else. They're toned for lifting and I feel that maybe weight-lifting should be a part of this program, but it should be, as I say, a part of it, not the complete program. I really feel that this would build a man's confidence, it would also build his appearance. We wouldn't have so many officers who couldn't handle a situation because they're just not physically capable of handling it.

The other officer involved in our incident also seems to feel that the turning point in the interaction occurred when physical force was used on the civilian. Force was used when the suspect's hands were removed from his pockets, and it was employed again when the arresting officer slapped his prisoner unjustifiably in order to quiet him down:

Subject: He started yelling in the car. He was quiet before, hadn't been loud, although he had refused to cooperate. There's a lot of people, and he is yelling so loud that M. told him to be quiet. We wanted to keep the situation a littler bit calmer, had handcuffed him, and we finally ended up uh . . . M. had gone back and slapped him, not hard. Slapped him, trying to calm him down in the back seat, and he was yelling even louder. So we finally ended up taking him down to get him away from the address.

But the second officer has an entirely different interpretation of the suspect's feelings from that of the first officer. He sees the civilian's reaction mainly as a means of saving his self-image in the face of a humiliating affront. The officer says,

Subject: As far as him yelling and becoming violent, I think it was mainly . . . a method for him to save face. Because he'd been put in an embarrassing situation, 'cause he'd been taken down and searched and handcuffed; and it was the only way, I guess, he thought he could do anything to bring himself back up.

At another juncture in the interview, the officer makes this interpretation more explicit:

Interviewer: You say he was trying to gain face, regain face?

Subject: Well, I'd say, well, yes.

Interviewer: Was he doing it for himself, or was he pointing it toward the crowd there?

Subject: No, not to the crowd. I don't know whether he's trying to draw one or not, but he seemed to be awfully concerned at the time about being abused or being brutalized and, "Go ahead and hit me again, go ahead and hit me, and do what you want," and sounded like a bit of a martyr.

Interviewer: For his own benefit, basically, you say?

Subject: Yeah, probably.

What of the civilian? His description of the encounter brings out two important details. First, he reveals that the officer had already classified him as a "Black Muslim" at the point of initial contact. Second, he indicates that he merely perceived himself as dispassionately insisting on his rights, up to the moment where the officer resorted to physical contact, at which juncture he became very angry:

Subject: I was sitting in the driveway on the fender of my car, and the policeman come up and asked me what hap-

pened. I said, "I don't know." I didn't even know that
they had been called. So they went and talked to her,
and came back and was talking to me. I had a beard
. . . he asked me was I a Muslim? And I asked him,
"Have you ever seen a Muslim wear a beard?" So then
he asked me to get my hands out of my pockets. I
said, "Well, am I under arrest?" He said "No." So I
said, "I don't see why I should have to take my hands
out of my pockets. I'm not in the street and I'm sitting
in a private driveway." And the next thing I know,
they grabbed me. So they took me . . . each one of
them had one of my arms twisted behind me, and they
took me in the car. And then this one came around
from the driver's side. . . . Came around and slapped
me. Up until that time I didn't get angry or lose my
head or anything, till then.

The man also comes to see the situation at the point of
physical contact as a challenge to a duel. He tells us that in
the squad car, when the officer grabbed him, he shouted at
the officer, "Why don't you stop the car and try that?" There
is also some evidence that after the episode involving the
removal of his hands from his pockets, a certain amount of
baiting and challenging occurred:

Interviewer: Now, can you think of any reason at all why this officer
would just come up and slap you?

Subject: Yeah, I think I know what. When he had my arms
behind me, as I said before, I didn't get angry. Until
he had slapped me. And I must have gotten angry
when he put me in the car, and I said something to
him and he said something to me, and he came around
the side.

Interviewer: Do you remember what you said?

Subject: No, I don't remember.

Interviewer: Was it cussing him out or threatening or something
like this?

Subject: I told him he was a stupid bastard.

Interviewer: At the point that they put you in the car, what were you thinking?

Subject: Well, when they first grabbed me and put my arms behind my back, you know, the first thought that came in my mind was if I had a chance, you know, to get loose from them, you know. Then I would have, probably most likely would have took them.

The motivation for the civilian's provocative behavior appears to have coincided with the interpretation of the nonparticipating officer. There is a question of self-image, in that the man places considerable weight on his manliness and inviolability. He is affronted both by the condescending aspect of being ordered around and by the fact that the officer initiates a physical contact without affording him an opportunity for retaliation:

Interviewer: Looking back on it now, if this were to happen again— if you and your wife were to have an argument, and she were to call the police and they drove up, how would you handle it now?

Subject: I don't know. If they came up and talked to me in a sensible way and I'm a man. Later I would probably cooperate, even though I felt that some things they asked me to do was unnecessary. If it was done in a mannerly way, but if I was approached the way that they approached me . . .

Interviewer: Let's take the part where you were sitting on the car with your hands in your pockets, and one of the police said, '"Take your hands out of your pockets." How could he have put the message across, you know, that he was afraid you had a knife in your pocket, in such a way that you would have complied with it? Or was this alternative open to him?

Subject: If he asked me to take my hands out of my pockets, I would ask him again why. And if he told me that he thought I had a weapon or something, or if he wanted to search me to see if I had a weapon, I would take them out. But he just said, "Take your hands out of your pockets." And I said, "For what reason?" And he said, "Just because I told you to." Then I would probably do it the same way.

Our man relates several other incidents in which he became involved because someone touched him, or because he was given an order, or because someone did not sufficiently acknowledge his manly status. Although the man's role in the episode with the officers was relatively passive, his perception of the officer's initial act and his intense feeling of being violated does represent a reaction which is far from purely situational. Just as the officer reacted to the civilian because he pre-categorized him as a challenge to law and order, so the civilian classed the officer as the type of individual who deliberately emasculates his fellows. And as a result of these pre-categorizations, each man was inspired to play a part which precisely corresponded to the misconception of his opponent.

We have tried to suggest in our discussion so far that the violent incident is cumulatively created by persons involved in it. As each sequence progresses, it takes on violence-prone connotations, and it displays reactions to match. We have also suggested, however, that violence-prone connotations do not spring out of the incidents themselves, but pre-exist in the shape of unconscious assumptions. We have shown that these assumptions are both personal and social: They are personal, because they embody stable frames of reference; they are social, because they relate to other people. We assume that such assumptions take characteristic forms in the minds of Violent Men. What are some of these forms? We turn to this question in our next chapter.

5

The Violence-Prone Person: A Typology

A ccording to our paradigm, we ought to be able to make sense out of a violence-prone person by studying his or her involvements in violence. We should be able to reconstruct personal dispositions that are stable over time from a sample of violent acts. Why? Because we expect the situations that get a person to react violently to be superficially or nonsuperficially similar. We expect aggressive acts to be guided and shaped by needs they subserve. We expect them to mirror character-istic models of conduct, salient feelings, and special sensitiv-ities and needs. We expect them to express the individual's "personality," in the technical sense of the word.

This view entered into our analysis of police incidents in Chapter 2, and we have tried to add flesh to it with illustrations linking encounters to persons in Chapters 3 and 4. In Chapter 4, we tried to show how the violent incident can become an arena in which the recurrent concerns of two violence-prone persons can compete. In Chapter 3 we suggested that if only one participant in an incident is violence-prone, he or she would most likely shape the incident; it would be he or she who would feel provoked by the other person, and it would be he or she who would interpret the problem posed by the encounter as calling for a violent solution.

We now arrive at the point where we are ready to test and expand this thinking through an analysis of the information obtained from our samples of violent offenders. These statements derive from individuals who, as an aggregate, constitute probably the most prolific originators of violence of any group its size. This small number of people had been collectively responsible in the course of their lives for an immensely disproportionate share of the interpersonal aggression that was of concern to the state of California. Unless such trends could be reversed, many of these persons would continue to generate strings of violent incidents to enrich our hypotheses and to provide us with newspaper headlines.

We interviewed 75 persons in our inmate and parolee samples. Four sets of the interview tapes became unavailable (could not be processed, could not be adequately identified, or were technically imperfect). The remaining 71 interviews were transcribed into a standard format, consisting of incident diagrams and checklists. Each such package was then submitted to a "study group" of the kind described in Chapter 1. The "study groups" questioned the veracity of two interviewees, but summarized the information for all 71 persons. The summaries took the form of personality sketches or pattern descriptions, in which the objective was to provide an informal but systematic picture of each interviewee's approach to his violent involvements, as it emerged from facts he had provided us.

Our last task was to try to evolve a typology that could reliably and validly accommodate the patterns of individual interviewees as we saw them. The typology, which will be described and illustrated in this chapter, was derived through a process of grouping and content analysis. Preliminary definitions came into existence deductively, were revised through cumulative classification of pattern summaries, and were then conceptually refined. The final definitions were applied in a formal analysis of the sample, with each interview assigned to the category which appeared to best describe it. These categories became the "primary themes" of the violent persons being classified.

In a second review of the pattern summaries, we assigned subsidiary categories to any case in which additional classification appeared to enrich the description (where the "primary theme" did not completely exhaust the pattern description). Such subsidiary categories proved useful in less than half (29 out of 69) of the cases, and appeared indispensable to none of them.

The reliability of our classification was tested by submitting a stratified subsample of 36 out of our 69 cases to a research psychologist for independent coding. Since we wanted to simultaneously test both of our grouping methods (the "study group" summary as well as the typology) the data were re-analyzed in the form of interview data rather than of pattern descriptions.

The Typology: A Preliminary Characterization

Our classification, which is outlined below, consists of ten categories, each describing one approach to interpersonal situations that promotes the exercise of violence. The total code is intended as a catalogue of ways of relating to people which carry a high probability of degenerating into contact of an aggressive nature.

We can characterize one group of our categories as encompassing essentially *self-preserving strategies*, with violence used to bolster and enhance the person's ego in the eyes of himself and of others. Our second group of categories may be described as encompassing behavior in which *approaches that dehumanize others* are used by persons who see themselves (and their own needs) as being the only fact of social relevance. Other people are viewed as means to an end, rather than as persons whose needs must be taken into account (or must be countered or anticipated).

Both types of approach can take many forms, and we shall merely sample them here. Our classifications include

Self-Preserving Strategies

- *Rep-Defending*: A category comprising persons who are allocated by public acclaim a role that encompasses the exercise of aggressive violence.
- *Norm-Enforcing*: A self-assigned mission involving the use of violence on behalf of norms that the violent person sees as universal rules of conduct.
- *Self-Image Compensating*: Various types of compensatory

relationships between low self-esteem and violence, comprising:

- *Self-Image Defending*: A tendency to use aggression as a form of retribution against people who the person feels have cast aspersions on his self-image.
- *Self-Image Promoting*: The use of violence as a demonstration of worth, by persons whose self-definition places emphasis on toughness and status.
- *Self-Defending*: A tendency to perceive other persons as sources of physical danger which require neutralization.
- *Pressure-Removing*: A propensity (largely resulting from limited interpersonal skill) to explode in situations with which one is unable to deal.

Approaches That Dehumanize Others

- *Bullying*: An orientation in which pleasure is obtained from the exercise of violence and terror against individuals uniquely susceptible to it.
- *Exploitation*: A persistent effort to manipulate others into becoming unwilling tools for one's pleasure and convenience, with violence used when other people react against this effort.
- *Self-Indulging*: A tendency to operate under the assumption that other people exist to satisfy one's needs—with violence as the penalty of noncompliance.
- *Catharting*: A tendency to use violence to discharge accumulated internal pressure, or in response to recurrent feelings or moods.

Table 5.1 lists the distribution of primary themes among the 69 members of our sample whose data were deemed valid. The categories are relatively evenly distributed over the institutional and parolee samples, and in the discussion that follows these subsamples are pooled. Among all four groups of interviewees, incidents of violence within institutions and violence in the street were obtained, but in the prison samples the ratio favored intramural incidents. This fact, which is partly a function of the emphasis of our interviews, proved irrelevant to the classification of individuals, although it may affect the relative distribution of types. Before we turn to this problem, however, we can describe our typology, and present one or two illustrations of patterns classified under each type. For this purpose, we can follow the order suggested by the ranks in Table 5.1.

Varieties of Self-Image Compensating

Self-Image Promoting

Fully one out of four members of our sample could be categorized as a "self-image promoter" in our classification scheme. According to our scheme, a self-image promoter is a man who works hard at manufacturing the impression that he is not to be trifled with—that he is formidable and fearless. He goes out of his way to make sure that people understand how important he is and how important it is to him that he is important.

His fights are demonstration matches, and they are designed to impress the victim and the audience. The impression left is presumed to govern future interactions with him. He is worried that if he does not follow this course of action he will be mistaken for a weakling or a coward. He also suspects that,

Table 5.1

Classification of Types of Violent Persons: Primary Themes Only
(N = 69)

In rank order	Frequency
Self-image compensating	
Self-image promoting	19
Self-image defending	9
Total	28
Rep-defending	10
Pressure-removing	8
Exploiting	7
Bullying	4
Self-defending	4
Self-indulging	3
Norm-enforcing	3
Catharting	2

if he did not "come on strong," he would be a logical candidate for victimization. Since he is so afraid of the possibility of being seen as weak or insignificant, one deduces that he suspects he is, in fact, weak.

The self-image promoter equates manhood with the advertised desire or willingness to fight. He involves himself in the affairs of others (usually uninvited and sometimes against overwhelming odds) because he sees such occasions as proving grounds and because his exaggerated self-esteem tells him he is needed. He tests people to see what he can get away with. If they fail to react, he concludes that his word is law; if they fight, he feels accepted among those who settle their differences at high noon on Main Street. But since he is unsure of himself, his efforts are frantic; he irritates others deliberately and pounces on them over-eagerly when they respond. He does not permit retreat or peaceful resolution of conflicts.

The self-image promoter may sometimes merely defend his self-image, but the affronts he responds to are prearranged. In other words, he manufactures situations in which his involvement or his status are likely to be questioned. The distinguishing feature of this type is that he behaves in such a way that predictable objections must arise to his behavior. When he is psychotic, his delusions assure him an unacceptable superior status. In his blander guises, he self-righteously steps on people's toes or demands unwarranted respect. This game not only risks conflict but invites it.

Ideally, for the definition to apply, the person who is being classified ought to go out of his way to become known as an individual of considerable toughness and potency. At the same time, he ought to leave the distinct impression that he himself is not convinced of his own worth. The following word portrait reveals the sense of inadequacy of the self-image promoter more clearly than most of our cases. This case summary, like all the others transcribed in this chapter, was prepared by a group comprising social scientists and nonprofessionals. The procedure for arriving at these summaries is the one we have described in Chapter 1.

> This man has been flooded all his life with strong feelings of not being able to be what he should be.

He hasn't been able to phrase in any positive sense what he ought to be, but he has done a tremendous amount of thinking, verbalizing and struggling with what he wasn't.

He has particular difficulty in handling verbal exchanges—as he sees it. He has also been very scared, especially as a youth, that if he got into physical combat he would not be able to take punishment. It seems at least plausible to assume that a great step took place in his life when he was actually able to start challenging people and to engage in physical conflict. He talks about a phase when he almost knew that he was going to get licked and usually did get licked, but that he became man enough to take the beating. He feels that here he was able to express something rather than just play the coward.

In this kind of involvement, it got so that he was able to win battles. He could then anticipate that with some selection one was able to win. It was a shift from trying to get some feeling of adequacy out of purely negative performances.

The chorus is important to him. There has been a series of involvements where he has to some extent sought a reputation. There is a further element in the violence that gets back to his earlier preoccupation—a feeling of guilt, of being scared and of a lack of worthwhileness. It bursts forth, at times, in expressions of violence.

He remarked: "It drives me wild that I ain't any good or ain't the guy I ought to be"—and he tries to prove himself wrong.

He proves himself wrong by going out of his way to provoke fights to show he isn't afraid. He tackles the first "bully" he meets in a juvenile institution; he calls another one "punk" shortly thereafter. He arrives at a party mad at one of his friends and proceeds to show him how well he could have licked him by assaulting the first man he comes across; he bluffs a pressure clique in prison to demonstrate how brave he is, even though he confesses intense fear. And in every instance in which his little demonstration succeeds he feels great. As he puts it in relation to one victim, he was tempted to stand on the man's chest and "yell like Tarzan." There are a few moments of regret—such as after he has beaten his wife knowing she was right, but by and large he feels good both after picking a fight and after stomping his opponent.

We speak of "promoting" one's self-image, to distinguish this type of person from the man who merely "defends" his self-esteem; however, the distinction is often difficult to apply. In practice, the blustering tough is often the man who most easily reacts when his performance is questioned by the audience. But such reactions are not really passive; where they are not engineered or initiated, they are certainly welcomed, in the sense that the man sees conflicts as opportunities to be eagerly encountered. Following is a case of this kind:

> We have an awfully powerful young man here who conceives of himself as something of a human tank—who feels that he is undamageable and that anyone who tackles him is going to go out of commission. Picking on him means several things, depending on the mood he is in. If he is angry or tense or depressed, it takes very little to pick on him. In other instances, he may give the person an awful lot of latitude, particularly if he defines the person as the sort of individual he feels it is beneath his dignity to clobber, such as a diagnosed sex pervert.
>
> He attacks when he feels that some aspersion that counts is being cast on him as a person and as a tough person. This happens, for instance, where after his arriving at a prison (while relatively young) he is whistled at in the yard. Following this encounter, he goes and broods for awhile and then comes out seeking the people who whistled at him, making them confess that they are sorry, and then beating them up.
>
> In various incidents that he tells us about he is quite specific about the fact that he just doesn't teach people a lesson—he puts them out of commission. He doesn't just vindicate himself—he destroys people. Even in one case where somebody comes and stabs him in the arm, he is very proud of the fact that with his bare fists he reduced this person to a condition where he had to be carried away in a stretcher. In several instances where someone foolishly tried to hurt him, he tells us that he immediately turned around and broke the person's jaw.
>
> It sounds like a broken record, "I turned it off, and broke his jaw." There isn't much time wasted here on verbal discussion. By and large the sequences are, "somebody says something to offend me, I provide the person the oppor-

tunity to challenge me to a duel and then I make mincemeat out of him." In other words, he puts the other person in a position where he can justify viciously attacking him. He very seldom feels sorry for what he has done, including killing his father's common-law wife in an argument or beating and knifing his father. He feels no remorse because he has already decided to his own satisfaction that violence is not only justifiable but necessary.

One statement he makes which might tell something about what goes on in his mind as he approaches these situations, is the statement that he has "never lost a fight." It is obviously quite important to him not to come out at the bottom, and he starts his fights knowing that he will come out on top. He is apparently compensating physically—where he knows that he can come out on top—for any encounter where there is some question about his being the victor.

Several of our self-image promoters appeared to be swimming against the tide, in the sense that they were either consistently unsuccessful in creating a favorable impression or seemed unable to assess the odds against them. Some demonstrated a propensity to challenge the wrong man at the wrong time all the time. In other instances, the promoting effort itself had a somewhat pitiful appearance, in that much thunder and grandiloquence appeared wasted on minute issues. Prisons, of course, are notoriously productive of this type of relationship between form and content. In depriving inmates of standard sources of identity and self-esteem, prisons vest trivial substitutes with disproportionate emotional connotations. It is for this reason that "staring" at a fellow inmate can prove fatal in prison or that lives are taken over two packs of cigarettes. It is thus also possible to find inmates whose existence revolves around games of domino, as in the following case:

We have two images we can invoke for this man. First, there is an element of the wild and woolly west about him. There is some swaggering and drawing. Secondly, somewhat inconsistent with the first, we have the image of a young man who is trying to keep his head above water. What happens specifically is the following: Our man has the image of people here and there in the world around him who are likely to pick on him and who are not fair. In the face of such people, he feels it incumbent upon him to rise to the challenge and to provide a good show. Now, admittedly, the people whom he fights don't appear to be particularly vicious, nor do the issues appear very monumental. These are really not Main Street duels but side street duels. The most prominent of the fighting issues is cheating at dominoes. Typically, we have a situation where our man spots the evil one in the shape of another person cheating and he promptly calls the man's attention to what is happening. Then he decides that he isn't going to let it pass. His feelings are hurt, and you have a kind of spiral in which he stages a fight. A small fight will do, and when it has taken place he walks away reasonably satisfied because he has made his point.

One or two other reasons for fights which are equally trivial are, for instance, an occasion in which he has occupied somebody's seat in the television room and where the other person comes along to reclaim it. He assumes that an unreasonable request is being made of him. Again he decides that this is the occasion for a duel and he attacks as the other person makes a move toward him.

Another occasion arises where we have him receiving a request that he can't meet, but he answers it in such a way that the other person feels victimized. When the man comes back to clarify the matter he gets the usual wild west type treatment, and the fight is on.

There is an involvement of others in this man's fights in the sense that there is some need that the show-down should be public and that everybody realize that our man is a fighting champion. But then the amateur battle takes place where there are bound to be few persons, because it is really a type of symbolic act.

By "symbolic act" we mean that the point of the fight is to demonstrate to our man's own satisfaction that he cannot be crowded, monkeyed with, challenged, cheated, unfairly treated, pushed. When he feels that someone is thus playing unfair, he feels that he must take a stand, that he must fight in order to show himself that he is no one's fool. There is no need to hurt, draw blood, do damage, destroy. A gesture suffices.

The duels are small time—they have a "spitball or marshmallow at thirty paces" flavor. But then, the issues are small. And this is the case, because our man lives in a world of minor detail. Where the world of others includes momentous battle grounds for matters of valor, power, prestige, or love, our man plays dominoes. He plays dominoes full-time, and it matters to him that no one should pull anything sneaky on him in this serious, important game. If someone does, he draws attention to it testily, and makes sure that the other understands that the gauntlet has been thrown. We call him the "Domino Kid."

Besides self-image promoting, the other form of self-image compensating we found in our sample—also relatively frequently—was the pattern of self-image defending. We should stress again that we see these subtypes not only as being psychological cousins, but also as making up a continuum along with distinguishing marks are matters of emphasis. Thus, the "defender" as opposed to the "promoter" would be *primarily* responsive to slights, whereas the "promoter" would prefer to initiate conflicts demonstrating that he couldn't be meddled with.

Self-Image Defending

The self-image defender is a man who is extremely sensitive to the implications of other people's actions to his integrity, manliness, or worth. His violence arises in the form of responses to challenges, retaliations to slights, or reactions against aspersions to his advertised self-conception.

Some self-image defenders react at once—or even anticipate what they perceive as challenges or insults. Others first worry about the implications of what has been done to them. (During the delay, they may either work up courage or develop evidence to hang the victim.) But there are those who not only attack a person long after the offending incident has escaped the latter's mind, but may even do so repeatedly. Another variation is to let one or two affronts pass, while watchfully waiting for the decisive one.

The self-image defender fights duels in the medieval or duelling tradition. He may respond to challenges or may throw his glove at the offending party, sometimes to the latter's considerable surprise. In some instances, this type of person may even contrive a potential conflict situation to test the proposition that others will slight him. He can do so with full awareness, because self-image defenders are often conscious of their doubts, of their feelings of unworthiness, and even of their self-destructive moments.

When this type reaches psychotic proportions, the self-slighting part of the self may be compartmentalized and may take the form of voices that tell the person he is worthless. Another psychotic stratagem is to manufacture the cues that inform the individual that other people hold him in contempt. In summary, self-image defenders are perpetually on guard against the probability that others will denigrate or belittle them. And the reason for their stance is that they suspect that the point is really a valid one.

Again, there is a dimension of social skill that cuts across the type, in the sense that some individuals are more apt and successful defenders than others. In some cases, we have evidence that the person selects with care the individuals against whom to retaliate and discriminately picks the most strategic time and place for vengeance. In other instances, we see persons who almost seem to be at the mercy of their challengers or who show a distinct trend in the direction of choosing the wrong opponent and the least effective setting for survival. Following is an instance of successful self-image defending, if success is measured in terms of the ability to commit aggression with a minimum of risk:

> This man makes a great deal out of not much in the way of unusual incidents. One has the feeling that he is careful about with whom he makes much out of a trivial incident. Part of it is in sizing up the ability and intent of the potential opponent. He tends to make a fuss over the way the other is acting, and arranges a great deal of verbal exchange without violence ensuing. In such a case, he will continue to crowd the exchange, but when there is a threat of violence he will back off. It seems, however, that this leaves him with a sense of disturbance, of not being the person he should be—so he can't just leave the situation. In one in-

cident, he waited six months before he finally went back and took the victim by surprise. The violence resulted from the initial situation, which made him look somewhat of a coward in not responding to the challenge that was offered.

In almost every incident, there is a backing off and then a sort of skimming around with this, before he eventually does something, provided he can fix the time so that he can get away with it. One possible exception to this occurs when he is stalking a man and the man turns around and punches him and makes him look quite bad. But here it seems plausible that he himself actually came from behind. Even so, this is a clear incident where he crowded the other person because he couldn't let the thing go, in terms of his concern about not being the coward which he seems to demonstrate fairly frequently that he is. He wants to show that he is not backing out. "I am tough, but this isn't the time or place," is the line. And then, eventually, he strikes.

In one instance, he is victimized because something is stolen and it is returned, but he doesn't let it go. In the second incident, he is accused of staring at somebody whom he has not been staring at, and when the person makes an issue of it, he proceeds to escalate the matter until he has challenged the person. In another incident, he victimizes somebody else and a third person intervenes. He backs off, as he always does when the going gets rough, and then subsequently challenges the person who intervenes. He postpones the fight but ultimately attacks the person with fists. So, what we have here is a series of delaying moves, a fencing method, a lot of hoopla and noise and a lot of talk surrounding what essentially ends up in a back-stabbing.

By contrast to this description there is the pattern we sometimes refer to as "small-time defending," which is extremely unproductive, if not completely self-defeating. In the following case, it occurs with an individual whom we have cross-indexed as primarily a self-image defender, and secondarily, a self-image promoter. The reason for this cross-classification is not so much ambiguity as the fact that there is a preliminary step of "throwing one's weight around" preceding episodes that are essentially clumsy reactions to perceived affronts. We also note that this individual shows a mixed pattern in the temporal nature of his defending acts; at times he reacts instantaneously, whereas on other occasions he broods and works himself up to his act of vengeance:

> This man is a not very astute, small-manner retaliator. He tries to throw his weight around and he doesn't have much, and when he is challenged in terms of not being treated as someone who has considerable weight, he resorts to immediate violence. It appears to be difficult for him to try to handle things verbally or even to try to pace his act of violence so that things will be to his advantage. Instead, he reacts immediately to the experience of degradation, initiating the violence himself without any apparent notice of the likely consequences of his being overpowered and seriously hurt. And he does tend to prolong these kinds of involvements—which in one case actually leads to his killing somebody. Specific incidents that illustrate the pattern include the following contrasting situations: A. The type of situation in which somebody says something to him which he can conceive of as degrading, such as throwing him out of the room or telling him to be quiet. Here he attacks, even in instances in which his own somewhat clumsy handling of the preceding events almost invites the other person to degrade him. B. The type of situation that we have referred to as involving time; the best illustration of this, combined with clumsiness, is a series of encounters with an officer who calls him a degrading name—calls him "Sunshine" in spite of the fact that he shows the officer the name that's printed on his I.D. card. Only after this has been going on for some time, and after a final precipitating situation in which the officer refuses to let him take a shower in the gymnasium, does he proceed to an encounter with the officer by walking past him without showing his I.D. card, thereby inviting certain self-destruction. Obviously, in a situation like this, it can be argued that the person is out of control. Once the gauntlet has been thrown at him, once he has engineered the situation in such a way that the gauntlet is thrown at him, he feels compelled to charge in— and he charges in with considerable anger. He charges into certain, intense difficulties, as in the situation with the officer, and in battling a person much larger than himself. And this appears to deflect the intensity of his reaction to

the flaunts that trigger these incidents, and the intensity of his feeling of shame and degradation.

The following case again illustrates the stewing and brooding that precedes retaliation among several of our men. In addition, the pattern shows the continuity we often observe between abnormal and normal reactions in the same person. In some cases, "sane" and "insane" violence seem to serve the same ends; in other instances, forms of abnormality are used as part and parcel of the person's standard reactions to the world. In the following case, for instance, the "self-image defending" includes a heavy component of paranoia, which feeds "evidence" to the man that he is being affronted or slighted:

> The man states himself that he has paranoid feelings. He cites a series of incidents in which, without any provocation from the other party, he gets the impression that he is being laughed at or belittled in different ways, and he invariably responds with violence to defend himself against the belittling. In one particular incident, in which he leisurely fights before a crowd, he then turns on the entire group as if to demand reassurance and to ask if anyone thinks what he did was foolish, with the obvious intent to beat the hell out of them if they did think anything like that. Although he claims to feel relief after any given violent incident, he retains long time grudges. His vendettas tend to go on interminably with at least some of the parties with whom he's had violence.
>
> We have a rather consistent picture here of his getting the feeling that people have contempt for him, or have a lack of respect for him. He wants to do something to try to handle this lack of respect, and the *one* thing that he does is to resort to violence. He admits to a series of fights where he was just sitting somewhere and imagined that someone was staring at him; there are other instances in which the thing which was questioned by the victims was his manliness. This occurs, for instance, in one situation in which he has just told his girl that he's not going to supply her with money to gamble with and a person at the same bar offers her money—thereby implying that he cannot take care of his woman; there is another incident, for which he served

a great deal of time, in which he killed the girl he was living with because he felt he had evidence that she was unfaithful to him. There is a whole string of incidents involving a young man who had informed on him, and in this case not only did he assault this individual (like he did his other victims) without any warning whatsoever, but kept on doing this time after time, until the victim finally apologized and said he wouldn't repeat his infraction. So what seems to dominate him, among other things, is a kind of need to save his self-image and a need to hurt anybody who in any way whatever could cast aspersions on it.

Rep-Defending: Violence as a Social Obligation

The next most frequent pattern we find in our sample is that of *rep defending*, where violence is the fate entailed in a role; in other words, where the person commits violence because his social position, physical size, or group status obligates him to do so—a matter of "noblesse oblige," so to speak. This sort of person is expected to have violent involvements, and he has therefore come to expect the same of himself; he is aware of his role and of the need to defend it or to sustain it or to live by it. He knows he must champion his people, execute the guilty, and put on a good show. He may not derive much joy from this special awareness; some gang leaders, for instance, may try hard to negotiate, and some muscular "gorillas" may discourage aspiring youngsters who feel impelled to challenge them. But the assumed obligation pursues such persons relentlessly and hard.

Some "rep defenders" contribute actively to their own destiny; they may enjoy the spotlight, arise with alacrity when summoned, do their job with an extra dash of vigor, and take more bows than the audience demands. They may, at the slightest provocation, pull out and display their collection of accumulated scalps. But even where the "rep defender" goes out of his way to follow his star, his various involvements tend to remain a corollary of an assigned role rather than an expression of an internal need. Violence occurs on behalf of the role, or to maintain it, or in terms of obligations implicit in it.

From the description we may note that in superficial details the rep defender resembles the self-image defender. The rep defender rises to challenges and sees himself as the bearer of the sword in situations in which others are content to sit on the sidelines. The distinguishing feature here, however, is that this conception or self-definition originates externally, in society, rather than within the person. And the rep defender plays from a position of strength rather than of weakness. He starts with a knowledge of his own charisma, of his social support, of his loyal following and acknowledged physical power. Although his violent actions strengthen his "rep" or establish it, this reinforcement is a by-product of the violence, rather than its aim. The intent is to comply with social obligations or to satisfy the audience.

It is in the case of the rep defender that the "chorus" is uniquely important as a cause of interpersonal conflicts. In some instances, we have evidence that in the absence of other people, a particular rep defender may even show a distinct pacifistic streak. Following is a case in point:

> This man can be described as a somewhat reluctant and pussy-footing champion. There is a rep motive in his action, but it is pursued cautiously, and in some instances, half-heartedly; and it appears as if in quite a few of these incidents he has to be pretty well pushed, or in one or two situations even tricked, into fighting.
>
> The pattern is one of trying to avoid fights, and he does appear to consider the probabilities of successful completion of his fights in deciding what action to take. The situation occurs repeatedly that he is either outnumbered, or that the odds don't look favorable. And in such instances he tends to arm himself or to get reinforcements. In one or two cases he tries rather clumsily to prevent the fight from occurring by restraining one or another of his more enthusiastic followers.
>
> He has one incident which takes place in an institution, in which he goes through a series of steps in response to somebody having made a racially derogatory remark to him, and then finally the fight breaks out in a situation in which

the chorus is present. In this same sequence where potentially a fight could break out, it doesn't. It appears that at
least one reason for this is because he and the other person
are alone at this point.

There are several gang fights here. And these are not the
stereotyped kind of gang fight (in which two groups of
people challenge each other, and then proceed to make good
on their challenges), but rather take the form of an initial
effort to get along and one or two misunderstandings which
finally result in a fight. In an instance in which the other
gang does take the aggressive role in a somewhat under-
handed fashion, the fight never really does get off to much
of a start before the police arrive.

In summary, what we have with this gang leader is an
effort to do the very minimum of fighting that is necessary
in order to maintain his position in the gang, and a reluctant
effort on his part to follow through on the aggressive over-
tures of his followers—when he has no other choice.

Most rep defenders seem less passive and hesitant and less
dependent on direct social reinforcement. The individual defender will carry his obligations with him into situations in
which members of his group are not involved.[1] The "chorus"
is implicit and invisible—its strains may be heard in the background, but it need not be present; the actor has adopted his
role, and he plays it without support or acclaim.

The man appears to be defending his status as a gang leader,
which in turn is expressed in his defense through violence
of the integrity of his gang (which is his racial group of
friends). There is no effort, as in many other situations of
this kind, to try to justify violent acts in terms of some kind
of code of justice. In other words, he does not argue that
people are taking advantage of his friends, therefore, he
fights. Rather it is that they are his friends, and he needs
them, therefore, he fights. He is undoubtedly seen as a
source of strength and support and is willing to help create
and keep this image as a tower of physical strength for the

---

[1] Redl describes this process among delinquents, and refers to it as "the
playing of the peer cassette."

group. It does appear, though, that he's not just a strong-arm-member of the group, but is actually a leader, and this leadership is maintained through his ability to use force to help the boys—to help protect his boys.

Part of the man's role, which he maintains and defends, is to be someone who backs up his word—or rather, the game that he is in. He also maintains an image for his friends to the effect that he'll back up the games they are in. In keeping with this, he doesn't do much that one would consider sneaky (such as backing out of involvements in order to retaliate later). In his case, there is an ability to, or commitment to meet challenge with physical action. There's only just enough delay here to suggest that the man isn't completely foolhardy in trying to handle himself.

Even in the one or two instances where this man is not fighting for or with his gang, the pattern remains the same. He feels protective (a friend tells him that a bully has been beating up his little brother in prison); he determines to intervene and fight (he vows to settle the matter once he is imprisoned again); he goes about making good on the resolution (having been imprisoned, he locates the guilty party, arms himself, and invites the other man for a conference in the men's room); he plays fair (when the other man asks that the matter end at this stage, he agrees), but firm (when the other man then arms himself to turn the tide in his favor, he stabs the other man).

On the border between rep-defending and self-image compensating are persons who have acquired some reputation, but who are sufficiently unsure of it or of themselves to feel the need to stretch public acceptance and credulity. Here is the "small-time" leader who seeks "big-time" acclaim and the acknowledged amateur pugilist who promotes a reputation of professional championship.

Following is an illustration of the pattern.[2] Here is a man (classified as primarily a rep defender and as secondarily a self-image promoter) whose reputation is a stepping stone to

---

[2]The reader interested in inputs that shape pattern descriptions can compare the group summary with the communication excerpted on pp. 15–16.

more grandiloquently shaped fantasy. The man's past reputation—which is inherited (his father is a distinguished Indian chief)—carries him only to a point, and it is here where
pathetic efforts at self-aggrandisement begin to affix patches
to his frayed mantle:

> We have decided that this man is a gunsel—an individual
> who plays kid's games in a man's world, where others are
> playing for keeps. The man is an Indian and is known to
> have had some status in the Indian world before he came
> to prison—and he spends considerable time and effort to
> capture some status in prison. When he can't do this with
> actual confrontations he is not above embroidering those
> situations he has been involved in—in order to impress us
> with his importance.
>
> Some of his incidents sound highly implausible; for in-
> stance, it always takes six guards to subdue him when he
> has gotten out of line. Those incidents that do have some
> plausibility about them involve his punishing somebody ac-
> companied by at least one and usually several friends. In
> other words, it appears that he does want the reputation of
> being tough and violent, but when it comes to actually
> getting involved in violence he sees that he has sufficient
> reinforcements at hand so that he can get the reputation of
> being tough, without the risk.
>
> There is absolutely no question that this man is recog-
> nized as somewhat of a leader by the Indians in prison, and
> he is using these Indians to help him accomplish his purpose
> by helping him to acquire a reputation for toughness. He
> can do this, because Indians as a group are known as tough.
> This is not to say that some of the Indians who have been
> used by him don't recognize this, or that they may not use
> him for the same purpose. But it does mean that he plays
> this game consistently, single-mindedly, and better.

Where we have admixtures of rep-defending and self-image
promoting, as in our posturing chief's son, it is the historical
sequence which may determine the primacy of one category
or the other. If the individual first "builds" a reputation, which
is next accorded him and which he then defends, one would
have to define him as primarily a self-image promoter. To the

extent to which the person starts with an assigned role, which he tries to convert into a more substantial one, the classification should credit him with the advantage of his starting capital.

Pressure-Removing: Panic in the Corner

Probably a majority of violence-prone persons may be classed as deficient in verbal and other social skills. In some instances, violence is clearly related to clumsiness, as in cases of armed robbery where the bluff is unconvincing, or in situations where forcible rape substitutes for courtship and seduction.

The most general and direct relationship between vulnerability and aggression is possibly that found among persons who use violence as an expression of helplessness, or as a last-minute effort to obliterate situations to which they are unable to respond. This type of violence is interpersonal when the "sore loser" wants not only to tear up the game but also the winning player.

Such is the case with our *pressure remover*, the type of person whose repertoire of available interpersonal strategies is limited, or at least insufficient to cope with some situations. Where others may be able to solve a problem through nonviolent techniques, such as verbal persuasion, the pressure remover feels himself smothered, walled-in, or subject to overwhelming odds. He may try to cope with this dilemma with brief, desperate, half-hearted, floundering moves, but it is usually clear that he had arrived at the bottom of his resources before he started.

The object of violence is to remove the horns of the dilemma, or to destroy its source. The dominant feeling tone is one of irritation, helplessness, panic, or blind rage. The violence has a desperate, lashing-out character.

The victim is told that he has been crowding beyond the limits of what is bearable or what can be coped with. He may have received a prior warning (such as "stop!" or "I refuse to argue!"), but this may appear innocuous despite its undertone of despair. The victim may not even realize that his plausible arguments or reactions are being perceived as nagging or pushing or boxing-in or threatening. The "discovery" comes at the juncture where, in lieu of an expected countermove, there blossoms an effort at complete physical annihilation.

The simplest version of pressure removing is the effort of verbally unskilled persons to terminate altercations in which they feel unable to respond. Here violence not only expresses frustration but also represents a brusque and inadequate summary of the argument the person cannot verbalize. In addition, it constitutes an effort to suspend the offending level of interaction.[3] The following pattern contains several instances.

> The object of this man's fights is to eliminate a source of irritation, which generally consists of verbal materials. The reason this kind of material proves irritating to him is because he himself seems incapable of handling his end of the argument. Now, even when the action that precedes the fight is initiated by him he can't follow through. As, for instance, in a situation in which he has issued a command to a homosexual to curtail his sex life—the next step being an encounter with a friend of the person to whom he issued the command. And in this situation the only means he has at his disposal to cope with logic and the effort to persuade him to desist is to tell the friend to stop arguing with him. And he does this in various ways, including turning away. It is only when the other person persists in talking to him that he gets angry (as he invariably does in such situations) and hits the other man. In some instances, our man is subjected to all kinds of talk, which gradually builds up an irritation to anything. In other instances, there are only relatively short conversations where he simply doesn't know how to respond other than to hit the person. In some cases the argument isn't even directed at him, or at least not by the party who finally gets involved in the violence. The most unusual instance of this kind is a situation in which his wife subjects him to a great deal of irritating talk about her ex-husband and he finally is very murderously inclined. He explodes, but not at his wife so much as at the ex-husband, whom he hunts out and shoots. In a relatively

---

[3] The most famous incident of "pressure removing" on record is probably Billy's attack on Claggart in Melville's novel *Billy Budd*.

minor incident of the same kind there is a conversation which is not directed at him but in which he feels involved.

What happens is not necessarily that he wins the resulting fights, because his anger is such that he doesn't really sit back and calculate the odds. Despite the fact that he is a very large man, he in one instance attacks an individual even larger than himself, and in at least two other incidents he tackles a person who has a great many friends, and as a result gets hurt. But the satisfaction for him—irrespective of the physical outcome of the fight—is always the removal of the irritation. There is the fact that where a response might have been expected from him it is now silent and peaceful again, and he can go about his business.

More complex versions of this pattern are characterized by diversified settings for helplessness. The range of situations in which the person feels impotent may be so wide that at first glance the pattern may seem nonexistent or obscure:

The group doesn't really have awfully much to say about this man, possibly because his pattern, if any, is somewhat evanescent. The one common denominator in his incidents appears to be that he acts violently when he perceives himself in a corner, or when somebody's doing something to him that threatens him. He reacts to threats which come in different shapes. The first incident, for instance, involves a situation in which he and a partner are burglarizing a motel room, and discover it is occupied by a woman. When she screams, they try to quiet her down by administering a well-placed blow on the jaw. This doesn't do the job, so they keep on beating at her (with the same objective in mind) until they have pretty well beaten her to a pulp. The obvious purpose of this action is not so much to hurt or to retaliate as it is to get this disturbing agent to stop disturbing.

The same kind of flavor permeates an incident which takes place in the institution, in which the victim keeps on nagging at our man, trying to make him admit that he made a mistake in placing a bet on a sports event. And it gets to the point where he doesn't see any way of stopping this verbal incursion except with force.

In three instances money is involved; in one case he has placed a bet, and in the other one he's appropriating money in a burglary, and in the third case, he has money being taken away from him while he's playing drunk in a bar. Again, this is an occasion in which he uses force because he doesn't know how else to get out of the situation (where his money is being taken).

It looks as though the reason why he uses force in order to extricate himself in situations like this, is because he does not dispose of the verbal skills that would constitute alternatives to force. This holds for the motel room scene, for instance, in which probably some less drastic ways of quieting the lady might have been attempted. It holds for the situation in which he finds the other man with his hands in his pockets, and it certainly holds in the situation where he's having the slight altercation with his friend.

We would like to note that the money element is present even in a relatively dramatic incident that occurred two weeks after we interviewed this man. Here he obtained some publicity; what is involved is his common-law wife shooting him after an altercation which dealt with financial matters.

It is interesting to note the ironic twist to the events referred to at the end of this summary. Obviously, lack of social skill can be a two-edged sword; not only can it produce violence as a substitute for talk but it can also inspire explosions directed at the inadequate person by other people who find themselves unable to reach him in more conventional ways.

Exploiting: The Cost of Consuming People

Our typology contains several categories of persons who manipulate others as if they were objects. The most "normal" or "adult" form of this enterprise is probably that of the "*exploiter*," who is relatively mature because he does not take pathological pride in human suffering, nor adopt the social perspective of a suckling infant. Exploitation is an avocation, in which skill and energy are invested in convincing other people to supply commodities or services without reciprocation. Violence results from the unwillingness of at least some target-persons to freely enter into this type of transaction.

If a person wants to live a parasitic existence, in which he can enjoy the possessions and the labor of his fellows, he risks the possibility of having to resort to violence. Heretofore co-operative associates may rebel, and presumably easy marks may acquire new confidence and wills of their own. Well-meaning spectators and other busybodies may intervene to spoil a plot and complicate the game.

Exploiters are persons who actively engage in the enterprise of using others as objects to satisfy their needs. They are aware of the fact that their preferred relationship to people runs headlong into the needs of these people, so that radical techniques must be used to insure reluctant compliance. The exploiter makes no assumptions about the human universe rotating around him, intending to be of service. This does not mean, on the other hand, that the formulas evolved to circumvent the intended victim's reluctance need be successful. Often, the exploiter jumps over-readily at the assumption that his routine cannot fail; often, his routine is clumsy and should never have been permitted off the drawing board and past the rehearsal stage. The less socially adept and perceptive the exploiter, the greater the likelihood that he will have to invoke violence, or that he will meet unexpected violence which he must counter.

The exploiter characteristically also does not view violence as the necessary or desirable means to gain control over others; on the contrary, he stands on the threshold of conflict like the cook who has followed directions but who has burnt the roast.

The following pattern shows an exploiter who is sometimes assaulted by his victims and sometimes reacts with violence because he prefers to keep his manipulations confidential. He reacts to accusations which publicize his role as a clumsy cheat and does some self-image defending at this stage. The violence in these sequences is presumed to convince spectators that the accusations are undeserved; it is also obviously intended to punish the victim for spoiling the unilateral game:

> This man's pattern appears to be one of taking advantage of others through procedures such as cheating in gambling, short-changing, blatantly running out on his wife, inform-ing, and eventually using up his credit with the victims of

his cheating efforts. He tries rather clumsily to ward off any open attack or reprisal, but when cornered, does fight. Once he senses that he might have the upper hand in the fight, he becomes extra aggressive and extra vicious. There's some feeling there of having lost status by the fact that his cheating has been uncovered. He may be trying to get back some sense of his own manhood or some sense of his own worth by being over-aggressive in a situation where he can look somewhat powerful.

In the sequence of events, it seems that once he is caught and people are ready to accuse him, or it's blatantly clear that he's been cheating, he isn't able to confess or he doesn't just run off and terminate the game but still tries to deny his role, and this leads to his getting in a corner, becoming aggressive toward the victims, and promoting the ultimate conflict.

This aspect in the pattern comes out in the interviewing process also, because in most instances one has to infer the dishonesty from circumstantial evidence. For instance, the police mysteriously arrive after his wife has damaged two of his teeth with no mention of his having done anything to her, and in two cases in which he is attacked after having gambled, there's no mention of any possible provocation for these attacks, although it is obvious he must have been cheating. And in an incident in the prison stockade, the first indication we have of his having been an informer, is that somebody comes and calls him a snitch, after which, as usual, he gets vicious.

A somewhat more cold and calculated—almost chilling— version of the pattern is embodied in the following description. In this case, we have a cool practitioner of applied violence. There is strikingly little social awareness in this exploiter, in the sense that other people are viewed by him as manipulable objects, pure and simple. There is also, in this person, a self-consciousness about violence which (as in our other example) borders on sadism:

> This man is a user of violence as an instrument to achieve personal ends. These ends change from one incident to another, and they usually involve a victim who is not prepared and is taken systematically by surprise. In several of

the incidents, our man has gone about the business of exploiting other inmates—violence comes in when this situation degenerates. The most flagrant case involves a game which he and a partner play on loan sharks, in which they send their victim back and forth between each other when he asks to be paid, with the hope that payment need not occur. This apparently works in some instances but there finally comes a man who gets wise to what is transpiring—and he is promptly stabbed.

The coldest instance of instrumental violence in this interview is one in which our man wants to be transferred, picks himself another inmate almost at random and assaults him—and as a result gets transferred. In several of the incidents the inmate culture reinforces his role. This occurs, for instance, where our friend learns that a new inmate has informed on his brother and everybody is telling him to murder this man, in retaliation. He does end up stabbing the man—not with the intent to kill him but to bruise him. A couple of incidents are minor, but this doesn't deprive them of information value. For instance, it turns out that our man cannot just walk away from a situation in which somebody sat down on his chair in the television room; he has to use violence, he feels, because otherwise people may have contempt for him. He definitely feels that when he is standing as a look-out for a friend who is collecting debts it is his obligation to intercept and fight the victim when he flees.

It appears that with him violence seems necessary and proper. We have here a man who uses every opportunity for violence provided him. And he not only strikes first, but he is extra careful to be systematic in the preparation and execution of his violence.

Bullying: The Joy of Inflicting Terror

The most unpleasant type of violent person (both from the vantage point of society and that of the victim) is undoubtedly the *bully*, who goes out of his way to be unfair, unmerciful, and inhumane in his violence. Empathy with the bully's perspective is difficult because of the fact that he derives satisfaction from the suffering of others, and because he is intent on protecting his immunity to the point of cowardice. One generally assumes that this type of alien disposition must spring from very strong motives which push the person to abandon otherwise universally held premises and feelings. The most probable motivating force is intense fear. This seems reasonable because of the fact that it is fear that the bully goes about generating in other people, and it is fear over which the bully makes such a point of exercising control.

The bully is the artisan of violence, for whom force is a tool or an instrument self-consciously employed to inspire terror and to increase pliability. Violence is the coin of the realm, and the balance of trade is maintained in one's favor.

Bullies may espouse quaint power-centered theories and may claim to follow simplistic approaches to the process of influence, but the bully is really the man who enjoys the experience of exercising effective violence—and the clue to this disposition is the habit of invoking violence wherever it can make an impression to be savored. What is wanted is the physical and psychological effect of violence on other persons, which can cement the bully's conviction that there is nothing to fear in fear itself because it is, after all, always present in others.

Bullies are not calculating and cool, effective and impressive, although some of them occasionally give that appearance. The bully makes his own task easier by not risking even encounters; he picks on weak people because the effects of terror are most easily secured with them; he gives no quarter, because lenience takes away the edge or full measure of his enjoyment.

The pure bully uses violence to secure power, obtain goods and services, and keep others in their place or at a distance. Violence is invoked as a tool in a variety of situations, because the means are more important than the ends. This polymorphous exercise of violence distinguishes the pure specimen of bullyhood from the bully (exploiter), who has the same strongly motivated faith in violence, but who is more specialized and pragmatic. The bully (exploiter) uses violence to secure cooperation from his victims; he uses it exclusively for this end, and uses no other means. What makes such persons primarily bullies is not only that they go out of their way to use violence but that they reveal a disproportionate emphasis on its use. Thus, they will selectively approach victims who are particu-

larly helpless, or they will expend considerably more vicious-
ness than the "exploiting" part of the job requires. Bullying is
wasteful. What matters to the bully is not that violence "works,"
but that it impresses and damages and intimidates.

With the bully (exploiter) as opposed to exploiters (bullies),
the classification problem is one of emphasis. We have a person
classifiable as primarily a bully if he is primarily a dispenser
of violence—if bullying is his main dish, and the exploitation
is his gravy.

The following description of a "classic" bully not only contains all the elements we have mentioned (including those
suggestive of the dynamics of this pattern) but also illustrates
the relationship of the bully to some of our other types. We
see the bully as an exploiter who gets carried away with his
more drastic tools, but also as a perverted caricature of the
self-image defender. It is possible that the magnitude of the
bully's reaction reflects a degree of personal inadequacy much
more pronounced than the self-doubts of other violent persons:

> Without making a value judgment, we think it would be
> fair to say that this man is a consistent, unmitigated, low-
> level heel, who has never had what one could describe as
> a fair fight. The pattern in a variety of situations (starting
> with a few boyhood escapades, and terminating with adult
> felony assaults) involves his taking advantage, unfairly, of
> somebody who is in a weakened position. As a second step,
> he will, when the other person gives some indication of
> weakness (begs for mercy or asks him to stop), accelerate
> his violence, and he here describes himself as becoming
> angry. And at this point he resorts to walking over the
> person's chest, or stomping on his face, or doing any num-
> ber of other things that are obviously extremely cruel.
>
> One consistent pattern with him is that he will do almost
> anything to create a situation in which the other person is
> at a disadvantage before he strikes. He will use deception;
> he will maneuver the situation physically. And as soon as
> he has achieved the objective of being able to surprise the
> other party, or being able to place a blow which creates an
> immediate advantage for him, he proceeds—but not before.
> He will also use people other than his victims. There is one
> classic instance of this in which he makes a pact with a girl

to fight a person who is hunting for him, and then leaves the girl to do all his fighting. This episode not only illustrates his tendency to use people, but also exemplifies his outlook toward the female sex, where we even have two or three instances in which he shows no hesitation about fighting girls. And he assesses them pretty much like he does his male opponents.

The general way in which violence occurs with him is that he evaluates instantaneously a situation in which it becomes possible. It even occurs in instances in which the other person involved, the potential victim, is in the process of complying with demands, or is in a conflict with him in which he had previously obtained the upper hand, but now somehow the tables can be turned, and advantage can be taken of this. And this second type of situation is important in that before the fight starts he might have experienced fear, and part of the reaction may be against his own fear. As a matter of fact, fear is a kind of theme that runs through the sequences in a variety of ways. It occurs very directly in any situation in which the other person does, objectively speaking, have the advantage, and he can't do anything about it. Then he has no compunction whatsoever about running, about giving up. It occurs in that he initially fights, as we have indicated, when he himself has experienced fear, and it occurs very blatantly in a situation in which the other person shows fear; that is, in which there is this request for mercy, or some other indication that the other person is afraid of him; and then he becomes extremely furious, and he shows no mercy whatsoever. And what one might infer from this is that in all of these situations what he's really doing with his violence is handling his own fear. That is, he is a bully in the classic sense—a person who acts extremely unmercifully toward others because of the fact that he himself (as he introspects) feels terribly small and disadvantaged.

Self-Defending: The Omnipresent Threat

Whereas the bully goes to great pains to fight fear in himself, the next most frequent type, the *self-defender*, cultivates fear, and uses violence to deal with people he fears. This does not mean that some of the threats in the self-defender's life are not concrete, objective, and urgent; but, since they occur repeatedly, we must suspect creative effort. At minimum, the self-defender must have a propensity to appear in the most dangerous places at awkward junctures; more usually, he counters vague insecurity by locating it where he can grapple with it, among dangerous people who surround him.

Self-defenders commit their violence as a means of attaining safety, or refuge, or the neutralization of danger. They fall on a continuum from accurate probability-assessment to complete subjectivity. On the one end of the continuum lies the person whose ability to diagnose real danger is rivaled only by his skill in systematically coping with it; next comes the precipitant practitioner of the "first strike," who attacks first and asks questions later (often too late to profit from the innocence of the replies). There is also the individual whose obnoxious demeanor gives him a penchant for making enemies or for creating unfavorable social situations. Further along the continuum is the person who easily panics, or whose fantasy is peopled with powerful and aggressive enemies. Lastly, there is the "paranoid self-defender," who is engaged in a continuing battle against an awesome conspiracy of his own creation.

The strong element of fear as the person's almost exclusive motive is exemplified by every one of these patterns; it shows us how precarious the existence of the typical self-defender really is; he may secure momentary peace by coping with specific threats, but he always discovers another danger lurking around a nearby corner. The following is an extreme case.

This man shows a pattern which is dominated by basic fear of doom and the conviction that others are trying to kill him. He sees in many of the personal exchanges that he has become involved in threats upon his life. Once he perceives this threat, he panics. He becomes enmeshed in extreme violence in an effort to handle his panic. He seems to resort to violence as a way of being assured that the other party is not going to kill him—at least, that is the way he feels. It seems ironic that he engages in the very thing of which he is scared to death. Now, in the last incident, it almost looks as if there is a flaw in his pattern, because here is an incident in which he is almost convinced that he is going to kill somebody and he doesn't kill him but feels that the price that the other person pays for not getting killed must be to provide him with assurance, in the form of statements that can be believed, that the incident is concluded. The point is that he can be reassured here.

We have noted in this man the kind of game which occurs both inside and outside the institution. When he is young he charges his brother with a rock because he is convinced that his brother is going to kill him (with a small baseball bat). Also outside, he shoots and kills the wife of a candy store owner because she screams when her store is being held up. Again, he has the feeling that he is going to get killed, so he is going to get her first.

In prison, the same kind of thing happens when he gets the same feelings. Usually, of course, there is not really any occasion for him to fear for his life, but he gets the feeling that he is wronged and he reacts with anger and becomes very dangerous at this point. Even the slightest statement that could possibly signify the possibility of somebody having designs on him, mobilizes this very intense fear. He then feels the need to defend himself against his "attackers" and he charges in and commits violence.

Self-Indulging: The Liabilities of Adulthood

Whereas most of us learn at an early age to at least take into account what others want, some adults continue to base their lives on the premise that the only purpose of other people is to cater to them in every possible way. This type of orientation can eventually produce a tantrum, when the patience of even the most nurturing providers becomes exhausted in the face of patently ridiculous demands and expectations.

We call such persons *self-indulgers*, because they view the world from the vantage point of infants, and toddle about their way expecting to find a crib or breast around every corner. Unlike the case of the exploiter, there is no intent here of deliberately taking advantage of others. There is, rather, the view—which is held naively and in good faith—that one's own wishes must invariably prevail. This premise is given the status of a natural law.

The self-indulger thus proceeds good-naturedly on the assumption that his own welfare must be of primary concern to others. He deals with his acquaintances and relations on the basis of this assumption. There is no concern here with the needs of other people, because these are irrelevant to the basic scheme. Information about the views and desires of others is not perceived. Their discontent is never noted until it has blossomed into full rebellion.

When the moment of truth arrives, the self-indulger sees people suddenly and mysteriously turning on him and feels compelled to deal with unprovoked aggression. His indignant reply reflects the magnitude of his hurt. At long last he must assimilate—with wonder and indignation—evidence of the unreliability and perfidy of man.

The almost comically naive orientation of the self-indulger becomes obvious when we examine concrete incidents in their careers. The following pattern, for instance, includes the most casual defiance of all manner of social convention, with a reaction of pained surprise in the face of predictable consequences:

> This man is very much concerned that the world may not be a place which has reasonable respect for humanity in general and for some humans in particular; yet he appears to approach his own interpersonal relationships as if the world ought to let him do anything he wants, anyway he wants to do it, at any time he cares to do it. He becomes very upset when the world does not live up to these expectations. Incidentally, the way the world treats him would be much more manageable from the philosophy that he expresses about the way the world is, but it appears that, at least implicitly, he's upset when the Southern police don't treat him (a Black) as if he had extra privileges beyond his regular privileges. He double parks in front of them, threatens them, and crowds the system, to say the least. He's concerned when his wife finds him with another woman; but even when, as far as he knows, it's been his transgression, he becomes very upset at her being annoyed about this.
>
> Things do not seem to happen immediately but rather, over a period of time. There's some brooding, and some

working out of the position that there's been unfairness done him and that there is the need to punish. Then he gets into the violence trying to handle the fact that people are not treating him as a deserving privileged person. In addition to this procedure, there seems to be an overwhelming elephantine quality about him. He has a penchant for associating with ineffectual persons in futile efforts to commit unmanageable transgressions; then, when he gets himself into a corner, he tries to extricate himself in ways that are doomed from the beginning. But he somehow still manages to extract from these experiences nothing but a continuing feeling that the world is an unfair place. This feeling then leads him to act violently. He plays his clumsy acts on a great variety of stages; in prison he stupidly challenges two other inmates, and flouts the guards. In burglaries, it is both his partners and his victims; in his marital affairs, his wife. It appears that this man simply has a penchant for doing the wrong thing and has the nerve to punish others for his overwhelming awkwardness.

Norm-Enforcing: The Burden of Dispensing Justice

There are some persons whose violence is ostensibly in the public interest and in the service of society—although the service is rendered informally and voluntarily, sometimes over the protests of its beneficiaries. This type of person—the *norm enforcer*—acts as a one-man posse, who feels that he knows when rules have been violated; his conception of how violators must be dealt with is primitive and direct, and invariably involves his active participation. There is a superficial resemblance to rep-defending in this pattern, because violence ostensibly occurs on behalf of others or in the common interest. The real parentage of this type, however, is the self-image promoter, who feeds his self-esteem by drawing attention to himself. When he interferes in the affairs of others he advertises his role rather than their problems. "Justice" serves as a convenient excuse for ostentatious interference. Unfortunately, this often is the only motive on record, and we must infer the self-doubt which we assume really inspires the performance.

Whereas rep defenders are elected to responsibility, "norm enforcers" enter their career on a self-appointed basis. Strictly on their own, they undertake the task of becoming the conscience of society and the insurer of its integrity. They exercise violence as a matter of principle rather than as a social obligation. They do not require others to come to them for help or for advice (no one does); they do not need anyone to nominate them as champions or to recognize them as spokesmen for their people (no one does); they are convinced that the job needs to be done and that they must do it.

These men perceive themselves as arbiters of disputes, as slayers of dragons, as protectors of the weak, and as dispensers of justice; they define themselves as policemen, prosecutors, judges, and executioners. They patrol their beat alertly searching for black knights carrying off maidens. They attack any abuser of power or violator of decency they spot, often without much prior notification. And although they may view themselves as exercising whatever due process is due, this is seldom the way they are perceived by others.

Their public image is that of unpredictable aggressors and of interlopers in the affairs of their peers. Because their entry onto the stage is unplanned and unannounced it leaves the villain abused, the onlookers confused, and the hero or victim ungrateful.

The following illustration shows the norm enforcers may sometimes operate in private encounters (involving relatives and acquaintances), while at other times they pretend to arbitrate relatively public and large-scale conflicts:

> This man appears to fit the "defender of justice" pattern; particularly for friends and for his own brother. He perceives himself as having a reputation to maintain as one who does not let people take advantage of his special friends and family. As soon as he perceives that the other party is going to resort to violence, he sets out to arrange the situation so that he will get in the first blow. He does not necessarily start every incident with the instigating of violence. He does make an effort to establish his reputation as a defender of justice on a verbal level. His first effort would be to get the other party to plead guilty. If such happens, then no vio-

lence need result. But if the other party will not plead guilty, and admit that he had committed an injustice to his friend or brother, then the man will set up the situation in rather elaborate form so that he is almost certain to win and so that he will have the opportunity for the first blow in the violent exchange. He also (to be consistent with his reputation) goes to extreme lengths to make this move so as to be referred to as an executioner. He is a protector who uses real violence and does not hesitate when the consequences of this violence include actual murder.

In one of the incidents, he is in one institution, and his brother in another. A new inmate arrives, claiming to be the brother's friend. Subsequent information reveals that the man is not only making a false claim, but that he even owes the brother money. When our man demands to be paid, the other puts him off; he also goes about the place asking for a knife. Despite the fact that the evidence indicates that the knife may be intended for other creditors, our man takes no chances; he invites the other for a cup of coffee, and—once safely in the crowd milling around the dispenser—he stabs him.

Catharting: Aggression as Emotional Release

Our final type consists of *catharters*, who attack others to release accumulated emotions, so that the identity of the victim becomes a matter of incidental importance. Cues and incentives to violence are in the "catharter's" mind, and the external occasions for it are arbitrarily selected; in this sense what goes on seems to fit the traditional picture of the indiscriminate exploder, for whom violence liberates accumulated tension. But this is not completely true as a statement of what occurs, because the timing of violence is always tied—and systematically tied—to specific feelings and needs; moreover, this kind of violence is purposive violence: The "catharter" is a person who has learned that by becoming aggressive at key junctures in his life he can successfully cheer himself up.

In other words, for "catharters" violence is not really a social response. Violence satisfies a personal need, rather than being a way of reacting to others. A precipitating incident generally starts when the person notes in himself urges and moods that he interprets as a call to arms. He then sets out in search of conflict, and generally finds some, because he will go to any length to manufacture a situation in which he can claim that violence is appropriate. "Appropriate" here can mean as little as that someone walked by him and made himself available as a victim, but it can also entail an elaborate ritual of "picking a fight" or justifying aggression.

The feeling tone preceding this game may range from depression and tension to boredom and desire for excitement. It may arise out of disappointment and frustration, or emerge out of a slow or eventless evening. The resulting conflict tends to be emotionally tinged to match. It can vary from grim and intense to devilishly lighthearted and "fun and games." To the victim, of course, the distinction is academic, because he faces the problem of being attacked without apparent cause. He—as well as most bystanders and observers—usually concludes that they have experienced flagrantly irrational behavior by an obvious maniac. However, the reason why the play is cryptic is simply because the aggressor is the only surviving member of the original cast and because the rest are hastily hired understudies who have not been supplied with the script.

The following illustration represents the "lighthearted" extreme of the type, in which the motivation for violence is boredom and the desire for entertainment. Other forms of the pattern feature more negative emotions, such as extreme tension and bitterness. No matter what the feeling, it impels the person to aggressive activity, because he has come to associate this with relief and peace of mind.

> It looks as if the main fights, or at least the most dramatic sets or sequences of fights, occur with this man when he wants to amuse himself, or himself and others, by spontaneously attacking casual victims whom he happens to encounter. One fairly spectacular sequence of this kind consists of him pulling drivers out of cars that patronize a drive-in and assaulting them physically. And a second sequence occurs as he and a friend go from one party to another on a weekend, antagonizing people. In the course of this expedition they assault gas station attendants, their host at one of the parties, and a set of guests who happen to arrive on the scene at another.

While in prison, our man appears to be somewhat careless in baiting several people in succession in such a way that by the time he's finished, his situation looks precarious to an outsider.

The role of others in this man's involvement is not always the same. In some situations there is teamwork involved and he appears to enjoy a kind of camaraderie with another violent individual. And there is some team spirit in this kind of sport. In other situations he's an entertainer, acting for an audience. In still other instances he gets himself into a violence-prone situation, counting apparently with the support of people who, assessing this same situation, decide that they don't wish to become involved. And then he proceeds anyway; since he has, at this point, no real option. There also appears to be some tendency for him to gain an unjustified feeling of immunity. That is, it looks as if he does not take very careful stock of the odds in several of the situations in which he encounters violence.

Another point is that after the sequence of events begins, he won't back out, he won't change his strategy until he's either knocked out or the fight's over.

It also appears as if, in at least some of the situations with this individual, the word "strategy" isn't as applicable as the word "fun." That is, there is a kind of spirit of enjoyment and levity about the proceedings. And it is as if he doesn't take account of the fact that the victim may not share the enjoyment as much as he and his friends do. (Although in at least one instance, the enjoyment was so infectious that one victim got into the spirit of the game before he was flattened.) There appears to be some evidence here that at least in the majority of instances violence for this man might be an end in itself. The clearest situation where this occurs is at a party where the guests discover that another set of guests is arriving, and our hero announces that whoever they are, he's going to lick them. And as soon as the first of the new group of guests arrives, our friend hits him in the face with a mop that he happens to have been mopping the floor with.

Problems of Validity

Do the classifications we have proposed correspond to real clusters of dispositions? The question is fair, but it is difficult to answer. Typologies, after all, are invariably fictions. Whenever we group complex configurations, such as people, we bring together only some of their attributes. With respect to other features, the in-groupers may differ as much as do their fellows at large. Moreover, the properties a typologist honors are the properties he or she thinks are of interest. These qualities may not stand out in the eyes of other beholders—or in the eyes of the individuals being typed—as essential or central.

The aim of our study was to make sense out of dispositions to aggression; our typology classifies people in terms of their propensity to violence. True, violence here is part and parcel of a person's social orientation; but that does not greatly change the matter. Although we record general characteristics, these are always characteristics related to violence. This means that other qualities are neglected, and some of these can be important. Any of our types can bring together saints and sinners, idiots and geniuses, schemers and obsessed persons. The types can be pure in our terms only, while being conglomerates with respect to more important matters.

Granted this fact, one can ask whether we have successfully accommodated our objective. Have we accurately classified people in terms of personal dispositions that promote their involvement in violence? Again, our reply must be inconclusive. For one, violence (like any other form of human conduct) is a brew of many causal ingredients, all of which in some sense shape it. We have focused on some information only—the type of information that documents the sort of explanation we favor. Ours is a typology of interpersonal orientations, because such is our theory. Our portraits may look plausible to someone who shares our view of aggression as a byproduct of social conduct. But anyone who feels that violence is born only in childhood, or that it is organizationally determined, may question the validity of our characterizations.

Theory and potential controversy enter elsewhere also. Clearly, our types are not merely groupings of observed facts. Frequently, they describe relationships among facts, and they even postulate causes for observed behavior. The validity of such clinical inferences can be only indirectly established, and it cannot be substantiated by pointing at the data we have collected.

We stand on more solid ground when we defend the integrity of individual classifications. Within the limits of our categories, we have some safeguards against arbitrary assignment of persons to types. We benefit from the fact that our typology is derived from case materials prepared by professional and nonprofessional staff. This method insures against narrow preclassifications. Nonprofessionals have intimate acquaintance with the context of the data, which permits them to screen out characterizations that are theoretically plausible enough, but that are incompatible with the experienced acts of comparable people in comparable situations. (Such "real life" experiences, of course, are not necessarily generalizable, and social scientists can help guard against the temptation of making too much of unrepresentative encounters.)

But what about the "facts" we have collected—the data themselves? Can we assume that these are valid? The chances are probably excellent. Our peer interviews were designed to gain the trust of informants, and we have evidence that the procedure worked. Often, our nonprofessional researchers learned that their presence made interviews possible. Many of our subjects were candid to the point of self-incrimination. The sample included offenders of notoriety, who had in the past proved impervious to official questioning. One such inmate spent several days regaling us with detailed descriptions of unrecorded transgressions, some of which we informally verified later.

In most cases, our code-numbered interviews and the coded record transcripts were found to supplement each other. As a rule, an interviewee would furnish us with at least one or two incidents already noted on his dossier. The details on record, to be sure, rarely provided information to fully explain the person's violent involvements. Causes were noted, but they tended to cover information needed to attach and to gauge blame, or to arrive at a casual understanding of precipitating interactions. Thus, the record often tended to give an impression of heterogeneously and malevolently motivated violence where we found more sophisticated patterns.

But we did encounter instances where the official record was factually more accurate than our interviews. Some rapists and chronic sexual exploiters would not talk with us at all. Several who did exercised prudent censorship in describing their involvements. They tended to limit their narratives to episodes less shocking and reprehensible than those on record. We found in such cases, however, that the interview accounts reflected the same exploitive orientation that permeated the material on the record—and usually the victims proved similar in kind. The following case concerns one of these persons, whom we classified as an exploiter (with a secondary theme of self-indulging):

> Here is a man who unmercifully takes advantage of women, and then gets extremely indignant when they show the slightest resentment. His record, which he does not discuss with us, is a long and redundant series of episodes in which he sexually assaults a collection of women ranging in age from kindergarten to senescence. (And in which, in a large proportion of instances, he also has the gall to extract money from his victims.) In addition to this he has another game that he plays with married women, forcing his attentions on them and then extracting blackmail money from them by threatening to tell their husbands that they submitted. The episodes he does discuss with us show the same patterns in a slightly less blatant fashion. In the first of these sequences, he ostensibly helps a female in distress by evicting her common-law husband, but then it turns out that his real motive was to move in as a substitute, and when this scheme is unsuccessful he becomes extremely annoyed with the intended victim.
>
> In another instance of unmitigated gall that he relates, he steals his current flame's complete bankroll, gambles it away, becomes indignant when she questions him on the subject, beats her up and then lies down to sleep on her bed. Here he is painfully surprised in more ways than one when he wakes up to find himself cut to ribbons.
>
> A similar episode takes place in another context, involving a lady whose acquaintance he made and in whose case there is a more attractive and younger niece residing at the same address. And as soon as the lady goes to the kitchen to prepare coffee for him, temptation lurks and he gives in. That is, when she returns from the kitchen, she finds him in the process of seducing her niece. Again, of course, he

is the object of some indignant attentions which he fails to understand.

In other words, there is a consistent tendency on his part to view women as objects for exploitation. And then the added factor that any resistance whatsoever on the part of his victims is viewed by him as provoking and as unjustifiable. It is of course one of the consequences of the kind of game he plays, that he has repeatedly come to the attention of authorities. However, there are many episodes that precede each of the unsuccessful encounters that end him in prison.

We have excluded from our typology the two interviews whose validity was questioned by our nonprofessional colleagues, and whose substantiation through recorded information was not satisfactory. Following is the text of the study group summary of one of these two interviews:

There are three indications that this man was fabricating most of the information he supplied us with. First, this is the impression of an interviewer, who records that "it was too bad this guy was such a liar": the interviewers felt that here was a blatant effort to impress them. Second, we would expect serious displays of public violence of the kind claimed by this man to be matters of public record—and we don't have a single incident officially noted in his parole file. Third, there is the internal evidence.

This man claims to be a vicious kind of superman, an avenging killer. The image he traces for us is that of the man who in cold blood avenges injustice at its source, by putting a gory end to those responsible. He walks into a juvenile institution—he says—and is nudged by a guard. Next thing he is standing in the Warden's office, explaining to the Warden about necessary changes. The Warden pays insufficient attention to the message, and is knifed. The rich fantasy life behind this episode of grand vengeance also permeates other stories. For instance, there is the gang fight, ended by our man with a shotgun—brutally used on the leader of the rival gang. Again, the image he conveys is of a definite, cold-blooded, brutal act.

He also claims to enjoy violence, and he certainly enjoys talking about it. He endows his incidents with an almost orgasmic quality, and builds up to the climax in a series of delicious delays. The violence, or the telling of it, is exciting.

There is one incident which rings true out of the group, and here the man admits stabbing someone by mistake. He assumed a knife that was being manufactured was intended for him, and it wasn't. The suggestion also is, judging by the mass of scar tissue on his face, that his experience with violence may not be that of the conquering dispenser of Justice, as he claims—but rather of a man who repeatedly has been taught the error of tackling the wrong people.

It would be hasty to discard this type of information as useless, even though our facts are probably largely fictitious. In dealing with this person, it is no doubt important that his fantasy life is peopled by acts of cynical brutality and bloody retribution against authority. There is directionality and pattern here which rests as securely on psychological foundations as would the bloody acts being described. In fact, the sense of inadequacy and some paranoid flavor are highlighted by the need to fabricate the information. By virtue of the individual's membership in our sample, we know that he has been involved in acts of violence; we can presume that these have a far less lofty aspect and definitive outcome than those with which the person credits himself. The discrepancy is one which could be of considerable diagnostic and therapeutic importance in more intensive work with this individual.

In other words, even fabrications, when subjected to the type of analysis we have suggested, can provide testable hypotheses and potential tools for the production of personal change.

And What About Reliability?

Our entire picture, of course, would fall into the realm of poetry if an independent judge could not duplicate the classifications. At best, our typology might constitute insight without applicability; at worst, it could imply that we had focused on irrelevant or idiosyncratic variables.

The independent rater (Dr. Jeanne Block) did not find the

classification task a particularly easy one. She reported that the coding did not resemble other types of judgment; although clinical experience was applicable, it had to be refocused, because the person's use of violence—rather than his general orientation—was at issue. Dr. Block also reported that the choice of one primary category was in several instances a difficult one to make.

Thirty-five interviews were independently typed. The results of this operation showed 7 out of 35 judgments to yield major discrepancies; in 16 instances, the types corresponded exactly, and in 12, closely related or functionally equivalent categories were used. This last group requires comment and has the most important implications for the nature and scope of our typology. We shall, therefore, discuss it first.

More than half of the twelve "related" classifications involved two categories; the first of these is that of self-image defender, which in four out of six instances was transmuted by the coder into self-image promoter. In one of these cases, the classification read "norm enforcer (self-image promoter)," but we can include this in the group because of the fact that norm enforcing is clearly a specialized subclass of promoting.

The preferential use of the "promoting" label indicates that our rater saw in most self-image compensation some initiative in the shape of readiness to fight, or some extra satisfaction with the opportunity for violence. Whereas this does not invalidate the conceptual distinction between advertised pugnaciousness and overeager responsiveness to slights, it does show that this distinction is hard to apply. The self-image compensator is rarely a pure defender or a pure promoter; if he tends to *react* to slights, it is also true that he does so with alacrity, so that the initiative for the conflict becomes difficult to assign; further, response to perceived challenges tend to add up to an aggressive stance. Conversely, challenging involves goading people into reactions that can be "defended" rather than "promoted." Finally, there is coder preference. Our rater seemed oriented toward initiative on the part of the self-image compensator; she thus placed the weight primarily on the promoting effort, rather than on the defending acts.

The second group of functionally related discrepant classifications involved pressure removers, three of whom were converted into "self-indulgers (pressure removers)" or, in one case, into a pure self-indulger. The link between these themes is a chronological one. By and large, pressure removing is the last resort used in self-engineered dilemmas. Most often, the type of person who operates at a level of maturity in which he expects others to comply with his needs (or at minimum, who assumes that they will refrain from being obstacles in his path) is most apt to blindly explode when he encounters what he sees as non-amenable and non-cooperative people. Our original classification focused on this final act, whereas the rater placed heavy emphasis on its presumed antecedents. Again, the discrepancy revolves around differential attention to the actor as against the incident, in a standard chain of related psychological events.

Patterning Problems: The Complex Violence-Prone Person

We have noted that in 7 of our 35 cases, independent classifications produced pictures at variance with the original coding. In some instances this difference was clearly attributable to different weights assigned to different aspects of a given person's violence. Thus, two of our rep defenders were seen as bullies (by the rater) because in both cases victims were manhandled and were fairly thoroughly and systematically destroyed. The type of individual classified here unquestionably took his rep-defending sufficiently seriously to raise the possibility that it provided him an excuse for the joy he derived from administering punishment. In a case like this, a secondary theme is not a standard solution, because the question is one of ambiguity rather than of intersecting motives; what is at issue is whether conflicts are imposed on the person and he *then* gets carried away, or whether he gets carried away in situations that he can legitimize as a product of his "rep." Such alternatives would have to be resolved through appropriate interview questions.

In addition to divergences such as these, which result from ambiguities in the data, there are others that seem produced by the fact that the violent individual is a man of unusual and considerable complexity. Here we have the rare person who with each stone kills several motivational birds, so that it becomes virtually impossible to pinpoint and isolate one motive for his violence.

The extreme is furnished by a member of our sample who also happened to be one of our research workers. His original classification (based on a "study group" summary prepared with his own participation) was self-image promoter, with secondary themes of bullying and rep-defending. The rater, however, decided that the man was a pressure remover, with admixture of exploiter. In other words, half of our typology was ultimately invoked in attempting to describe this one man's violence.

How is this type of classification phenomenon possible? We turn to our study group summary, where we find the following excerpts:

1. (Self-image promoting): There was—the group noted—a persistent theme "of coping through force (and force here means essentially a show of force) with people who haven't sufficiently caught the point that here is someone that one doesn't want to mess with." Again, "one factor in our man's violence is hostile spectators who are warned 'here is someone you don't meddle with,' and people who are to be impressed in terms of recognizing the status of this kind of activity."

2. (Bullying): The group noted that in many of the fights "the terrorizing can become fairly drastic, and can take the form of physically neutralizing the opponent and continuing to harm him beyond what is necessary to put him out of action." Furthermore, "there is also the continual presence of the weapon, combined with the way in which fights are set up, both of which seem to indicate that the effort is really to physically harm the other person—not to permit him to escape by saving face in some fashion or by concluding the matter peacefully."

3. (Rep-defending): The group noted a "secondary" aspect to the man's violence, "which consisted of protecting the members of the clique, or members of the team, or the extended family, or simply friends if they require strong arm protection." There was also mention of an omnipresent "chorus of friends

who receive the impression that their interests are being adequately protected."

4. (Pressure-removing): The rater noted that our man "can't stand people crowding close," and that he "doesn't know when and how to stop." The group also recorded this second reaction and located it principally in youthful or early acts of violence; in these early incidents (according to the group) "the action degenerates because, after the terrorizing, he is really somewhat clumsy"; the resulting violence is thus "unintended." The group and the rater both saw the subject angrily responding, in unscheduled ways, to accumulated pressure. The group, however, felt that the pressure represented crowding behavior come home to roost.

5. (Exploiting): The rater pointed out that the subject "exploits his friends and sacrifices them to his needs . . . three times his friends are hurt as a result of his acts." The group also noted these facts but attributed them to a propensity for clumsiness and an inability to control self-demonstration efforts. Thus, the group described one youthful adventure, in which our man went out of his way to carry a gun to a party, where "he unnecessarily uses the weapon and finds himself hurting several people who strictly speaking didn't have to be hurt," simply in order to carry through.

We here find that part of the reason for discrepant classifications is a difference in interpretation and weighting of identical facts, including instances in which the rater concentrated on a theme prevalent in some incidents which appeared to drop out in others. This possibility points up the variable of change over time, which in a few of our violence-prone persons could make it desirable to permit a more complex classification, with successive stages in the development of one individual's violence represented as overlapping but different categories.

The picture also suggests that there are some violence-prone persons whose complexity demands a relatively multidimensional categorization for accurate representation. Although most persons in our sample appear to be adequately covered by means of one (or, at most, two) recurrent themes, there are a few whose games are more sophisticated. Here a more generous catalogue of themes can both increase validity and insure that the type is as reliable as is the person it represents.

Result of the Reliability Study

Clearly, the major moral of our re-classification venture has been that our typology can be communicated and that it can yield defensible results in diverse hands. Given the complexity of the concepts involved, one could probably live comfortably with more than seven errors out of 35 classifications.

Of course, when we speak of "seven errors" we assume that we can concentrate on the phenomena referred to rather than on the labels we use for them. We can thus accept our coding nuances in the classification of self-image compensating, and we can accommodate the career-oriented versus incident-oriented variations we have found in the classification of the self-indulging–pressure-removing sequence. The transition from one such label to the other could easily be bridged with one or two explanatory phrases, or by standardizing the instructions, or by awareness of the coder's bias, or by increasing multiple-classification. The point is that the labels are functionally related and that the concepts referred to are the same, so that the transition is provided for.

A different situation exists in the seven negative cases we referred to. In some of these there is recognizable ambiguity, and the remedy here would be to suspend classification until questions could be clarified with the interviewee. (If the ambiguity is not obvious, two independent codings would make it so, as in the above cases.) The remaining instances seem to consist of persons who make violence serve more purposes than the one or two that are characteristic of the average violence-prone individual. These multi-variate practitioners of violence need not be confused with men of polymorphous violence, as envisaged in the "indiscriminate exploder" model. Whereas the traditional conception of violence denotes an exploder, the person we refer to makes violence serve objectives; whereas the traditional violent man is unpredictable and random, our complex practitioner replicates his violence, with the diverse elements that comprise it. Rather than being the exception that proves the rule, this problem child is the exception that embodies the rule, and does so with such a vengeance that he makes rules difficult to apply.

6

The Anatomy of Violence

In Chapter 5 we presented the substance of the typology used in this study. We cannot maintain that the types we isolated exhaust the universe of violence, but it can be expected that an extension of the classification would not alter its nature.

What is the shape of violence-proneness as we have begun to describe it? And how is the type of violence we have described related to other forms of violence? What bearing does this description of violent personalities have on collective violence, such as riots? What are the similarities, if any, between people who are recurrently violent and those who explode insanely once in a lifetime? In the following pages, these questions will be explored. We shall attempt thus to extend the findings and to place them in context.

First, we shall consider the nature of the beast we have isolated and its place in psychological functioning.

We have suggested that two types of orientation are especially likely to produce violence: One of these is that of the person who sees other people as tools designed to serve his needs; the second is that of the individual who feels vulnerable to diminishment. These two perspectives, when we examine them more closely, become faces of the same coin: Both rest on the premise that human relationships are power-centered, one-way affairs; both involve efforts at self-assertion with a desperate, feverish quality that suggests self-doubt.

Of course, this description does not fit all cases. Some of

the rep defenders, for instance, initially respond to a draft, instead of promoting their own reputation; some self-defenders react to a human jungle in which they are unfairly asked to survive; pressure-removing sometimes represents little more than feeblemindedness. But even in these instances, experiences with violent encounters teach the person to respond overeagerly, suspending the dictates of equity, ignoring the norm of reciprocity, and asserting personal autonomy at the expense of others. Such, it appears, is the nature of the violence-prone game.

The violence-provoking incident typically consists of several stages: First there is the classification of the other person as an object or a threat; second, there is some action based on this classification; third, the other person may act—if he has the chance—to protect his integrity. At this juncture, the violent incident reaches its point of no return. The initial stance of the violence-prone person makes violence probable; his first moves increase the probability of violence; the reaction of the victim converts probability into certainty.

The extent to which violent incidents are predetermined depends on how aggressive the aggressor feels. If his violence-propensity is substantial, he may insist on conflict; if his requirements are modest, the victim may be left with pacifying moves. For instance, a mildly scared individual can be reassured; a person who feels somewhat inadequate can be satisfied with flattery or a show of humor. But if the aggressor's ego demands blood, the victim may find himself pursued remorselessly, no matter what he says or does. Hemingway illustrates this in an episode involving two professional killers (Max and Al) toying with a restaurant owner (George) and his patron (Nick):

> "You're a pretty bright boy, aren't you?"
> "Sure," said George.
> "Well, you're not," said the other little man. "Is he, Al?"
> "He's dumb," said Al. He turned to Nick. "What's your name?"
> "Adams."
> "Another bright boy," Al said. "Ain't he a bright boy, Max?"

"The town's full of bright boys," Max said.

George put the two platters, one of ham and eggs, the other of bacon and eggs, on the counter. He set down two side-dishes of fried potatoes and closed the wicket into the kitchen.

"Which is yours?" he asked Al.

"Don't you remember?"

"Ham and eggs."

"Just a bright boy," Max said. He leaned forward and took the ham and eggs. Both men ate with their gloves on. George watched them eat.

"What are *you* looking at?" Max looked at George.

"Nothing."

"The hell you were. You were looking at me."

"Maybe the boy meant it for a joke, Max," Al said. George laughed.

"*You* don't have to laugh," Max said to him. "You don't have to laugh at all, see?"

"All right," said George.

"So he thinks it's all right." Max turned to Al. "He thinks it's all right. That's a good one."

"Oh, he's a thinker," Al said. They went on eating.

"What's the bright boy's name down the counter?" Al asked Max.

"Hey, bright boy," Max said to Nick. "You go around on the other side of the counter with your boy friend."

"What's the idea?" Nick asked.

"You better go around, bright boy," Al said. Nick went around behind the counter."[1]

The probability of violence in violence-provoking incidents is tied to the extent to which the aggressor indulges in pre-classification or selective perception. For instance, many of the participants in our police incidents scan human contacts assiduously for the possibility of threatening implications. They do so with varying degrees of intensity and with differing abilities to "spot" suggestive information. The actions of other

---

[1] Reprinted with the permission of Charles Scribner's Sons from *Men Without Women*, pp. 378–379, by Ernest Hemingway. Copyright 1927 Charles Scribner's Sons; renewal copyright © 1955 Ernest Hemingway.

people are eventually classified as either non-challenging (safe) or as challenging (requiring action). Because the consequences of error matter, the scales are far from evenly weighted: With greater or lesser distortion, potentially harmless encounters become transmuted into offensive acts by monsters or degenerates. And at this point, the time-worn formula of the weak ego prescribes an aggressive confrontation. If this confrontation consists of direct aggression, it ends the incident; when it does not, the other person must somehow cope with the affront to which he has been subjected. His response is likely to lead to violence, because it usually feeds into the hypothesis that provides the aggressor's rationale for offensiveness.

For several reasons, the probability of violence in personal encounters increases with each new act of aggression. Violence is habit-forming. Aggressors discover that they can satisfy new and unsuspected needs by becoming aggressive. They also learn to view themselves as participants in violent games. Most importantly, they start seeing elements of past violent encounters as they approach fresh situations and begin to respond to them. They seek and find consistency of self at the expense of their victims. Richard Wright illustrates this phenomenon in his description of the murders committed by Bigger, the hero of *Native Son*. Both killings were motivated by panic and by the desire to escape danger. The first—which was almost accidental—resulted when Bigger tried to quiet a drunk girl, to avoid being discovered in her room:

> Mary mumbled and tried to rise again. Frantically, he caught a corner of the pillow and brought it to her lips. He had to stop her from mumbling, or he would be caught. Mrs. Dalton was moving slowly toward him and he grew tight and full, as though about to explode. Mary's fingernails tore at his hands and he caught the pillow and covered her entire face with it, firmly. Mary's body surged upward and he pushed downward upon the pillow with all of his weight, determined that she must not move or make any sound that would betray him. His eyes were filled with the white blur moving toward him in the shadows of the room. Again Mary's body heaved and he held the pillow in a grip that took all of his strength. For a long time he felt the sharp

pain of her fingernails biting into his wrists. The white blur was still.[2]

The second murder was in many ways parallel to the first. Like the first, it was designed to rid Bigger of a girl who threatened to impede his escape. Again, Bigger had nothing against his victim and merely wanted to insure his safety. And the danger was the same, with the discoverer of the first incident still perceived in the shadows of the second.

Bigger, however, had changed. Having killed once, he now saw himself as a taker of life when the occasion demanded it:

> A sense of the white blur hovering near, of Mary burning, of Britten, of the law tracking him down, came back. Again, he was ready. The brick was in his hand. In his mind his hand traced a quick invisible arc through the cold air of the room; high above his head his hand paused in fancy and imaginatively swooped down to where he thought her head must be. He was rigid; not moving. This was the way it *had* to be. Then he took a deep breath and his hand gripped the brick and shot upward and paused a second and then plunged downward through the darkness to the accompaniment of a deep short grunt from his chest and landed with a thud. . . . How many times he had lifted the brick and brought it down he did not know. All he knew was that the room was quiet and cold and that the job was done.[3]

Evolution of the Violence-Prone Premise

Although the logic of violence may emerge from the practice of violence, it probably originates most frequently in interpersonal relationships early in life. Thus, manipulative efforts mark the failure of socialization somewhere between unbridled infancy and the assumption of social responsibility. Self-assertiveness or defensiveness suggests that one's upbringing has been deficient in stability and emotional support, thus

---

[2] R. Wright, *Native Son* (New York: Harper, 1949), p. 74.
[3] Ibid., pp. 200–201.

making it difficult for positive self-perceptions to develop.[4] In both instances, brittle egos spend their adult years in belated efforts to buttress themselves at the expense of other people, and these efforts become productive of violence.

Of course, a brittle ego is a relative construction; some situations can shatter selves of steel, while others cater to the lowest levels of maturity. The young police officer out on his first beat faces all kinds of problems with which he is unprepared to cope. And what of the "fish"—our Sam, for instance—entering the prison yard for his first time, expecting to be terrorized into a state of emasculated slavery? And what of the fact that both the young officer and the young fish have learned that they are entering a world in which power is the only voice that carries, and in which attention to the feelings of others is a dangerous weakness?

Situations promotive of violent reactions undoubtedly exist; individuals are faced with human relations problems of almost insoluble complexity and serious personal import. These problems awaken fear and a sense of inadequacy; violence-prone solutions advocated by persons who are presumed to be experienced and sophisticated are persuasive. It would almost follow that these solutions would be adopted.

It would *almost* follow, that is, except for the circumstance that these solutions involve violations of the integrity and the aspirations of other people, and that this circumstance can be plainly inferred. It is obvious that the mythology of violence-proneness at minimum requires the short-circuiting of rules of procedure, or calls for precipitous aggressive action with little inquiry into its justification. And it is because violence is primitive that the most successfully socialized persons among those exposed to a potentially explosive situation will resist premature acceptance of the violent formula of survival.

---

[4]The extreme form of this relationship is that of the phenomenon known as "the cycle of violence." Many victims of child abuse are found among known practitioners of violence. Children who are abused grow up and brutalize their own children, who can become child abusers themselves. This sad and paradoxical correlation can result from a combined effect of self-destructive modeling, an impact of traumas, and internalization of a "hurt-or-be-hurt" premise about how society works.

The willingness to adopt the violence-prone mythology of survival distinguishes the members of our sample from other inmates or police officers or slum children or unhappily married men. It distinguishes them as persons with a starting capital of insecurity or egocentricity available for investment in violence-promoting premises.

Unfortunately, as the game of violence unfolds in our interviews, it appears to be insidious in its cumulative character. Once a person discovers that the ego can be buttressed at the expense of others, the discovery seems to be recurrently applied. The routine, moreover, gains from both success and failure; its stability rests on the fact that it feeds on personal insecurity, rather than on the reactions of victims and the sanctions of authority. The task of re-educating the violence-prone person is thus one of considerable magnitude and a challenge worthy of the best the social sciences and helping professions can offer.

The Subculture of Violence

We have made much of the role of violence-prone premises or assumptions in the creation of violent incidents. We have seen that persons who tend to interpret situations as threatening, or goading, or challenging, or overpowering can turn harmless encounters into duels, purges, struggles for survival, or violent escapes.

To be sure, the propensity satisfies personal needs; it resolves doubts about self-importance, it brings social prominence and respect, and it preserves a consumer role in personal relations. But these ends can be achieved in other ways—sometimes with considerably less risk or consequence.

Violence-prone premises tie neatly into immature personality patterns, but the connection is not inevitable. Some use violence as a crutch, and others do not; some use violence as a weapon, and others do not. The question is, what accounts for the difference? Where do violence-prone assumptions have their social origin—where are they invented? One explanation would be that violent alternatives may be accidentally discovered and that, once violence has been exercised, the experience transfers to successive encounters. But this explanation is too related to chance. It seems easier to assume that in some segments of our society violence-prone premises at some juncture become widely accepted and available for adoption by susceptible individuals.

This type of explanation has been advanced by Marvin Wolfgang, and has been expanded in Wolfgang and Ferracuti's treatise *The Subculture of Violence*.[5] The basis for the idea is a statistical one: It rests on the finding that in some groups members of the group are more prone to use violence to solve their problems than are members of other groups. For instance, Sicily and Sardinia have several localities in which it has been customary to retaliate against private affronts, and in parts of Colombia and Mexico citizens have been apt to settle their disputes with physical combat. In the United States, young men who have grown up in urban ghettos are disproportionately among dispensers (and victims) of violence.

Such situations can be assumed to reflect the impact of "subcultures of violence" because they imply that there is some sort of code which prescribes violent conduct and which is passed on—through word and deed—from one generation to the next. The question arises, Why is violence thus prized, particularly among young men? One widely accepted explanation was advanced by Talcott Parsons in an essay about aggression in Western society.[6] Following Freud, Parsons discussed a need among young male adolescents to evolve a masculine identity. Where fathers are conspicuously absent or relatively unimpressive, this process is impaired. A compensatory "compulsive masculinity" orientation can evolve, which emphasizes traits perceived to be unfeminine, such as toughness and aggressivity. American and Mexican slums, for instance, contain many homes in which the mother is of considerably more consequence than the father, who may be rarely in evidence. In such homes, the masculine role may not seem

---

[5]M. Wolfgang and F. Ferracuti, *The Subculture of Violence: Toward an Integrated Theory of Criminology* (London: Tavistock, 1967).

[6]T. Parsons, "Certain Primary Sources and Patterns of Aggression in the Social Structure of the Western World," *Psychiatry* (1947), 10: 167–181.

imposing, and growing boys may feel compelled to evolve physical means of demonstrating their worth. Violence here becomes one of the facets or vehicles of the well-known *machismo* syndrome.[7] In other subcultures, emphasis on violence can originate in transformed social customs or group relationships. Family feuds and tribal rivalries, for instance, can give rise to a tradition of retaliation, as in parts of Italy. Frontier justice can be transformed into a system for privately punishing presumed offenders.

Whatever the origins of the subculture of violence, it exists in the form of values, beliefs, and attitudes held by its members. These may relate to all manner of situations, and may prescribe appropriate conduct for them. Violence is one such form of conduct, and it is permissively viewed. That such a doctrine is prevalent does not mean, of course, that every person residing in a given geographical area will be equally subjected to it, nor that everyone exposed to these assumptions will adopt them. Violence-proneness is restricted to the select minority within the subculture who have used and distorted its violence-prone teachings and who live by them.

For these select persons, a wide range of situations would be defined as justifying aggressive responses. Violence-prone people do not merely espouse violence as a doctrine or philosophy, but they tend to see the world in violent terms and respond to it accordingly. In the words of Wolfgang and Ferracuti, "variations in the surrounding world . . . [would] have a greater chance of being perceived and reacted upon . . . as menacing, aggressive stimuli which call for immediate defense and counteraggression."[8] Among gang boys in the ghetto, for example, "a male is usually expected to defend the name and

---

[7] Most of the literature on *machismo* exists in Spanish-language publications. Erich Fromm has established the relationship between assertion of masculinity and mother-dominated homes; see E. Fromm and M. Maccoby, *Social Character in a Mexican Village* (Englewood Cliffs, NJ: Prentice-Hall, 1970). Among American delinquents, the masculine "toughness" value has been described by Walter Miller: W. B. Miller, H. Geertz, and H. Cutter, "Aggression in a Boys' Street-Corner Gang," *Psychiatry* (1961), 24: 283–298; also, by U. Hannerz, *Soulside: Inquiries Into Ghetto Culture and Community* (New York: Columbia University Press, 1969).

[8] Wolfgang and Ferracuti, op. cit., p. 157.

honor of his mother, the virtue of womanhood . . . and to accept no derogation about his race (even from a member of his own race), his age, or his masculinity. Quick resort to physical combat as a measure of daring, courage, or defense of status appears to be a cultural expression. . . ."[9]

Members of the subculture of violence perceive themselves as proactive; they see opportunities for violence in the world around them, and they play stereotyped violence-prone games. An example of stereotyped violence is the procedure known as "playing the dozens," which is popular in the slums and in prisons. "The dozens" is a form of verbal interaction designed to test one's own equanimity, to produce rage in one's opponent, and to build up a rationale for physical violence. Ralph Berdie describes one form of this interaction as follows:

> One of the tormenters will make a mildly insulting statement, perhaps about the mother of the subject, "I saw your mother out with a man last night." Then he may follow this up with "She was as drunk as a bat." The subject, in turn, will then make an insulting statement about the tormenter or some member of the tormenter's family. This exchange of insults continues, encouraged by the approval and shouts of the observers, and the insults become progressively nastier and more pornographic, until they eventually include every member of the participants' families and every act of animal and man. . . . Finally, one of the participants, usually the subject, who has actually been combating the group pressure of the observers, reaches his threshold and takes a swing at the tormenter, pulls out a knife or picks up an object to use as a club. That is the sign for the tormenter, and sometimes some of the observers, to go into action, and usually the subject ends up with the most physical injuries.[10]

---

[9]M. Wolfgang, *Patterns in Criminal Homicide* (Philadelphia: University of Pennsylvania Press, 1958), p. 188. A systematic study of this pattern is described in J. F. Short, and F. L. Strodtbeck, *Group Process and Gang Delinquency* (Chicago: University of Chicago Press, 1965).

[10]R. F. Berdie, "Playing the Dozens," *Journal of Abnormal and Social Psychology* (1947), 42: 120–121, p. 120.

Stereotyped violence-prone games appear in many forms in subcultures of violence. They also have elements in common. A striking parallel to "playing the dozens" for instance, is the dueling among German university students, and jousting among medieval knights. The character of the latter is evidenced by the prescribed sequence of insults preceding each encounter. T. H. White amusingly makes this point in describing the clash between King Pellinore and Sir Grummore, in *The Once and Future King*:

> "Suppose we'd better have a joust, eh, what?"
>
> "Yes, I suppose we had better," said King Pellinore, "really."
>
> "What shall we have it for?"
>
> "Oh, the usual thing, I suppose. Would one of you kindly help me on with my helm?". . .
>
> As soon as they were ready, the two knights stationed themselves at each end of the clearing and then advanced to meet in the middle.
>
> "Fair knight," said King Pellinore, "I pray thee tell me thy name."
>
> "That me regards," replied Sir Grummore, using the proper formula.
>
> "That is uncourteously said," said King Pellinore, "what? For no knight he dreadeth for to speak his name openly, but for some reason of shame."
>
> "Be that as it may, I choose that thou shalt not know my name as at this time, for no askin'."
>
> "Then you must stay and joust with me, false knight."
>
> "Haven't you got that wrong, Pellinore?" inquired Sir Grummore. "I believe it ought to be 'thou shalt'."
>
> "Oh, I'm sorry, Sir Grummore. Yes, so it should, of course. Then thou shalt stay and joust with me, false knight."
>
> Without further words, the two gentlemen retreated to the opposite ends of the clearing, fewtered their spears, and prepared to hurtle together in the preliminary charge.
>
> "I think we had better climb this tree," said Merlyn. "You never know what will happen in a joust like this."[11]

---

[11] Reprinted by permission of G. P. Putnam's Sons from *The Once and Future King* by T. H. White. Copyright 1939, 1940 by T. H. White; © 1958 by T. H. White.

The subculture of violence can prescribe certain rules for the exercise of violence and also equips its members with motives, attitudes, and perceptions which produce the games in which these rules apply.

Fannin and Clinard, who studied the self-images of lower-class and middle-class delinquents, report that it is usual for the lower-class boys to see themselves as tough, powerful, fierce, and fearless. It is also usual, according to them, for these boys to want to become even tougher, harder and more violent than they are. The boys further feel that their prestige depends on advertised ability and willingness to fight, on physical superiority over others, and on general fearlessness. The interesting point is that the delinquent boys do not uniformly live up to the prescription, nor do they have similar conceptions of their own activities. Fannin and Clinard explain:

> The range of such conceptions appeared to run typologically from the "bruising marauder" to the "fearlful warrior." The former is a boy who is constantly proving his toughness by fighting unrelentingly at the slightest provocation, or who initiates brawls because he "likes to fight." His perception of ridicule, or the merest hint of disbelief about his masculinity, is extremely acute and he will settle the matter immediately by force. He is looked upon with respectful apprehension by his peers as a "nut," "crazy bastard," "a real goner," and as "dangerous" because he is always stirring up trouble; he is, in short, a disliked deviant.[12]

How does this observation relate to our typology? We assume that the dedicated, responsive, violence-predisposed member of the violent subculture—at least in the American slums— would be comparatively rare in real life. We know that even persons with common backgrounds are somewhat differently reared and that individual preferences always govern suscep-

---

[12] L. F. Fannin and M. B. Clinard, "Differences in the Conception of Self as a Male Among Lower and Middle Class Delinquents," *Social Problems* (1965), 13: 205–214, p. 211. A more detailed portrait of the self-conceptions of aggressive delinquents is provided in J. Katz, *Seductions of Crime: Moral and Sensual Attractions in Doing Evil* (New York: Basic Books, 1988).

tibility to general norms. The subculture of violence should thus consist of individual variations on subcultural themes. These variations should reflect both the subculture and the private views and problems of each individual. Wolfgang and Ferracuti themselves indicate that "differential personality variables must be considered in an integrated social–psychological approach to an understanding of the subcultural aspects of violence."[13]

Personality can intersect with group norms in one of several ways. For one, personal needs will dictate how well subcultural teachings are assimilated. Ultimately, it is the individual who decides whether violence is to be eagerly adopted, casually rehearsed, or totally avoided. And given the primitive prescription, weak egos are apt to assimilate best violence-prone lessons. Moreover, neighborhood definitions can leave considerable latitude for excitability thresholds, for preferences in roles, for variations in rationalizations, and for individual styles of response. Cultural definitions can reflect all manner of personal sensitivities and can accommodate every stage of maturity in interpersonal dealings. Thus, subcultural prescriptions for violence may not specify whether insults should be sought out or reacted to, whether aggression should take delayed or sudden forms, whether the individual should lead or follow in matters of aggression. Whereas the subculture of violence condones violence, it does not prescribe specific encounters of individual members. The nature of the person's violent acts can therefore reflect both the spirit of the times and the unique contribution of his individual predilections.

This is especially the case with persons who take to the justifying norms of the subculture with more alacrity and enthusiasm than their neighbors. It is these individuals, who meet the norm "thou may be violent" much more than halfway, who best personify the sociopsychological model of subculturally induced violence. For it is these persons whose needs are most felicitously responded to by the license to destroy which they feel is furnished them. And ultimately, these per-

---

[13] Wolfgang and Ferracuti, op. cit., p. 160.

sons carry violence to such an extreme that even their sub-cultural coreligionaries will classify them as violence-prone.

Collective Violence

No form of violence is more accepted and more damned, more ignored and more feared, than collective violence. On the one hand, the carnage of war—terrifyingly standardized and de-humanized and organized—has become an almost noncon-troversial feature of the human landscape. Except for a mi-nority who are often viewed as starry-eyed, civilized society condones the violence of war and rewards and decorates in-dividuals who have distinguished themselves by inflicting death and destruction on the battlefield.

On the other hand, we encounter apprehension bordering on hysteria in relation to such forms of domestic violence as urban riots. It is these displays of rage, with their sniping and arson and looting, which first made of violence a public policy issue in the sixties, and inspired the first of several inquiries into the causes of violence. It is these events that also produced contrasting simplistic explanations, which either emphasized the irrationality of collective behavior (a view favored by con-servatives) or the frustration that results from oppression (the liberal perspective). The dominant formula emphasizes eco-nomic or historical determinism, though studies by the Pres-ident's Commission on Civil Disorders (1968) have pointed to some of the complexities in the motivation of collective vio-lence.

The riot commission listed five "powerful ingredients" as "catalysts" of riots: (1) frustrated hope, generated by the civil rights struggle in the North and South; (2) a climate heavy with "approval and encouragement of violence"; (3) the frus-tration of feeling powerless to move the system; (4) a new mood—particularly in the young—of "self-esteem and en-hanced racial pride"; and (5) the view of police as a symbol of "white power, white racism and white repression."[14]

---

[14] *Report of the National Advisory Commission on Civil Disorders* (New York: Bantam Books; Dutton, 1968), pp. 10–11.

Clearly, these factors comprise a package of sorts. Increased hope creates increased bitterness as institutions are found unresponsive; enhanced self-esteem can generate a determination not to accept disappointments as answers; alternative solutions can be sought, and these can take the form of increasingly self-reliant measures (especially, given the premise that legality is a cloak for oppressors). It is also understandable that if conventional justice and conventional society are perceived as unjust and hostile, "antisocial" violence can come to acquire a positive, rather than a negative connotation.

According to this view, rioting is a last resort. The person or group has problems, seeks relief, obtains no satisfaction, and becomes bitter. Since direct demands yield no result, one is forced into increasingly indirect, affect-laden, protest-oriented action. The Commission points out that riots are preceded by incidents that dramatize unredressed complaints or affronts. A Cincinnati disturbance, for instance, followed a period during which, "without the city's realizing what was occurring . . . protest through political and non-violent channels had become increasingly difficult." The Commission points out that "to young Negroes, especially, such protest appeared to have become almost futile."[15] In pre-riot Newark, "Negro constituents and their white councilman found themselves on opposite sides of almost every issue"; anti-police charges were made, but "no complaint was ever heard of again"; against opposition by Blacks, the city determined to name a White secretary to the board of education.[16] Such stalemates, according to the Commission, "were linked in the minds [of rioters] to the pre-existing reservoir of underlying grievances." The recurrent picture is one of a "cumulative process of mounting tension that spilled over into violence when the final incident occurred." The precipitating incident—usually involving the police—could then be of a relatively trivial nature, and yet trigger rioting.

The type of explanation offered by the Riot Commission is that of a "chain," in which unhappiness leads to unsuccessful

---

[15] Ibid., pp. 47–48.
[16] Ibid., pp. 58–60.

efforts at redress, which in turn cumulates in despair, anger, and a sanctioning of violent solutions. Interviews with riot participants and sympathizers tend to confirm this view. By and large, statements at the scene of a riot are catalogues of unresolved grievances and cumulated feelings, and the riot emerges as an expression of impatience and an emotional discharge.

The Phenomenology of an Urban Riot

A review of press quotations from Watts rioters may serve as illustration of the feelings described by the Commission. Remarks made to Black reporters during the Watts riot tend to cover a relatively small number of themes, some of which are the following:

Police brutality. The rioters frequently referred to feelings against the police as the motive underlying their violence. They often talked of the police as their enemy, and they were bitter in discussing police-related grievances. It seemed as if the police had come to connote all manner of humiliations and mistreatment suffered at the hands of racist officers. One young man who had participated in the burning of a supermarket, for example, ventured the opinion that "the riots will continue because I, as a Negro, am immediately considered a criminal by the police, and if I have a pretty woman with me, she's a tramp—even if she's my wife or mother." An unemployed man, who admitted having repeatedly thrown rocks at the police officers, declared, "Maybe the people of Beverly Hills would riot too if they spent most of their life with a cop's club in their face. Or if they had to get out of an automobile with their hands over their heads to be questioned for doing nothing at all. We're not safe from police brutality even in our own home."[17]

The various rumors circulating about the incident that triggered the riot illustrate the extent of anti-police sentiment. Thus, one young rioter recalled that "the police struck a lady—

---

[17] *San Francisco Chronicle*, Aug. 18, 1965.

and she was pregnant—and they broke her nose."[18] A young mother, standing outside her Watts residence, related, "I heard they beat an old woman over there—them police beat her half to death." She added, "You can't sit and take it forever, can you?"[19]

Retaliation against White exploitation. This was the motive implicit in most of the spontaneous remarks made by rioters in the course of their destructive activities and probably the most prevalently voiced rationale. Stores with windows carrying signs that identified their owners as "Negro," "Soul Brother" or "Blood Brother" were generally not looted or burned;[20] among White-owned stores, the first targets were reportedly those "whose owners had a reputation for gouging Negroes or for foreclosing mortgages."[21] And in the course of looting, "the first thing they [the rioters] went for is the credit records."[22] A female resident of Watts explained: "They're fed up with these whites cheating them out of their money—you know it ain't easy for people like us to get jobs, and we got to work hard for everything we get. Why should we let them cheat us out of what little we got? Let 'em lose a little bit now. Ain't it about time?"[23]

The rioters, in discussing the White Watts merchants, alleged that the commodities offered for sale in the ghetto were rejects from outlets in White areas, including stale food. These items, according to the rioters, were generally sold at much higher prices than elsewhere. Considerable resentment against White landlords was also voiced. One man declared while he was watching a burning building, "I wouldn't give a goddamn if they burned my house down as long as I could get this. Mine ain't worth a damn nohow. He's the one with everything to lose."[24] In general, the mood prevailing among those engaged in the destruction of White property was described as

---

[18] Ibid., Aug. 16, 1965.
[19] *San Francisco Sunday Chronicle*, Aug. 15, 1965.
[20] *Los Angeles Sentinel*, Aug. 19, 1965.
[21] *San Francisco Chronicle*, Aug. 21, 1965.
[22] Ibid., Sept. 3, 1965.
[23] Ibid.
[24] *Life*, Aug. 27, 1965.

one of joyful vindictiveness. The anti-White "warfare" aspect of the proceedings is also evident from the fact that Black nonparticipants were frequently informed that their inactivity implied treasonous partiality to "The Man."

Unemployment. Lack of jobs was frequently mentioned as a motive for the riot, as evidenced by Governor Brown's complaint that when he asked people for the reasons behind the destructiveness, they "gave me no clues to the reasons, although they did describe the economic problems."[25] A speech by Martin Luther King in Watts was interrupted with the shout, "'I had a dream, I had a dream'—hell, we don't need no damn dreams. We want jobs."[26] Many Watts residents indicated that they believed unemployment to have been the chief cause of the riot. The *New York Times* quoted a young Watts mechanic as proclaiming, "We've come to life. You get me a job and pay me—we're satisfied. If you don't—well, we're not going back to slavery" (Aug. 17, 1965). A woman explained that "this wasn't no race riot. It was a riot between the unemployed and the employed. We are tired of being shelved and being told we don't want to work."[27]

Hopelessness. This feeling was mentioned by some as a contributing factor to the riot. A young mother of four put the case very eloquently, when she told Governor Brown, "I feel buried here in Watts with nothing to look forward to. . . . Everyone has a deep feeling of lostness. There's no hope out here in Watts, we're stranded. We want something to look forward to. It's no fun cashing a county welfare check every week."[28]

A number of Watts residents discussed their past hopes and failures. A young man who had migrated to Los Angeles from Texas with his wife and three children explained that he was working as a dishwasher. "People come here looking to better themselves," he said, but "it ain't here for you." A female evangelist interviewed by the same reporter indicated that "when

---

[25] *San Francisco Call Bulletin,* Aug. 20, 1965.
[26] *Newsweek,* Aug. 30, 1965.
[27] *Time,* Aug. 27, 1965.
[28] *San Francisco Call Bulletin,* Aug. 20, 1965.

the government says it's going to help, but then there ain't
nothing, it's disheartening to people."[29] Louis Lomax wrote
that "Negroes in Watts have a pathology of failure—they failed
in the South and failed to find the promised land in Los Angeles."[30]

Anonymity. This appeared to be a condition which for some
was dispelled by the riot. In one encounter a young Watts
citizen asked Brown, "Had you planned to come down here
before this?" "No frankly, I hadn't," Brown replied."[31] Another resident declared, "I don't believe in burning, stealing,
or killing, but I can see why the boys did what they did. They
just wanted to be noticed, to let the world know the seriousness of their state in life."[32]

Rioters felt that as a result of their actions, they would achieve
collective and individual visibility. The one is exemplified by
the statement of an old man, who said, "The only way we
can get anybody to listen to us is to start a riot." The other is
implicit in the claim of an unemployed young man that "Negroes are ready to die for respect."[33]

Lack of identity. A feeling of pride was produced by the
riot, according to some participants and observers. A Black
graduate student who had returned to Watts at the time told
a former teacher, "As a riot, it was a masterful performance.
I sense a change here now, a buzz, and it tickles. For the first
time people in Watts feel a real pride in being Black. I remember, when I first went to Whittier, I worried that if I didn't
make it there, if I was rejected I wouldn't have a place to go
back to. Now I can say: 'I'm from Watts.'"[34]

James Farmer asked one young rioter how he felt, and the
boy replied, "Baby, I feel like a man." Another told him, "Man,
this is instant renewal."[35] A Black psychiatrist described the
rioters as having developed "a feeling of potency." He said

[29] *New York Times*, Aug. 26, 1965.
[30] Ibid., March 20, 1966.
[31] *San Francisco Call Bulletin*, Aug. 20, 1965.
[32] *San Francisco Chronicle*, Aug. 18, 1965.
[33] *Newsweek*, Aug. 30, 1965.
[34] *Life*, Aug. 27, 1965.
[35] *San Francisco Sunday Chronicle*, Sept. 3, 1965.

that "they feel the whole world is watching now. And out of the violence, no matter how wrong the acts were, they have developed a sense of pride."[36]

Riot-Generated Motives

It is clear that this type of testimony does not provide a full picture of riot motivation. For one, it omits or embroiders socially less desirable or constructive needs, such as the satisfaction obtained from destruction for its own sake, or from the use of violence to obtain property. Such statements also underrepresent the motives that are born from the riot situation itself. For instance, there are those who join destructive activities because of excitement generated by collective action, or as a means of entertainment, or as a response to opportunity.

In relation to one of the disturbances following the murder of Martin Luther King, *Time* magazine observed,

> The majority of plunderers and burners in American cities last week were about as ideologically motivated as soldier ants. Many, to be sure, were venting the longstanding resentment of black Americans in a white society. But the Negro looters were predominantly driven by a combination of self-help and help-yourself. What of Martin Luther King? "His death just gave us an excuse," said Ronald Rudolph, 22, in Pittsburgh. "I never did dig the man much when he was alive." When a well-provisioned Harlem "liberator" was asked why he was stealing, he cried: "It's because they killed what's-his-name!" "You know why people loot?" explained one young rioter. "Because they ain't never, so long as they live, gonna have enough money to buy a color-television set. Man, I got big ambitions, but not much will power."[37]

The influence of other rioters is an obviously important factor in riot motivation, especially among people who become in-

---

[36] *Time*, Aug. 27, 1965.
[37] Ibid., April 19, 1968.

volved as the disturbance expands. Although latecomers might be motivated by grievances, these predispositions would be more likely to remain latent if it were not for the presence of an ongoing disturbance. It is a truism that an individual could never riot. The availability of like-minded companions and the example set by riot-initiators often facilitate the translation of despair into destruction and explosion.

One reason why violence comes so easy to rioters is that they can derive it from a common cause. They can see themselves individually laboring toward group ends. They can feel themselves partners of a joint enterprise. They can conceive of their own acts as defined and sanctioned by a larger effort. Every solitary marauder can come to regard himself as a member of a crusade.

In this sense, every riot is—in extended form—a violent incident of the sort we have described. The game is played between members of a frustrated group and the agents of White society. In the opening moves, Black Citizen A makes demands and requests of White Social Agent B; these strongly felt aspirations are defined as entitlements or psychological requirements. The game revolves around A's discovery that his aspirations cannot be satisfied. Presumably, A can make a variety of efforts to gain his ends before he concludes that B will remain unresponsive. Moreover, he can make such efforts on various fronts. Thus, he can look for a job, and not find one; he can stand on street corners, and be chased off them; he can appeal police actions, and be rebuffed. Ultimately, he concludes that the agents of society are his tormentor, and that he must act accordingly. When many persons arrive at this conclusion, a collective move to act in its spirit can be expected.[38]

The target of collective violence thus symbolically represents persons and agencies who have remained unresponsive to human aspirations. In the Watts riot, we have seen the police as a prominent enemy, because police action is visibly repressive and because personal awareness can most easily focus on

---

[38] H. Toch, *The Social Psychology of Social Movements* (Indianapolis, IN: Bobbs-Merrill, 1965).

the sort of humiliation experienced in police contact. Moreover, the police have inherited their connotations from their role as instruments of power already perceived as repressive.

A more general reaction, similar in kind, is the second theme we have mentioned. At the height of a riot almost any White person can be perceived as an enemy. This is the case because the riot participants have come to ascribe goal-squelching policies to the authorities with whom they have dealt. Frustrating agents not only have been seen as anti-Black but have become viewed as the spokesmen for similar sentiments among White people at large. Hence, the broad retaliatory theme in the Watts riot.

The remainder of our list describes the substance of the discrepancy between expectations and failures. In the case of Watts, the list includes low status and the non-availability of means of advancement. This fact suggests that participants in the riot felt that they could look back on a very broad range of downgrading experiences. It also suggests that specific economic measures (such as the creation of jobs) would not now address the core of their problem, much of which revolved around self-esteem and the desire for psychological rewards.

One dimension of riot motivation which tends to be obscured by summaries of grievances is that of the permutations that these grievances achieve in the individual histories of rioters. The Watts riot no doubt contained individuals who stood as classic examples of the sort of sequence described by the Riot Commission. Persons who found no access to medical service; swindled consumers; frustrated job-seekers; subjects of police searches; forced school dropouts; commuting menial workers—such men and women could point to reservoirs of experiences that found direct expression in rioting. In other instances, the sequence might have been similar, but based on more unrealistic aspirations, including immediate access to a life of luxury and leisure. We also assume that frustrations totally unrelated to racial themes could become displaced in retaliatory violence, giving the Watts riot more psychological and existential overtones.

Obviously, some participants in group violence will be more conscious of its social objectives than others. But it is hard to conceive of any rioter who could be totally oblivious of the grievances shared by his fellows. Such a non-socially-motivated destroyer must at last be a self-conscious hanger-on to social protest. He must know that he is riding the crest of a wave which provides him with the respected cover of a large-scale revolt.

At the initial juncture of collective violence, the Riot Commission isolated a group predisposed to action by many unredressed grievances. Such persons arrive at the situation with a level of outrage sufficient to fuel their participation. The motives impelling them to rioting, however, are not yet born. In the words of Ralph Turner, these are an "emergent norm."[39] They must be created, in the sense that the anger must attach itself to the precipitating event and must convert it into an unacceptable affront. Here it matters little that the sparking situation may be a proper exercise of police power or a jury deliberation. The event is interpreted as symbolically related to grievances—hence, as the occasion for action. The ideal type of situation for this purpose is one of ambiguity, and it is filled with confusion, discomfort, excitement, rumor-spreading, and tension. The illusion which is created converts the discrete event into a collective insult, or into a reminder of past insult or humiliation. If this view is sufficiently prevalent, violence can be legitimized. A crowd becomes a mob, and the frustration–aggression formula gains potency. And when this occurs, the intrinsically innocent situation has become transmuted into a time and place for destructive retaliation—into a "violent incident" of gigantic proportions.

The Precipitating Incident in Collective Violence

The Watts riot shows the role of pre-existing motives in shaping the perception of incidents that precipitate collective violence. It also highlights the fact (which we shall discuss later) that violent persons can contribute to the genesis of large-scale explosions.

The Watts tragedy took place during the week of Wednes-

---

[39] R. H. Turner, "Collective Behaviors," in R. E. L. Faris (Ed.), *Handbook of Modern Sociology* (Chicago: Rand McNally, 1964), pp. 382–425.

day, August 11, 1965. The context and background fit the Riot Commission's prescribed pattern: Watts consisted of small, congested, pre-war rental homes, and, in terms of living style, the Watts resident was only slightly better off than his peer in New York's Harlem, who typically lived in a cold water tenement flat. Statistics confirm the underprivileged, but not rock-bottom, status of the Watts Black; 30 per cent of the children in the area came from broken homes; the drop-out rate in Watts schools was more than twice the national average; only one-third of the residents had started high school. The majority of the persons living in Watts were migrants from the South, and most were unskilled. Not surprisingly, the Watts unemployment rate was more than triple that of the White community; more than half of the Black families of Los Angeles were on relief; and 20 per cent of Black families in the area earned less than $3,000 a year.

The riot occurred during an unusually hot period toward the end of the summer; for four days preceding the explosion, a heat wave combining temperatures of 90° to 100° and very high humidity had prevailed through the area.

On the national scene, the hopes of Blacks had been recently raised: For at least three years, the civil rights movement, with its sit-ins, marches, and other demonstrations, had been in full swing. Black voter registration in the South was initiated the very day on which the riot began. Locally, hopes had been squashed. For example, President Johnson's anti-poverty program had not become active in Los Angeles, in part because the mayor had been unsympathetic to some of its provisions. A hard-won state fair housing act was repealed in 1964 by a public referendum.

At the time of Watts, rioting had already occurred elsewhere—most dramatically in New York and in Rochester, the preceding year. Models were therefore available. Some local observers had pointed to Watts as a potential riot scene for several months, because of the resentments and bitterness encountered there, closely comparable to those in other riot areas.[40]

---

[40] *San Francisco Chronicle*, Aug. 16, 1965.

The events that triggered the Watts riots began with the arrest, on a drunk driving charge, of a young man named Marquette Frye. There were spectators to the arrest; their mood was one of amusement. If anything, their sympathies extended to the officer, who was clearly justified in making his case. Everything went lightheartedly until the trooper and his partner tried to place Frye into physical custody. The young man reacted with panic. Robert Conot reports that as the officers started toward Frye, he broke down completely:

> As he spoke to his mother, his voice broke. He was almost crying. Spotting the officers, he started backing away, his feet shuffling, his arms waving.
>
> "Come on, Marquette, you're coming with us." [Officer] Minikus reached toward him.
>
> Marquette slapped his hands away. "I'm not going to no sonofabitching jail!" he cried out. "I haven't did anything to be taken to jail."[41]

As Frye's fear increased, so did his awareness that he was exposed in the eyes of his neighbors. Shame produced resentment, and resentment brought memories of past humiliations: "What right had they to treat him like this? 'You motherfucking white cops, you're not taking me anywhere!' he screamed, whipping his body about as if he were half boxer, half dancer."[42]

The incident had been converted into a tense, violent confrontation, and it was acquiring connotations susceptible to more general interpretations. Conot reports that the witnessing crowd—now including mostly persons who had only just arrived on the scene—became sympathetic to Frye. Frye's situation seemed to be that of a victim, and his fate mobilized feelings of indignation grounded in a common underprivileged past:

[41] From *Rivers of Blood, Years of Darkness* by Robert Conot. Copyright © 1967 by Bantam Books, Inc.

[42] Ibid., p. 14.

The officers were white; they were outsiders; and most of all, they were police. Years of reciprocal distrust, reciprocal contempt, and reciprocal insults had created a situation in which the residents assumed every officer to be in the wrong until he had proven himself right, just as the officers assumed every Negro guilty until he had proven his innocence. The people began to close in on the three highway patrolmen.[43]

As the situation degenerated (Marquette's brother, Ronald, had become engaged in the dispute), another police officer arrived. This officer, like Frye, was a man susceptible to panic— a person who seemed prone to precipitantly aggressive action. Conot describes his entrance into the sequence in the following terms:

> Officer Wilson, as he arrived on the scene, riot baton in hand even before he had the kickstand of the motorcycle down, was confronted by an image of blurred chaos . . . he went into action with no more opportunity to assess the situation than those Negro spectators who had arrived late and assumed from what they saw that there was violent conflict between Marquette and the officers. . . .
>
> Rushing toward Ronald and Lewis, and without speaking to either, Wilson jabbed the riot baton into the pit of Ronald's stomach. As Ronald doubled over, he jabbed again. Ronald rolled to the ground.
>
> With one adversary dispatched, it was but a half dozen steps to where Marquette was fending off Minikus. Wilson swung the baton. He caught Marquette with a glancing blow to the forehead, above the left eye. As Marquette turned instinctively to meet him, Wilson jabbed him hard in the stomach. Marquette doubled over.[44]

At this juncture, Ronald's mother, seeing her sons painfully beaten, indignantly intervened. As a result, the crowd was treated to the spectacle of an old lady forcibly pushed into a

---

[43] Ibid.
[44] Ibid., pp. 15–16.

patrol car. One member of the crowd later declared, "When that happened, all the people standing around got mad."[45] Conot reports that there were isolated shouts of "Come on, let's get them!" "Leave the old lady alone!" "We've got no rights at all—it's just like Selma!" "Those white motherfuckers got no cause to do that!"[46]

The situation degenerated even further after one officer complained that a young lady in the crowd had spit at him. Several other officers converged on the girl, and they apprehended her after considerable resistance. The picture of the girl's helpless struggle against overwhelming odds symbolized, for many in the crowd, the hopelessness of their own fate. This feeling, and the resulting impotent rage, is vividly described by Conot:

> In the manner with which the police had handled the girl the people saw, or thought they saw, the contempt of the white man for the Negro. They felt, collectively, his heel grinding in their faces. They were stricken once more by the sting of his power.
>
> "Goddam!" a woman called out. "Goddam! They'd never treat a white woman like that!"
>
> "What kind of men are you, anyways?" another challenged. "What kind of men are you, anyways, to let them do that to our people?"
>
> "It's a shame! It's a pitiful, crying shame!"
>
> "Blue-eyed white devils! We is going to get you! Oh, shit! We is going to get you!"
>
> "Motherfuckers!" It came from all sides of the crowd. "Motherfuckers!"[47]

The Riot Commission's "cumulative chain" had reached its last link. An incident had been generated which symbolized for those present every ounce of humiliation, every nuance of hopelessness, every hurt to pride, self-esteem, and loyalty possible. The fruits of past frustrating experiences had taken shape: They had become sensitivities which turned private

---

[45] *Time*, Aug. 20, 1965.
[46] Conot, op. cit., p. 16.
[47] Ibid., p. 21.

conflict into public issue, which converted disputants into Oppressors and Oppressed; which metamorphosed a minor exercise into a morality play that promised intolerable victory to unspeakable evil.

To be sure, the transformation was not inevitable: Some actors played their parts too well; some pawns proved ambitious, and hastened the plot. Frye's fear impelled him to present himself as a frenzied martyr; Wilson's pugnaciousness converted him into a caricature of arbitrarily exercised power. Tragedy might have been averted if one impulsive girl had been permitted to escape into the crowd. And there might have been no riot if one man had not felt more humiliated, more resentful, more excited, more impotent, more shamed, more desperate, more angry, and more compelled to act than his neighbors. It took one man, feeling what others felt and converting these feelings into action, to generate the last interpretation, the ultimate connotation, the irreversible inference—the crucial conclusion that violence was in order:

> Without conscious thought of his action he darted into the street and hurled the empty pop bottle in his hand toward the last of the departing black-and-white cars. Striking the rear fender of Sgt. Rankin's car, it shattered. And it was as if in that shattering the thousand people lining the street found their own release. It was as if in one violent contortion the bonds of restraint were snapped. Rocks, bottles, pieces of wood and iron—whatever missiles came to hand—were projected against the sides and windows of the bus and automobiles that, halted for the past 20 minutes by the jammed street, unwittingly started through the gauntlet. The people had not been able to overcome the power of the police. But they could, and would, vent their fury on other white people. The white people who used the police to keep them from asserting their rights.
>
> It was 7:45 p.m. Amidst the rending sounds of tearing metal, splintering glass, cries of bewilderment and shouts of triumph, the Los Angeles uprising had begun.[48]

---

[48] Ibid., p. 29.

Once collective action has been initiated, it acquires a momentum of its own; even if people did not suffer from grievances, riots would attract and recruit participants. They would do so because they appeal to boredom, anger, frustration, desire for adventure; because they provide a ready-made opportunity to discharge feelings; because they furnish festive activity with the sanction of peers and under the aegis of principle.

As violent crowds form, bystanders are invited to join; many resist, but others fill gaps in the ranks. Streets become an arena for heroism, a proving ground for bravery, a stage for vendettas. Boys can achieve manhood heaving rocks or defying police officers; men can acquire purpose through guerrilla warfare; groups can gain meaning through riot-connected projects such as raids on commercial establishments and hit-and-run expeditions. Benefits are provided to so many persons that there are few left to disapprove. Violence becomes a way of life until postriot sobriety supervenes.

Shared Violence and Personal Violence

In our discussion so far, we have only been able to hint at the relationship between collective violence and personal violence. At first glance, the two types of violence differ. Whereas the violent person approaches his encounters as a solitary agent, the rioter becomes mobilized as a member of a group; whereas the violent person has affinity for aggressive action, the rioter is a product of contagion; whereas the violent person provokes violence, the rioter seems to respond to a situation created to provoke him. The appropriate kind of analysis differs: While in personal violence we expect to find consistency within the individual, in collective violence we assume that people respond uniformly to a sequence of frustrating experiences.

But these divergences are less sharp after we examine the motivating patterns in riots. For one, we see that violent incidents must come into being to provide a focus for grievances. In the genesis of such incidents, individuals with violence-prone personalities play roles similar to those which they play in their other encounters.

We have seen that in a riot the man in the street can gain benefits usually reserved to the Violent Man. He can gain these benefits by availing himself of ready-made opportunities, which make violence possible for him. Riots contain provisions for the replication (in miniature) of several of our violent types. A person may become a rioter to promote his self-image, or to defend his status, or to remove pressure, or to release pent-up feelings. And the quality of riot participation is probably to some measure dependent on such preferred modes of adjustment, or on favored styles of relating to others.

On the other hand, the motives and perceptual content of a riot are restricted, compared to the rich tapestry of free lance violence. Many rioters are self-defined revolutionaries; many of them see rioting as vengeance; other rioters are inspired by the fellowship of their comrades; and in all instances, they have a mythical, collective conception of the Enemy. We have also seen that in the development of riot motivation, economic grievances and social disappointments are prominent in the awareness of rioters.

Riots gain uniformity from the fact that reactions are partly spread through contagion and partly institutionalized: The Ghost of Riots Past hovers like a friendly specter over each new outbreak; it provides historical sanction, and it furnishes vivid images of how and why to proceed. This kind of advance prescription reduces the room for individual initiative.

This does not mean that personality cannot express itself in riots. There is occasion for the display of personal style, and opportunity for the satisfaction of personal needs. Riot participation can be lighthearted or grim; it can be angry or playful; it can be fearful or calm. And the riot situation can be viewed in many different ways: Rioting may thus be an act of revenge for some, and an emotional discharge, or an act of rebellion, for others. Violence may serve as a vehicle to personal identity, or as a means to power or material gain. A riot can be many things to many people; some of its meanings may run deep or may extend far back into time.

In this sense, riots are less psychologically confining than are some other forms of collective violence, such as war. In battle, violence is committed because the individual's military vocation demands it. The soldier is instructed to follow destructive routines (such as shooting at moving targets or pressing a button that operates equipment to release a projectile), and he largely complies because he has learned to do so, because he respects his superiors, and because he accepts his role as defined for him. Typically, he gains no satisfaction from violence beyond those of efficiently discharging his obligations and of participating in the collective destruction of a consensually defined enemy.[49]

There are soldiers, to be sure, who seek out blood and gore beyond the call of duty and who gain considerable reward from the administration of death and destruction. There are those who volunteer for elite killer units that operate behind enemy lines and engage in assassinations or sabotage; there are others who prize assignments as snipers or scouts; and there are figures of heroic stature with a penchant for single-handedly launching offensive operations in defiance of sensible odds. It is within the ranks of soldiers such as these that we find our violence-prone persons, those driven by the desire for physical action, those who seek a new identity or a bolstered image in the eyes of themselves and others. And it is these individuals—praiseworthy though they may be from the viewpoint of the military—who must be monitored and eventually resocialized for membership in the civilized community.[50]

---

[49]The extent to which mechanized and impersonal violence characterizes modern warfare is illustrated in the following description of an American bombing mission over Vietnam:

Harris lined up the target in the luminous cross hairs of his screen, threw two switches that opened the bomb bay and armed the load of 108 bombs. Over the radio, the impersonal voice of a SAC ground controller announced "seven minutes to 'hack' (bomb release point)." The count droned on until at hack, when Harris punched a black button and 30 tons of high explosives cascaded toward the ground more than 30,000 feet below us. There was no shock, no noise, no sight of explosions. Only the impersonal voice of the controller: "Bombs in the target area. That was a good run, fellows. Have a nice ride home and see you another day." Thigpen banked again and we were on our way back to Guam, six monotonous hours and 2,600 miles away. In a small oven in the cockpit the men began heating TV dinners. They had not seen their target, their enemy, or the effect of their mission. (*Time*, Aug. 2, 1968)

[50]J. Hersey, *The War Lover* (New York: Bantam Books, 1960).

Front Page Violence

Among persons who engage in violence, there are some who fill the public mind with special dread and revulsion. These individuals stir the imagination, displace headlines, and inspire draconian legislation. And these people are not those who account for the bulk of violent damage, nor are they necessarily those who engage in repeated acts of destruction. They are, rather, the unexpected authors of violence that is irrational and senseless—the perpetrators of acts that are invariably blood-curdling and sometimes bizarre.

One type of offender that gives us pause is the casual violence user who seems to lack empathy for other people and who kills or maims without provocation and with studied indifference. Most of us understand the workings of instrumental violence—muggings, for example, in which necks are scraped where chains or pendants are torn off. But a stabbing that gratuitously follows a mugging strains our credulity—and so does the predatory offender who shows neither remorse nor concern for his victim, or emotion of any kind. Such reactions have strained taxonomies since the inception of clinical schemes, and have earned pejorative labels such as *moral imbecility, moral insanity, psychopathic inferiority, psychopathic personality, sociopathic personality,* and *antisocial personality disorder.* The psychological attributes that have been assigned to this constellation have varied over time, but they tend to include hedonism, limited time perspective, absence of conscience, and the inability to form relationships. A propensity to violence is not a standard assigned symptom of the disorder, but the tie-in is generally assumed.

A second type of violence that mystifies the public is that of persons who act in apparent response to delusional ruminations or hallucinatory commands, assaulting their victims suddenly, out of the blue, with no plausible rationale. Such persons strike fear for several reasons: For one, they cast doubt on the sanctity of life, because they assault victims who have done them no harm and who are frequently unknown to them; they raise questions about the meaningfulness and predictability of human motives, because their lives often do not foreshadow their tragic fate. Frequently, their violence seemingly emerges "out of the blue." Frequently these are the mildest, gentlest souls, immune to anger and unconcerned with their surroundings. Frequently, they are shy, brooding, and shadowy, unnoticed until the moment when they explode into horrible prominence.

The most noteworthy feature about these persons may be their extreme nonviolent disposition. Edwin Megargee tells us,

> In case after case the extremely assaultive offender proves to be a rather passive person with no previous history of aggression. In Phoenix an 11-year-old-boy who stabbed his brother 34 times with a steak knife was described by all who knew him as being extremely polite and soft spoken with no history of assaultive behavior. In New York an 18-year-old youth who confessed he had assaulted and strangled a 7-year-old girl in a Queens church and later tried to burn her body in the furnace was descried in the press as an unemotional person who planned to be a minister. A 21-year-old man from Colorado who was accused of the rape and murder of two little girls had never been a discipline problem and, in fact, his step-father reported, 'When he was in school the other kids would run all over him and he'd never fight back. There is just no violence in him."[51]

This sort of picture represents, in many respects, the opposite of the pattern we found among typical violence-prone persons. Whereas the average Violent Man becomes aggressive in a wide variety of situations, the type of individual described by Megargee does not; in fact, he is calm and unresponsive in situations that would make most of us angry. It is as if he saved his rage and resentment until the pressure becomes unbearable, and until the dike of his self-restraint bursts. Although incidents that finally trigger violence may be provocative, their role is often minor. In fact, the precipitating incident may be irrelevant and the victim incidental. It is useless

---

[51] E. I. Megargee, "Undercontrolled and Overcontrolled Personality Types in Extreme Antisocial Aggression," *Psychological Monographs* (1966), 80: Whole No. 611.

to study actual explosions to understand this type of violence. Instead, one must focus on potentially violent encounters in which no reaction takes place. It is among these nonviolent incidents that we can expect to find the self-destructive patterns that ultimately burst into the open. And we expect these patterns to be of a different order from those encountered in other violent persons. Rather than comprising simple feelings and monolithic urges, these patterns should simultaneously feature irreconcilable and opposing needs. They should promote violence and restrain it, and require unsatisfactory and unstable compromises.

A fine example of this sort of pattern is the case of a wife-killer reviewed by LeRoy Schultz. The man (Jim) carved up his second wife, who had subjected him to an endless series of unreasonable demands. Jim's previous marriage had included the following sequence of events:

> Then Jim came home by surprise one day and discovered his wife in bed with a neighboring farmer. He said he did not know what to do and merely closed the door and returned to the fields and cried. He added that he could have done "something" as there was a loaded rifle in the room adjoining the bedroom. Jim never brought up his wife's infidelity and she, seeing so little objection, became more bold in her affair. The paramour began staying for meals and on several occasions stayed overnight. Jim voiced no objection and even lent the paramour money, seed and farm equipment, as well as labor. Finally, after this arrangement had gone on for three years, the paramour took a truck to Jim's farm while the latter was away, loaded up the household goods and livestock, as well as Jim's wife and four children, and took them away. Jim, though surprised at his wife's and children's absence, did nothing to find out where she was or to attempt to bring her back, nor did he ever approach his wife's lover.[52]

Jim murdered his second wife after she informed him that

---

[52] L. G. Schultz, "The Wife Assaulter," *Journal of Social Therapy* (1960), 6: 103–111, p. 106.

she also had acquired a lover. This act not only placed her in the position of evoking rage in her own right, but also of inheriting the suppressed resentment of Jim's past. The pattern was more complex, however, because Jim did not marry his wives at random, nor did he treat them in a random fashion. Instead, he found domineering women, and he clung to them with desperate possessiveness. It was as if he demanded self-destruction on one level and resented it on another. He thus created both his aggressors and his potential victims.

Jim had problems with the way he handled his feelings, particularly sexual and angry feelings. But there are deeper and more bizarre meanings to Jim's game. Freud would suggest that Jim had formed a love/hate attachment to his mother, and that he attempts to reenact it as an adult. He has assigned his wives a role in this displaced play, as The Seductresses that Betray You.

The meanings that seriously disturbed aggressors such as Jim assign to their victims are not only inaccessible but rarely available to the aggressors themselves. What they present are punchlines or sums of calculus—delusional beliefs or hallucinations (usually voices) that prescribe violence. Sometimes we see even less, as in the following examples:

> The offender enters a laundromat armed with a knife and encounters a stranger. The stranger leaves the laundromat and is followed by the offender, who stabs him in the back and throws bottles at him. The offender tells the victim, "I'll kill you if I see you [again] on this street."
>
> The offender peeks through a window and sees a woman taking a shower. He enters the house, picks up a knife and knives the victim in the arm, neck, and back, subsequently indicating he has "no idea why" he committed the offense.[53]

If there is anything in incidents such as these resembling a rationale (if, say, the offender attacks someone who works for a company that fired him), the link is private and overblown.

---

[53] H. Toch and K. Adams, *The Disturbed Violent Offender* (New Haven, CT: Yale University Press, 1989b), p. 126.

For psychotics, victims are repositories of long-term resentments and far-fetched obsessions that derive elsewhere. Such violence is a solitary game in which the opponent is a creature of imagination.

Neither victims nor spectators of such incidents of violence can do anything to change self-generated fantasies, and this makes the incidents largely unpreventable. The offenses also appear "unmotivated" because we cannot understand the violent games that the offenders play. Even when an offender tells us what was on his mind at the time of the offense (such as "a high-pitched voice told me to kill"), we cannot envisage this as a motive for violence.

Our reaction to disturbed offenders, as surprised spectators to their acts, is ambivalent. The offenders always inspire fear— more fear than do other offenders. On the other hand, standard (punitive) responses to their behavior seem inappropriate. The same dilemma is experienced by courts that deal with the offenders. For courts, punishability means culpability, which means that an offender knows what he does when he does it, and/or can avoid doing it if he wants to. The question "Is this disturbed person responsible?" is raised through standards such as those for the insanity defense. This defense permits a jury to acquit a killer whose delusional beliefs show obliviousness to reality or morality, or whose command hallucinations look peremptory. When a jury acquits an offender, however (particularly one who has killed a public figure), the citizenry gets upset, and legislators who set standards for acquittal tighten them another notch.[54]

But whether the insanity defense is used can become a moot

---

[54]There is a parallel in this connection between the cases of Daniel McNaghten (1843) and John Hinckley (1982). The former tried to kill the prime minister of England and killed his secretary; the latter injured Press Secretary Brady and President Reagan. McNaghten's acquittal upset the British House of Lords, which formalized the McNaghten Rule. Hinckley's acquittal disturbed Congress, which tightened insanity standards in the Federal Crime Control Act of 1984 so as to require "clear and convincing evidence" of incapacity and place the burden of proof on the defense. Hinckley's delusion revolved around a young actress (Jodie Foster), for whose benefit he staged his assassination. McNaghten suffered from delusions of persecution by the British government.

point for acquittees who must spend years in forensic hospital wings that are indistinguishable from prison tiers with mental health services. In both cases, the disturbed violent offender is dealt with as a set of two compartments, one that is mentally ill and one that is violent. Mental illness comes to be handled with medication, and violence brings confinement. In practice, treaters assume that mental illness must be treated and that violence must be punished, even if the two are interlinked in the same person who is sequestered in a mental health or correctional setting.[55]

In this context "treatment" means disease reduction (or amelioration) and it is subsumable under the medical model of change. Treatment is furnished by mental health workers in prisons because of society's responsibility for keeping inmates as healthy as possible. This obligation can entail providing an appendectomy for one inmate, dental work for another, and psychotropic medication for a third. Reducing the inmate's violence potential is a different sort of goal, which falls under the rubric of "rehabilitation." Offender rehabilitation is currently out of favor in this country.

Rehabilitation is in theory possible even if a person is mentally disturbed (provided he is in remission) or serving a sentence in prison. Punishment does not disqualify a patient from receiving medical attention, treatment does not keep an offender from being punished, and neither punishment nor treatment preclude rehabilitative efforts. Where problems are linked, approaches can come in packages that comprise medical, rehabilitative, and criminal justice interventions. It is the latter of these components (rehabilitative and criminal justice) that we turn to in our next chapter.

---

[55] The mental health system is not concerned about punishment but it is concerned about preventing harm to future victims from disturbed persons. The best predictor of future dangerousness is past dangerousness. Seriousness of offense spells risk, which affects the chances that one takes. This means that the mental health and the criminal justice systems can use similar criteria in deciding how long to sequester the offender. In one case the issue is future conduct, and in the second, the unregenerate nature of past conduct.

Chapter

7

Some Implications

During periods of enhanced concern about violence, eminent experts are typically convoked to tell us what to do in the light of The Latest Knowledge. Such exercises produce impressive compendia of data from different disciplines, which reflect fashions prevailing in social science at the time. In the sixties, for examples (when this book was first published), sociology was in the ascendance. In the nineties, genetic and biological explanations had become the vogue. In the words of Thomas Szasz, we had come to "look for the twisted molecule behind every twisted thought."[1]

Experts must decide how to collate variegated data and disciplinary views. The easiest way they can do this is to list as many perspectives as applicable. But some perspectives are more applicable than others, because they are more directly relevant to one's concerns. And laundry lists can become particularly useless for purposes such as ours, which involve explaining individual offenders and the causes of their behavior.

Explanations make no *human* sense if they take the form of catalogues. We are not helped when we learn that violence can be produced by biological, economic, demographic, cultural, and psychiatric factors. True as this may be, it poses

---

[1] T. Szasz, *Insanity: The Idea and Its Consequences* (New York: Wiley, 1989), p. 49.

questions such as, Where does which factor apply? How do causes A and C combine?

Are some offenders prisoners of genes and others of economics? Can equations be generated that quantify contributions to individual motivational variance? Can Offender A be a thirty percent product of a dysfunctional family and twenty percent peer pressure? Can B be a victim of neurological handicaps aggravated by violence on television? Such statements are hard to imagine and even more so when sequencing—A leads to B which reinforces C (or A)—is illuminated by longitudinal studies. Such studies flesh out theories that explain how problem behavior typically evolves, but individuals have their own varying sequences of experiences, and are ultimately unique products of these experiences. Lists of ingredients do not furnish recipes for human behavior, even if we can estimate the proportions and the order in which the ingredients have entered the pot. To study violence causation in an individual we must understand how he or she reacts to unfolding life experiences. Case studies that ignore this requisite typically contain details of questionable value or could apply to anyone who grew up troubled under disadvantaged circumstances.

What we need is information that permits us to understand motives for violence, and we must garner from records whatever helps us to understand these motives. Some personal history information may be relevant to this end, particularly if it illuminates nuances of the person's perspective or sheds light on the rapidity with which he explodes, or points to special sensitivities or specialized dispositions that he manifests in violent encounters. Unrelated facts can be distracting.[2]

We must keep in mind what does and does not help us to help the person, or permit self-help. If we cannot affect the variables the explanations point to, the explanations carry no

---

[2] Social scientists who belonged to the Progressive Movement in the late 19th century assumed that detailed case histories can somehow illuminate the genesis of problem behavior and suggest what remedial steps we can take on a case-by-case basis. As a result, even today human service clients tend to come with folders that contain both wheat and chaff, and no way for us to separate them. See D. J. Rothman, *Conscience and Convenience* (Boston: Little, Brown, 1980).

implications for action, and are unhelpful. We cannot rechannel water that has run under the bridge.

If explanations are multivariate, they can further discourage us. How do we address a multifaceted product of multiple causes that range from economic and cultural to biogenetic? The more variables enter into the product, the more hopeless the rehabilitative enterprise looks. And few problems spark more pessimism about what can be done about them than violence, and with more justification. We have made many mistakes in the past—such as overreliance on incarceration— which have brought us disillusionment and added cynicism. To stop making mistakes, we must learn to ask questions that help us target susceptible personal attributes with beneficent effect.

Violence and the Criminal Justice System

It is often brought home to us that we must know something about the personalities of offenders before we process them. We cannot subject to routine booking a psychotic or an addict deep in a dream world of his own making. We have discovered the risk of releasing into prison yards bands of predatory homosexuals and rival gang members.

If the goal of criminal justice is to regenerate people, the need to consider personality attributes becomes greater than if we are merely guided by concern for the smooth operation of our police stations, courts, prisons, and probation systems. Most correctional clients prove no major embarrassment, but by the same token they are neither helped nor changed. To accomplish the latter objective, one would have to have different programs available for different kinds of offenders, and one would have to distribute inmates to such settings on the basis of special knowledge about them. One would also have to treat people at such locations with the aid or more refined knowledge than is now used in making decisions about people in institutional settings.

In the case of violent offenders, the need for information is greater than it is in other offender groups. On practical grounds, violent persons are extremely troublesome. Many of them resist smooth handling, and when released, they commit the kinds of crimes that reflect adversely on our correctional machinery. To keep our system functioning, it is essential, in the case of these men, to separate them from potential victims. We have classification instruments that facilitate this task in correctional settings.[3] But the most logical step we could take next is to try to address the violence-related propensities of these offenders. And the regeneration of Violent Men is difficult without information about the nature of their violence and of its psychological meaning. Whereas burglars and sneak thieves can be treated without knowledge of their antisocial conduct, the nature of a man's violence relates importantly to the techniques we must use to discourage it.

If we do not face the task of regenerating the offenders we are reduced to labeling them, and to secreting them away for several decades. In prison, the Violent Man often becomes a custodial problem, and he may dispense his violence more lethally, if less visibly.[4] He creates a need for physical settings of a kind that had been regarded for a time as outmoded, such as maxi-maxi prisons, in which prisoners are locked in their cells twenty-three hours a day. He contaminates other inmates and staff by enmeshing them in his violent games. And he must eventually be discharged—usually as a more bitter and dangerous man. If the Violent Man is a model prisoner his relapse may or may not take place after his release. In such a case, we have accomplished a successful act of storage and segregation. This result may be modest, but it is admittedly positive. The difficulty, of course, is that this result is unpredictable. As long as we only know that a man is violent, we have no way of sorting the nonviolent inmate from the one who explodes in prison, or after leaving prison.

---

[3]The most widely used such instrument is described in H. C. Quay, *Managing Adult Inmates: Classification for Housing and Program Assignments* (Washington, DC: American Correctional Association, 1984).

[4]This point pertains to individuals with chronic violent dispositions, not to offenders convicted of violent offenses, who frequently lead exemplary prison existences. The most reliable predictor of prison misbehavior is age. Young inmates at the inception of their sentences incur the highest violation rates.

But are Violent Men not deterred by prison? Nothing in our picture suggests that they would be. To the contrary, in fact: Violence feeds on low self-esteem and self-doubt, and prison unmans and dehumanizes; violence rests on exploitation and exploitativeness, and prison is a power-centered jungle. It is true that we try to teach inmates that the use of force can only produce more difficulty for them, but we make this lesson far from convincing. If a man harms others in a prison, where else can he be sent? What extremity of discouragement can we furnish him? Many of our own interviewees preceded their discussions of particularly vicious acts with the declaration, "What the hell, I had nothing to lose!" It is an ironic commentary that prison violence is concentrated in the maximum segregation units, where violent inmates are sent for misbehaving in the yard.

The deterrence argument for long sentences sometimes has it that Violent Men will harken to the fate of their imprisoned comrades. This assumption is implausible. For one, violence is private and personal. Violent Men form no community, have no affinity for each other, join no unions. Where they are members of gangs or neighborhood groups, their status and prestige tend to rest squarely on their known propensity for violence. This fact is not neutralized by imprisoning other members of the group. In fact, enhancing the risk of violence would no doubt function to increase its prestige value, and hence, the benefits derived from its exercise.

The chief reason for doubting the impact of deterrence on Violent Men, however, lies elsewhere. It rests on the fact that destructive behavior is the least loss-and-gain motivated conduct of all antisocial activity. The rewards and punishments of violence are measured in increments and decrements to the ego rather than in terms of future well-being. The perspective of violence is short-term and impulsive rather than calculated and future-oriented. The Violent Man measures his worth by the distorted criterion of his physical impact, rather than by his ability to pursue a life plan. He has no career to be threatened, no stake to be impaired by prospective imprisonment. Of course, he desires freedom, and he would rather be at large than in prison; but his violence is neither stimulated nor inhibited by such remote and general needs. It is curiously true that deterrence is potentially most effective with those who least require its impact—with rational, career-oriented, future-invested individuals of the kinds who populate the ranks of the nonviolent, law-abiding middle class.

Of course, there are purposes to institutionalization other than storage and deterrence. Ideally, a closed institution furnishes the possibility of carefully controlling a person's environment and of providing him with continuing support and sustenance. It also makes it possible to monitor the person's progress on a day-to-day basis, and to adjust for adverse changes if they occur. Here, it is obviously important to provide constructive support and positive programming. There are no advantages to settings with custodial orientations. To multiply such facilities under the assumption that they can change Violent Men (other than by making them more bitter) is unrealistic.

Identification and Classification of Violent Men

A Violent Man is a person who has a propensity to take actions that culminate in harm to another. Such a person can be validly and reliably identified only on the basis of his record of violent acts. By "record", I don't mean his police "rap sheet," nor his list of accumulated convictions. Such documents are fragmentary and incomplete and are confined to unrepresentative acts that have come to the attention of authorities.[5] A man brought into court as a first offender may have initiated scores of violent incidents at home, in the school and in the streets; a repeat offender may have become, on one or another occasion, a victim of fortuitous circumstances.

On the other hand, many persons are currently classified as

---

[5]Chaiken and Chaiken emphasize that "information currently available from such sources as official arrest and conviction records does not allow criminal justice officials to distinguish meaningfully between the violent predator and other types of offenders." M. R. Chaiken and J. M. Chaiken, "Offender Types and Public Policy," *Crime and Delinquency* (1984), 30: 195–226, p. 197.

violent offenders who are not really violence-prone, in the sense of tending to inflict harm on others. For instance, the consummate robber may be a professional who is skilled at avoiding the use of the weapons he may carry. Such a man must be separated—for purposes of treatment—from the unstable robber who may shoot because of a propensity to be clumsy, boisterous, fearful, touchy, or sadistic. This type of person is a Violent Man, and he must be processed as such. For this purpose, he can be identified through systematic review of his conduct.

Our law enforcement agencies and our courts must thus make it their business to secure data about their clients' involvements in violence—without regard to the severity or the legal significance of the incidents that are uncovered. This information can be obtained through interviewing, through searches of school files, through field surveys and other fact-gathering techniques.

A long, diverse list of violent incidents can identify a person as a Violent Man. When such an identification has been made, it becomes important to secure detailed information about incidents, so as to categorize the person in terms of the nature of his violence. It is this information which makes sensible disposition possible—provided, that is, that relevant treatment is available.

The Objectives in the War Against Violence

Violence is not an isolated phenomenon, socially or psychologically. "Subcultures of violence" have attributes other than violence-proneness; Violent Men are blessed and cursed with diverse qualities, many of which are unrelated to their destructive potential. To reduce violence it is not necessary to remake people, nor to remodel society. Our assignment is to rechannel or to redirect specific propensities, without prejudice to the integrity of the persons involved. A more wholesale approach would not only be wasteful but might magnify the problem it seeks to eliminate. Violence feeds on low self-esteem, and it thrives on a sense of inadequacy. We have to make sure that we stress to Violent Men that they are not condemned as individuals but that our concern about their destructive behavior is ultimately governed by our regard for their worth as human beings, as well as by our feelings for the victims of their acts. We must make certain that every Violent Man understands that he himself is the victim of violence—not only because society reacts against him, but because violence is self-defeating. The history of each violent person contains ample documentation to support this case.

Reducing violence among "subcultures of violence" is a difficult process, and our research contains little information relevant to the problem. When people assume that certain kinds of violence are appropriate and legitimate, it is obviously sterile to combat this assumption by arguing the case that violence is undesirable. Sermons and speeches that decry violence are viewed as ludicrous and insolent by subcultural audiences. This is only in small part due to the fact that sermonizers and speechmakers belong to a society that itself sanctions violence (sometimes vis-à-vis the very persons who are told to decry it). The main reason for cynicism lies in the fact that excluding the use of force in situations that other people encounter takes no account of problems and needs that seem to require violence in the eyes of its practitioners. Nor does a blanket condemnation of other people's use of violence to solve what they see as problems take cognizance of the need to provide substitute goals and meanings. Ideally, other actions have to go hand-in-hand with efforts to reduce subcultural aggression. Wolfgang and Ferracuti have pointed this out:

> To intervene socially means taking some kind of action designed to break into the information loop that links the subcultural representatives in a constant chain of reinforcement of the use of violence. Political, economic and other forms of social action sometimes buttress the subculture by forcing it to seek strength and solace within itself as a defense against the larger culture and thereby more strongly establishes the subcultural value system.[6]

---

[6]M. Wolfgang and F. Ferracuti, *The Subculture of Violence: Toward an Integrated Theory of Criminology* (London: Tavistock, 1967), p. 299.

If the resources for direct attack on social problems that create recurrent occasions for violence are not available or not used, society is limited to the indirect strategy of rescuing members of violent subcultures from the common fate of their brethren, and of building them into groups that do not assume that violence is necessary for survival. In the words of Wolfgang and Ferracuti, "The personality must undergo a process of weakening of the subcultural ties by means of one of a variety of techniques until allegiance is decreased and a new value system can be introduced."[7]

This process, as I indicated, does not ever require complete transmutation of a person, nor does it always necessitate complete divorce from his or her erstwhile companions. Rather, it presupposes some change program directed at aims that are invoked to legitimize violence. At minimum, it involves furnishing substitute means (such as different approaches to dealing with interpersonal conflicts, constructive social action, or new career lines) for the achievement of these same objectives.

Unfortunately, the task of regenerating individual Violent Men is far from confined to their integration into nonviolent subcultures. Violent Men have propensities for violence that are built into their personalities and modes of functioning, and the difficult task we ultimately must tackle is that of reshaping or redirecting such propensities. The remainder of this discussion will address itself to this problem.

Strategies for Change

In planning strategies designed to change Violent Men, a number of considerations must be kept in mind:

1. The violence-prone person invites violence-prone interactions with other people. These interactions follow a pattern, in that they arise under repeatedly occurring circumstances, and in that they serve persistent ends. The object of change must be (a) to reduce the needs and incentives for such games, or (b) to furnish alternative expressions or courses of action.

---

[7] Ibid., p. 309.

2. Violence-prone games tend to be played by men who feel unsure of their status or identity, and by others whose orientation toward people tends to be egocentric or exploitive. Such basic dispositions must be specifically attended to.

3. Simultaneously, the task of the changer must be to provide each violence-prone person with insight into his conduct, in the sense of making him able to diagnose his own motives. Such insight must be accompanied with retraining, in that the person must be taught to respond to similar situations in different ways. Retraining must be accompanied by rigorous and reliable tests. As long as alternative behavior patterns are not firmly established, the person remains violence-prone.

4. It makes no sense to approach all Violent Men with the same remedial program; by the same token, it is unnecessary to tailor-make efforts at change individually. Violence-prone persons can be grouped in terms of the nature of their violence; persons who follow the same pattern of violence can be subjected to a common strategy of change.

5. Efforts applied to homogeneous groups of violent offenders are not only economical but may be designed to have enhanced impact where group pressure can be mobilized on behalf of constructive change, so that "outsiders" are not viewed as the change agents, and so that individuals can use each other to gauge their own condition and to measure progress.

6. On the other hand, violent games are interpersonal in character, and they can be best modified by involving in the change process not only the Violent Men themselves but also the partners of their games.

The Problem of Intervention

Two facts must be set against each other in considering the issue of when to deal with Violent Men: 1. If one confines efforts to convicted violent offenders, only few acts of violence can be prevented, because most Violent Men are at large and are unknown to us. 2. The formal treatment of people who have not been convicted, and who merely have a "propensity" to violence, would be grossly unfair and would force unpleasantness on a substantial number of persons whose future violence is merely hypothetical. The first statement implies that we must make an effort to extend our attention beyond the ranks of those Violent Men sentenced to prison; the second premise excludes the institutionalization of such persons and raises questions about any programs involving involuntary processing, manipulation, or restraint.

It is obvious that we must take steps to improve our prediction methods, particularly with respect to young boys who will someday seriously aggress against others. In the interim, we must deal with the violent youths whose propensities have been established, and explore retraining possibilities of a kind that would invite their participation and would not violate their integrity.

Consider the case of a mythical lad who delights in forcibly relieving his classmates of their lunches, setting animals afire, and otherwise showing his faith in a two-fisted approach to interpersonal relations. Currently, the boy's life may be studded with summonses to the principal's office, threats of reform school, and impending disciplinary dispositions that carry a heavy nuisance value.

It might be possible to offer such an individual the mild alternative of joining extracurricularly an activity or club involving contemporaries who have shown themselves similarly troublesome. In this setting, group discussions of violence could occur, formerly violent incidents could be rehearsed through role playing, anger reduction could be achieved, and behavior patterns could be generated that could meet the boy's requirements for self-affirmation, without its destructive consequences.[8]

The young man who shows that he can now handle conflict situations might be recruited as a hallway monitor or as a

---

[8] A great many conflict-reduction experiments of this kind have been introduced in schools across the country. For examples, see S. J. Apter and A. P. Goldstein (Eds.), *Youth Violence: Programs and Prospects* (Elmsford, NY: Pergamon Press, 1986); J. E. Lochman, P. E. Burch, J. F. Curry, and L. B. Lampon, "Treatment and Generalization Effects of Cognitive–Behavioral and Goal-Setting Interventions With Aggressive Boys," *Journal of Consulting and Clinical Psychology* (1984), 52: 915–916; J. E. Lochman and L. B. Lampon, "Cognitive–Behavioral Interventions for Aggressive Boys: Seven Month Follow-Up Effects," *Journal of Child and Adolescent Psychotherapy* (1988), 5: 15–23.

member of team sports activities, or as a teacher's aide. Such nonviolent involvements, when combined with self-analysis linking them to destructive motives, could be effective—especially at this early stage—in heading off the development of a Violent Man. And civil libertarian objections would not apply to this strategy as validly as to more formal therapeutic efforts.

In the case of adult offenders, in whom convictions require formal dispositions, limits must be set in terms of rehabilitative requirements. If finite sentences are deployed, these obligate us to insure (a) that the time is in fact used, and (b) that we do what we can in the time available to us. As soon as experience accumulates, success rates must be translated into maximum terms and paroles. Moreover, confinement must always be viewed as a last resort. Combinations of imprisonment and furlough time can be introduced to prevent stagnation, to ameliorate pain, and to test level of rehabilitation in real life.[9] This is especially important for offenders such as Violent Men, whose contact with social reality is deficient.

Building Mature Personalities

Probably the hardest task we face in the rehabilitation of Violent Men is that of developing their interpersonal maturity, or—in psychoanalytic parlance—of building their ego. Some reshaping of personality undoubtedly does occur if we simply teach people to be consistently nonviolent. We have seen that the exercise of violence has a cumulative effect, so that the violence-prone personality becomes increasingly warped over time. It would stand to reason that the continued exercise of peaceful options—if we could teach it—could lead to a less immature outlook on life. Moreover, if we could resocialize violent offenders in groups, as an experiment in living with others, one would expect some carry-over in the shape of a less egocentric orientation.

But more direct effort must be expended on the task of converting Violent Men into men in fact, into persons whose

---

[9]N. Morris, *The Future of Imprisonment* (Chicago: University of Chicago Press, 1974).

chronological maturity is matched by more mature outlook and conduct. Achieving this transformation entails supplying self-esteem and self-assurance to fragile selves that are domineering, blustering, self-advertising, and afraid. It includes the development of concern and consideration among individuals whose outlook on humanity is self-centered and exploitative.

This task probably requires the participation of clinical professionals who see violence problems as an interesting challenge, and who are not intimidated by the harm their clients have done. Precedents exist among skillful clinicians, who have demonstrated the ability to resocialize violent children.[10]

Institutional climates and routines can be designed to permit clinicians to provide support for immature personalities and to build into their patients the controls they need for civilized dealings with others.[11] This sort of climate must give every resident insight into his strategies for self-preservation at the expense of others.[12]

Group pressure and feedback can more than supplement professional skills in this area. Sociologists—and most notably G. H. Mead—first emphasized that the self is a social product. Interpersonal immaturity may be partly the result of deficiencies in the way other people have supported (and controlled) the growing person in his or her formative years. If the child is catered to or neglected, the resulting adult may view other people as instruments rather than as life-partners; if the child is unrecognized and unloved, the adult may be filled with self-doubt and may be convinced of his or her own inadequacy. Experiences of being brutalized are apt to teach us that survival requires that we use preemptive violence, and/or that no one can be trusted.

Deficits resulting from such deficient socialization should be

---

[10] F. Redl and D. Wineman, *Controls from Within: Techniques for the Treatment of the Aggressive Child* (New York: Free Press, 1952); B. Bettelheim, *Truants from Life: The Rehabilitation of Emotionally Disturbed Children* (New York: Free Press of Glencoe, 1955).

[11] For a superlative example, see V. L. Agee, *Treatment of the Violent Incorrigible Adolescent* (Lexington, MA: Heath, 1979).

[12] A model for a prison program that accomplishes this is described in H. Toch and K. Adams (with J. D. Grant), *Coping: Maladaptation in Prisons* (New Brunswick, NJ: Transaction, 1989a).

redeemable through the restorative acts of people bent on rebuilding each other.[13] Groups of Violent Men, given the task of reeducating each other, should be able to function as a "therapeutic milieu." They could do this by reinforcing each other's strengths, by helping each other to rehearse options, and by each analyzing the others' roles in the enterprises of their community.

The task can be facilitated by creating meaningful projects in which the men can jointly engage, in which they can demonstrate proficiency, and in which they can practice cooperation and interdependence.[14] The role of each person in such teamwork could be reflected in results obvious to him, as well as in the expressed esteem of his team members and supervisors.

Additional benefits could arise if the work assignments provided skills with market value outside the institution. And it is desirable for the work to be such that the men can build on existing aptitudes and experiences. Although this shrinks the number of available possibilities, it means that rehabilitation can start at the apprenticeship stage.

The Context for Retraining

Probably one of the most direct approaches to the task of retraining Violent Men is to undertake re-educational programs in the context of violence-centered research and program development. There are several advantages to linking study and planning with subject matter concern. For one, the focus remains on the relevant theme. If the program is intensive enough, each man can become violence-conscious, to the point of sleeping, eating, and living violence. A related advantage is that of

---

[13] D. R. Cressey, "Changing Criminals: The Application of the Theory of Differential Association," *American Journal of Sociology* (1955), 61: 116–20; O. H. Mowrer, *The New Group Therapy* (Princeton, NJ: Van Nostrand, 1964); H. Toch, (Ed.), *Therapeutic Communities in Corrections* (New York: Praeger, 1980).

[14] Maxwell Jones, the father of the therapeutic community, has repeatedly made this argument. See M. Jones, "Work Therapy," *The Lancet* (March 31, 1956), 343–344.

promoting self-involvement. Most violence-prone persons are opposed to violence in other people. A campaign against violence could be attractive to them and could constitute an acceptable means of entry into self-change.

This transition is not only seductive, but logically plausible. The awareness of the Violent Man often is populated with specters of negative pressures. These comprise power-centered relationships, omnipresent threats and fears, threatening and destructive intentions in others. The Violent Man assumes the necessity or desirability of violence in the sort of life in which he sees himself enmeshed. Attention to violence can help to sort this subjective component from social reality and can focus attention on the man's own role and his own contribution.

Another related benefit is the fact that in such an effort, the person can perceive himself as an expert as well as knowing himself the focus of inquiry. This role can give him pride, furnish him with elements of a new identity, and even provide him with a few marketable skills. It can also introduce new meaning, in the shape of end products that transcend the person's own resocialization. These end products, moreover, are badly needed: Case materials on violence are sparse, and the nexus between social environments and individual reactions to them is not easily bridged. Research into violence carried out by persons with experience in the world of violence can shape such materials.

Finally, inquiry is a respectable prelude to change; the transition is natural and easy. The first step toward self-examination is self-knowledge, and self-knowledge is tied to more general knowledge, encompassing the place of one's conduct in its social context. When such information has been acquired—not in the passive stance of the classroom learner but in the role of the information-gatherer and analyst—the next step, of applying the knowledge and of operationalizing its implications, can be more readily faced.

Another possible framework for the resocialization of Violent Men is that of social service work or human service activity. This type of enterprise might be especially helpful in the reorientation of bullies, exploiters, and other manipulative persons. It might help them make a transition from "doing to" to "doing for," without sacrifice of "doing." Self-centered orientations could be undermined, as the person learns to evaluate himself in terms of the quality of the services he renders.

It is obvious that in this as in other types of programs there exists some danger of co-optation. A power-centered view of social relations can be easily translated into social service, as patronage politics and some social work efforts demonstrate. This sort of tendency can be undermined, however, if client initiative and involvement are stressed. Psychodrama, roleplaying and other techniques can be used to insure that altruism does not become transmuted into a system for dispensing gratuities or for accumulating credit.

The Staging of Violent Incidents

One of the difficulties in devising strategies for changing violence-prone persons, and in monitoring their change, is the problem of simulating relevant situations. Obviously, we cannot afford to place Violent Men into the testing grounds of real-life incidents. By the same token, there must be clear relevance and transferability in the trial situations that we are able to devise. These must be subjectively equivalent to temptations and threats, goadings and pressures encountered in the tavern, the back alley, the home, and the prison cell. The stimuli must be intense, realistic, and convincing. The person must become oblivious to the make-believe character of the situation and to its role as a measure of his rehabilitation.

Several techniques are available at this stage. One of these is psychodrama with scenes drawn from violent incidents in the person's past, and from variations on these scenes. The person can replay his own role, both constructively and destructively, and also that of other participants in the same incidents. He can discuss the implications of his behavior, after he has experienced it from every vantage point. He can carry incidents back to various stages of their origin, and he can explore alternative courses of action and their consequences.[15]

---

[15] Psychodrama is a standard feature of therapeutic communities, including those designed for violent offenders. A general case for the method is made by Maxwell Jones, in "Acting as an Aid to Therapy in a Neurosis

Audiotapes, videotapes, and other mechanical aids can be used to keep reactions in awareness, and to focus on relevant aspects for discussion. Such records are also useful for gauging progress or lack of progress. The participation of other violence-prone group members can provide tools for comparative analysis of various kinds.

Stressing sessions can be tailored to create pressures that matter. These pressures can be intense, and they can be meaningful. Having lived and worked with other members of the group for a period of time, each man must regard the others as important to him, and he will have formed special relationships with some of them. Experiments carried out in such contexts can have qualities similar to incidents in the street.

Two types of test situations can be devised; one of these would revolve around working and living relationships, in which roles can be assigned (involving power relationships, conflicts of interest, and issues of prestige and reputation) that carry violence potential, whose consequences the group could evaluate. The type of stress situations used in OSS training during World War II contains models that could be adapted and used for this purpose.[16] Inquisitorial interviews and group problem solving ventures, particularly if they take place (relatively speaking) under frustrating conditions, constitute examples of mock stress. Leadership and followership roles in these kinds of exercises can be interchanged, and each task can be followed by a review of interpersonal conflicts and their resolution.[17]

Centre," *British Medical Journal* (1949), 1: 756–758; the application of psychodrama to dangerous patients is discussed in G. K. Stürup, *Treating the "Untreatable"* (Baltimore: Johns Hopkins, 1968). A more tailor-made approach to rehearsals to violence—using our pattern analytic techniques to design "social skills training"—is reported in K. Howells, "Interpersonal Aggression," *International Journal of Criminology and Penology* (1976) 4: 319–330. This work was done at the Broadmoor Hospital in England.

[16] OSS Assessment Staff, *Assessment of Men* (New York: Rinehart, 1948).

[17] Work situations were sequenced in this way among violent inmates who were examined for parole potential at two California stress assessment units. In typical sequences, menial jobs (with high structure) were followed by responsible jobs (with low structure). The program featured daily "living learning" group sessions.

Another promising type of test situation has been developed in self-help movements, such as Synanon.[18] Here groups convene in counseling sessions, and members subject each other to systematic cross-examination and prosecution. The substance of the person's defense against such tactics, and the nature of his reaction to attack can ultimately be subjected to constructive recapitulation. This second, reviewing phase (which is not prominently featured in the Synanon use of the technique) seems especially important, because it converts the interaction from one of unmitigated hostility to a constructive and didactic one.

Games as Violent Incidents

In several experiments currently under way in various institutions for juvenile offenders, simple retraining procedures based on principles of learning theory are being tried. These involve rewards for desirable conduct, such as completed work assignments, and they stress the use of praise and other signs of approval in conjunction with token economies.

Elsewhere, artificial reward systems may be effective if taken lightly. No person likes to be treated as a maze rat, but most of us like to gamble. This fact makes leisure time important, both as a period for lighthearted testing and as an occasion for playful training. All manner of games could be devised, for instance, to make violence tempting and to reward nonviolence.

In general, commercially marketed children's games tend to emphasize competitive, retaliatory, amassing and aggressive solutions, to a disquieting degree. Variations on some of these games could place the premium on more desirable conduct. The emphasis could be placed on negotiation, for instance, in situations in which warlike acts are standard options. Reality-

---

[18] L. Yablonsky, *The Tunnel Back: Synanon* (New York: MacMillan, 1965); E. Hampden-Turner, *Sane Asylum* (New York: Morrow, 1976).

testing could be encouraged in game form.[19] Self-defenders could be involved in a game of danger, for instance, in which gains are accumulated by acting in defiance of potential threat and discovering that harm does not exist, or, to be more accurate, that it most often does not exist. Games for self-image promoters and reputation defenders could stress the definition of force as a manifestation of weakness. Self-image defenders could be rewarded for non-retaliatory conduct in the face of provocatory moves, in games combining "Dirty Dozens" with alternatives featuring nonviolent resistance.

Equity, justice, and fairness could be built into some games. In many current games, for example, the elimination of weak opponents is routinely rewarded. This condition could be reversed in games designed primarily for bullies. Players could be penalized whenever they moved aggressively against a position of weakness and could be rewarded for protecting a weak partner against a strong opponent.

The number of variations on socializing games is potentially large and only limited by the ingenuity of the designer. Commercial toy manufacturers should welcome the opportunity of becoming involved in the production of constructive games. However, there is no reason why Violent Men themselves could not be involved in the creation and building of anti-violence games. If playing is psychologically involving, knowing the principle of the game should not impair its effectiveness.

Although procedures such as these may seem trivial and irreverent, they can perform a critical role in re-education. Violent Men play violent games because their nonviolent repertoire is restricted. Even when a violent person is aware of what he does, he rarely knows what he could do instead. In fact, such a man frequently assumes that violence is the only means available to achieve his objectives. Changing his needs

---

[19] A game featuring group feedback to the "players" has been developed for violent hospital inmates, and is currently in use, having met with client acceptance. The game is described in V. L. Quinsey and G. W. Varney, "Social Skills Game: A General Method for Modeling and Practice of Adaptive Behavior," *Behavior Therapy* (1977b), 8: 279–281.

is not enough; we must help him arrive at the discovery of new strategies for satisfying needs. Playful simulation enters here, because it represents a painless way to help the player abandon reactions that invite defeat or harm in favor of more constructive ones. Games may succeed where real-life situations fail, because there is little at stake, and there is small risk in rehearsing unfamiliar and untried moves. Simultaneously, games are ideal shorthand representations of life. They bring to the fore rewards and punishment that every Violent Man has encountered, whenever he is not immersed in his sub-culture of violence. And unlike life, games offer no opportunity to miss the point.

The Interpersonal Setting of Retraining

One of the ironies about Violent Men that we have repeatedly pointed to is that they not only play violent games but involve others in the playing of these games. Rep defenders *do* succeed in making innocent targets "lose their cool" and explode with undignified rage; self-image promoters *do* obtain responses in their efforts to challenge others to personal duels[20]; violent persons communicate their fear and resentment to substantial numbers of people and can thus be instrumental in initiating large-scale disturbances, such as riots.

Frequently, social environments are set up unwittingly to make the destructive task of the Violent Man relatively easy. Total institutions, such as prisons, often provide ammunition for the rationale behind violence; standard administrative procedures, such as police practices, can meet the Violent Man more than half way in his efforts to create an arena for violence.[21] Often, the role taken by persons representing the con-

---

[20] Thus teachers frequently become involved in violence-prone games with their students. See F. Wertham, "The Function of Social Definitions in the Development of Delinquent Careers," "President's Commission on Law Enforcement and Administration of Justice, Task Force Report: *Juvenile Delinquency and Youth Crime* (Washington, DC: U.S. Government Printing Office, 1967), pp. 155–170.

[21] H. Toch, *Peacekeeping: Police, Prisons and Violence* (Lexington, MA: Heath, 1976).

trolling authority may trigger the playing out of a game that ends in violence. This role, which emphasizes physical and social distance, minimal communication, and a we-versus-they attitude, makes it all too easy for the instigator of the game to ignore individual differences among persons in the controlling role, to view them in terms of preconceived stereotypes, and to justify his behavior in terms of the stereotype. We may recall one of our subjects, whose core concern was defending his reputation as a fearless leader. One cannot, of course, be seen as fearless unless there is an enemy—perceived by others as both threatening and powerful—to attack. This man's way of maintaining his reputation among the inmates was to challenge the staff periodically, in defense of his peers. Since challenge invites retaliation and punishment, his attacks on staff were a proof of his fearlessness and he was able to maintain an unchallenged leadership reputation among the other inmates. Staff reaction to his provocations did nothing to discourage the playing of this game. In fact, it only increased its usefulness to him and made him ready to play the game again when his reputation needed to be bolstered.

Other persons use violent behavior to manipulate the controlling authority in a specific way. In these cases authority's reaction, which focuses on the violent act itself and not on its antecedents in the instigator's current experience, is readily predicted. It is this reaction which is the goal of the violent act. For example, an exploitative inmate wants to get out of a situation in an institution in which his game of taking advantage of others has been just about played out. He attacks another inmate in a way that brings minimal risk of harm to himself through the encounter, but that makes certain the authorities will be informed. He knows the custody staff games sufficiently well to predict that this incident will get him transferred to another institution. He is right.

For still other persons, the low probability of being apprehended for a given incident built into the control procedures itself becomes an instigating challenge to play out some forms of violence-prone games. These games merely move around the authorities. If the instigator does not want to get caught while engaging in violent or violence-prone behavior, he can be assured that the probability of his being detected is (and even more importantly, is perceived by his peers as being) very slight. In our prisons, control staff admit tacitly (and sometimes openly) that they are not able to enforce regulations and to guarantee the protection of potential inmate victims. What they are able to do is engage in crude detective and spying intrigues with little chance of success for any given incident. The probability of "beating" the staff at any given time is therefore very high. Thus, the looseness within the control procedures and the lack of opportunity offered inmates to prove themselves as men in any other way than "beating the system" provides a climate in which those inmates concerned with proving their manhood rise to the challenge of playing out a violence-prone game.

What these facts imply is that training for nonviolence must involve not only Violent Men but also the standard partners in their violence-prone interactions, including peers, love-partners, authorities and officials. This extended definition of retraining has multiple benefits. Not only does it alert nonviolent persons to the violence-prone sequences in which they become enmeshed, but it also brings the partners of standard violence-prone interactions into new, more constructive relationships.

In establishing such training, it might be advantageous to work initially with staff and with violent offenders in separate groups, then bring them together as soon as the groups are reasonably comfortable with the method and its content. Such a procedure for working with separate interest groups with the intent of ultimately bringing them together has been used with wife batterers and wives if they wanted conciliation. It has also been used in community action programs.[22]

In any event, as training programs for violent offenders are set up—in juvenile settings or in special centers in penal institutions—it is desirable to involve mainline staff in them as participating observers. Career correctional staff are often suspicious of new programs that veer from a philosophy of

---

[22] H. R. Sigurdson, D. G. Dodge, A. Gromfin, and R. Sanfilippo, "Community Education for Delinquency Prevention: Santa Monica Community Study," in *Corrections in the Community: Alternatives to Incarceration*, California Board of Corrections Monograph No. 4 (Sacramento, 1964).

punishment and control, that appear to coddle offenders, and that seem to give scant respect to their own experience and training. Staff experience is as important as offender experience in the design of research and development. If program development is likely to involve shifts in staff functions and roles—and it inevitably will—then it is important not only that staff be involved in shaping the direction of new programming but also that self-development opportunities be opened for them through participation in programs.[23]

The War Against Collective Violence

In our discussion of riots, we suggested that collective violence tends to consist of retaliation against symbols of perceived unresponsiveness.

This fact does not invariably imply that we must deal with collective violence by meeting the aspirations of those involved. Some past race riots, for instance, were based on the desire to retain a monopoly on neighborhoods, jobs, and living accommodations. Lynching mobs have sought to retain a social system in which other persons would remain subservient, or (in the case of religiously motivated lynchings) in which one set of beliefs would be universally enforced.

Moreover, the rhetoric of a riot sometimes disguises needs of questionable legitimacy. Some student rioters in the sixties, for instance, couched demands for autonomy in language deploring every evil of twentieth-century existence. In other situations, the roots of collective violence are irremediable. For

---

[23]Two Canadian institutions have implemented this strategy. One (Penetanguishene) has created a staff "assault prevention training task force." The other (St. Thomas Psychiatric Hospital) has a "committee for the management of disturbed behavior." The programs are described in V. L. Quinsey, "Studies in the Reduction of Assaults in a Maximum Security Psychiatric Institution," *Canada's Mental Health* (1977), 25: 21–23; St. Thomas Psychiatric Hospital, "A Program for the Management and Prevention of Disturbed Behavior," *Hospital and Community Psychiatry* (1976), 27: 724–727. Also see M. E. Rice, G. T. Harris, G. W. Varney, and V. L. Quinsey, *Violence in Institutions: Understanding, Prevention and Control* (Toronto: Hogrefe & Huber, 1989).

example, a panic may stampede persons to death, where physical safety can in fact not be assured. In such instances, action must be confined to helping people address their tragic fate more constructively, if possible.

We have suggested that at the juncture of collective violence it is no longer possible to set the clock back to the initial steps of riot history. In 1992, for instance, an insensitive jury verdict sparked angry rioting. The situation of rioting included various results of frustrated aspirations, such as feelings of resentment, hopelessness, helplessness, low status, and lack of redress for injustices that had been done in the past, including the violence perpetrated by police. Such damage being done, the challenge now was to open up the system in the future, and make it responsive. It becomes essential to promote activities that permit maximum participation, increase status, and provide meaningful life goals.

Potential participants in collective violence must come to see other means of achieving their objectives, in the same sense in which this lesson must be learned by Violent Men. Like the latter, they can be enlisted in community improvement, and they can be taught that nonviolent resources are available that would result in more gain and less damage to self and others. This presupposes, of course, that nonviolent means *are* accessible. Once it becomes true that the police and other agencies remain impervious to reform, so that citizens continue to experience police brutality, the basis for such an assertion must be removed. Violence cannot be remedied when there is in fact no other way to achieve dignity and status.

One area of collective violence which requires additional exploration is the role of key rioters. Not only must we abandon the illusion that riots are created by "agitators", but we must face the fact that destructive influences are exerted among riot participants by groups such as gangs of juveniles within their ranks. Such centers of violence-proneness can be selected for special attention and can be converted or delegitimized.

I have stressed the Riot Commission's conclusion that precipitating incidents are crucial in the genesis of riots—which implies that such incidents are logical targets for prophylactic intervention. For example, increased flexibility in police handling of street encounters in hostile settings has clearly evolved. We know that the answer does not lie in rapid mobility for police egress and the availability of reinforcements; at such junctures, the violence potential of the sequence has often already reached a point of no return, and only the shape of destruction can be affected. The police now know that "backing down" or "standing up for the law" are not meaningful concepts for the assessment of strategy in the early stages of games of collective violence.

Police Retraining

The police have crucial roles to play on both sides of the War against Violence. Most obviously, they are our assault force and our first line of defense against Violent Men; less visibly, the police can become involved in violence-prone games, and sometimes actively contribute to bringing these to a head. Both roles are played in relation to individual and collective violence; both contributions are matters of prime concern to society and to the police themselves.

The concern with police violence is a longstanding one. A social scientist writing in 1968 quoted a police official who complained that "for three years, there has been through the courts and the streets a dreary procession of citizens with broken heads and bruised bodies against few of whom was violence needed to effect an arrest." This quote derives from a statement made in 1903, and the person who quoted it adds (in 1968) that "never before has the issue of police brutality assumed the public urgency it has today."[24] This same claim could have been made in 1991, as television audiences across the country stared in horror at a videotape featuring a large group of police officers in Los Angeles who stood watching two of their peers kicking and clubbing a helpless suspect. And it could be made in 1992 when acquittal of all the principals in this incident set off a bloody race riot. The commission created to investigate the Los Angeles incident points out that "what leaps out from the Department's own statistics—and is confirmed by LAPD of-

---

[24] A. J. Reiss, "Police Brutality: Answers to Key Questions." *Trans-action* (1968), 5: 10–19, p. 10.

ficers at the command level and in the rank-and-file—is that a 'problem group' of officers use force, and are the subjects of complaints alleging excessive or improper force, far more frequently than most other officers."[25] The Commission records, for example, that 63 officers had filed 20 or more Use of Force reports, which denote that serious violence had been deployed. Five percent of the officers accounted for one fifth of the reports.

Our research suggested to us that the ranks of law enforcement contain their share of Violent Men. The personalities, outlooks, and actions of these officers are similar to those of the other men in our sample. They reflect the same fears and insecurities, the same fragile, self-centered perspectives. They display the same bluster and bluff, panic and punitiveness, rancor and revenge as do our other respondents. To be sure, the destructiveness of these officers is circumscribed by social pressure and administrative rules; but it is also protected by a code of mutual support and strong *esprit de corps*.[26] And whereas much police violence springs out of adaptations to police work rather than out of problems of infancy, the result, in practice, is almost the same.

The Los Angeles Commission, for example, talked of "problem officers," but wrote that "the problem of excessive force in the LAPD is fundamentally a problem of supervision, management and leadership."[27] Elsewhere in the report they noted that the violence problem is also a problem of the police locker room, and of the way the Department relates to the community. In theory, aggressive police officers could be dealt with as dangerous deviants by their peers and by the administrators of their departments. Instead, they are seen as overly-forceful

---

[25] Independent Commission on the Los Angeles Police Department, *Report of the Independent Commission on the Los Angeles Police Department* (Los Angeles: Author, 1991), p. 32.

[26] Westley (1970); A. Niederhoffer, *Behind the Shield* (New York: Doubleday Anchor, 1969). Westley was the first to talk of a "Code of Silence" among the police, but the Wickersham Commission as early as 1930 observed that "it is an unwritten law in police departments that police officers must never testify against their brother officers."

[27] Independent Commission, op. cit., p. 32.

practitioners of a philosophy that comprises themes such as "lots of suspects are scumbags," "one cannot tolerate disrespect," "situations must be (physically) controlled," and "the real measure of police productivity is numbers of arrests." Such themes—which characterize enforcement-oriented departments and their locker rooms—are fatefully compatible with the perspectives of the officers. Given less hospitable settings, such officers would be disgruntled and unhappy, but the ranks would contain fewer Violent Men.

In addition to the dangers posed by Violent Men among police, a less dramatic but more pervasive source of difficulty is that of police partnership in the games played by civilian Violent Men. We have seen that in interpersonal situations, causation is often unrelated to motivation: A fair, impartial officer can become involved in violence by unknowingly playing a part in someone else's script—and he can do so frequently and reliably. Unexamined police procedures can contribute to the officer's fate. They can do so because of messages that they send, such as "making good arrests is the only thing that counts."

Some prevalent beliefs about the "police problem" are unrealistic, and they can lead to misplaced programmatic efforts. The most obvious such fallacy is the premise that the "problem" consists of personality disturbances among small groups of officers, who can be fired after psychiatric screening and psychological testing. A related fallacy is the supposition that the difficulty takes the form of racist attitudes that translate into discriminatory uses of force, and that the solution consists of "human relations" programs, including lectures on minority group history and urban problems, dialogues with black nationalists, sensitivity group sessions, social psychology courses, and the like.

It is doubtful whether Violent Men among police officers could be psychiatrically diagnosed as emotionally disturbed. Theirs is a specialized propensity—a gift for escalating interpersonal encounters into explosive situations. This sort of conduct can be reliably isolated only by on-the-spot observations of on-the-street interactions.

Such observations are best conducted during an officer's probationary period. Every recruit's patterns of social behavior could be examined to assess the degree of his violence potential and the nature of his approach to others. The critical question is, what next? If the man or woman proves tactless, or over-aggressive, or oversensitive on his or her maiden patrols, do we screen him or her out of the force? If we have no facilities for remedial training, this may be our sole option. But it is certainly not the ideal course of action. For one, there is the matter of due process. We cannot demand of a person that he display sterling conduct in an area where he has not been advised what he is doing wrong until it is too late. Worse, we cannot expect him to anticipate strong disapproval if he has been rewarded for the behavior ("go-gettem" toughness) that gets him into trouble. Moreover, since violence-proneness con-sists of habits and propensities, it cannot be treated as an indictment of a man's worth. On the other hand, the willing-ness to modify one's conduct is obviously meritorious. And if self-generated change occurs, we know that we can count on a promising officer, or at least, a sadder-but-wiser one.

Moreover, we must consider the fate of persons whom we are tempted to negatively assess and punish. It is inconceivable that such a course of action should not damage an officer's self-esteem—especially when we already have evidence of compensatory conduct. And one must worry about the impact of disciplinary actions on the officer's peers, who may suspect that he is unfairly singled out and that others are similarly vulnerable to capricious punishment.

Whereas the conduct of Violent Men among the police is at least partly due to dispositions brought into law enforcement from civilian life, violence-proneness in other officers is largely engendered by stress on no-holds-barred crime fighting, and by formal and informal indoctrination. Sometimes, omissions are critical. Steps or policies necessary for sound interpersonal relations may nowhere be spelled out. No one, for instance, may impress on the young officer the need to communicate to civilian spectators the import of his actions and the reasons for them. As a result, the officer may take the position that if he is asked to justify his conduct, he betrays his force unless he points to his badge in response. And he can someday provoke a riot by leaving in his wake an information vacuum in which rumors can circulate.[28]

Ambiguity in the definition of police powers is a perpetual source of difficulty. Often, an officer discovers that he has much discretion, but he received little guidance as to its exercise. He may be informed that he can use "reasonable" force, for instance, without being told what this means.[29] To no one's surprise, violent incidents described in police reports (which can be a mix of poetry and history) often terminate in the purported use of "reasonable force." An analogous problem exists when officers are instructed to request identification from suspicious civilians, but are not advised how to counter stubborn refusals. As we have seen, much violence results from indiscriminate requests for identification and information.

Police training (both formal and informal) occurs in the shape

---

[28]J. H. McNamara, "Uncertainties of Police Work: The Relevance of Police Recruits' Background and Training," in D. J. Bordua (Ed.), *The Police: Six Sociological Essays* (New York: Wiley, 1967).

[29]It is, of course, difficult to prespecify in detail a level of force that is "necessary" or "excessive" in specific situations. Some observers have maintained that the line is impossible to draw. Bittner (1970), for example, writes that

In sum, the frequently heard talk about the lawful use of force by the police is practically meaningless and, because no one knows what is meant by it, so is the talk about the use of minimum force. Whatever vestigial significance attaches to the term "lawful" use of force is confined to the obvious and unnecessary rule that police officers may not commit crimes of violence. Otherwise, however, the expectation that they may and will use force is left entirely undefined. In fact, the only instructions any policeman ever receives in this respect consist of sermonizing that he should be humane and circumspect, and that he must not desist from what he has undertaken merely because its accomplishment may call for coercive means. We might add, at this point, that the entire debate about the troublesome problem of police brutality will not move beyond its present impasse, and the desire to eliminate it will remain an impotent conceit, until this point is fully grasped and unequivocally admitted. In fact, our expectation that policemen will use force, coupled by our refusals to state clearly what we mean by it (aside from sanctimonious homilies), smacks of more than a bit of perversity. (E. Bittner, *The Functions of Police in Modern Society*. Washington, DC: National Institute of Mental Health, 1970, p. 38) of general principles, which are far from uniformly applicable in street situations. And verbalizations about police work, of the kind to which every new officer is subjected, are frequently misleading. Experienced officers may impress on the young recruit the need for a uniformly firm approach, or of differential approaches to pre-categorized types of civilians. Universal apprehensiveness about certain types of assignments may be communicated to the young officer, and they may induce panic in many situations.

The young officer may be brought up with myths in lieu of facts and may acquire prejudices under the guise of inside dope. Thus equipped, he may embark on self-destructive patterns of conduct that become established and cumulative.

Police structure can be improved with new definitions of criteria of conduct and with realistic preparation for life on the beat. Ultimately, such information must be communicated through directives and in-service training. The form of in-service training is important. Lectures, seminars, and other passive learning experiences, when transferred to the human relations area, are generally not very effective. In fact, they may increase bitterness and prejudice. More intensive and personally involving methods, such as transactional analysis and community–police confrontations, have more chance of impact, but their diffuseness makes them wasteful as violence-prevention techniques.

Situations that produce violence can be directly addressed, and their resolution can be worked out and demonstrated. Both idiosyncratic and prevalent errors can be subjected to analysis, dramatization, and correction. Simultaneously, successes in explosive situations can serve as positive training materials. (Creative prevention should be routinely rewarded. For instance, if an officer recruits citizens to his side in a conflict situation, or befriends someone who approaches him belligerently, or disarms a man without force, his effectiveness deserves commendation.)

Police training for violence prevention must vary with the cliéntele. For instance it need include only two or three sensitization sessions when its aim is to alert the average officer to a few violent games he will encounter on the street.

In all police training programs, the within-rank group co-hesiveness of police can be turned to advantage. To accomplish this end, training can rely on peer pressure, both inside and outside the classroom. Those who have been trained can be converted into a cadre for training others. Such emphasis is especially important for the violence-prone officer, who would feel isolated and threatened if he were singled out for indi-vidual attention.

In a sense, the problem of retraining violent officers presents fewer hurdles than does the rehabilitation of other Violent Men. A focus on police victimization in unnecessary confron-tations can counter officer resistances. The discovery of police contributions to violence can be made by the officers, and this discovery inspires a natural shift in project emphasis to the question of what can be done about this.

The Oakland Violence Reduction Project

After the first version of this book went to press, we decided to test these ideas (with National Institute of Mental Health sponsorship) in the Oakland Police Department. We secured the help of some of the officers who had served as subjects for the study.[30] We started with seven skilled officers, and they remained our close partners for the next four years. One of the seven officers had a chapter almost to himself in this book, and he became a star of our team. The subsequent impact of what we accomplished is partly a result of his efforts.

The design of the intervention was as follows: The seven officers (four of whom were violence-experienced) studied the problem of use of excessive force in Oakland. They then led three groups of seven officers (all of them problem officers) who were charged with designing new programs that could address the problems of the Oakland Police Department and

---

[30] Chief Charles Gain made the study and the intervention possible. The real names of the first seven officers (we use pseudonyms elsewhere) are John Dixon, Roy Garrison, Carl Hewitt, Larry Murphy, Mike Nordin, Robert Prentice, and Mike Weldon.

the community. The most substantial reform idea that emerged was the Officer Peer Review Panel (or Action Review Panel), which retrained violence-prone officers. The panel became a rotating group of patrolmen; many panel members had once served as panel subjects, and all were experienced officers. The panel's deliberations included pattern analytic exercises of the kind we have illustrated. In this case, they were designed to help problem officers gain insight into what they had been doing to promote violence. The panel worked with its subjects to evolve alternate approaches to street incidents.

We describe the project in detail elsewhere,[31] but a few highlights may help to convey some flavor of the sessions. Our first concern was with whether trust problems could be resolved. In the opening session of the first group, the following dialogue about this issue took place:

Officer:	Well, I'd like to be called Sam from now on. Because everytime he refers to Mills he's using my first name, and I'm the one that's going to get the ax.
Staff:	May we have it for the record that Joe is Sam.
Officer:	One thing that I heard several times tonight, and I'd like, of course, to express my opinion, was I think there's some doubt on the part of you gentlemen, not the officers, but the gentlemen who are conducting this program, as to our honesty, because of the trust we might place in whatever's going on. And I think that you're going to have as complete cooperation as possible. I don't think there's going to be any problems withholding information, not wanting to say something because you're afraid of what could happen. Going on to one of the points that Hiram made. . . .
Officer 2:	The name is Genevieve.[32]

Trust problems were resolved, and close relationships de-

---

[31] H. Toch, J. D. Grant, and R. T. Galvin, *Agents of Change: An Experiment in Police Reform* (Cambridge, MA: Schenkman, 1975); H. Toch and J. D. Grant, *Police as Problem Solvers* (New York: Plenum Press, 1991).

[32] Toch, Grant, and Galvin, p. 20.

veloped. During the last session of the first group, an officer (our research subject) offered the following retrospective:

> I don't know whether it's been a real pleasure or not. I think we said before, it's a hell of a lot easier to go out on the street for 16 hours and kind of do our thing on calls in a relaxed, nice atmosphere. Because this has been a lot of work. It's been a good experience for me, because I'm lacking in formal education and I probably got something here that I would never have gotten otherwise. And I am appreciate of everybody here, especially of the staff members. It's been a good association. There's been a lot of name-calling and a lot of kidding, and I think most of it has really been in jest on my part. My sardonic, morose attitude isn't bad all of the time. Generally I feel very close to you assholes, and I'm looking forward to seeing you again next summer.[33]

The Action Review Panel was designed by one of three second-generation groups. The idea, however, had come up before. During an early session, for instance, our group had interviewed several Oakland Hells Angels, including their leader. One of our officers noted that the Hells Angels had members who were equivalents of problem officers, and (according to their chieftain), were assisted by peers:

> He mentioned something to me that impressed me, that is diametrically opposed to how we think, how we act, and what we, in fact, do on the street. And that's when he brought up the fact that "when we see a guy out of line, we stop him, man, and kind of let him know that he's out of line." This is diametrically opposed to anything I've learned in six years, and it's opposed to what Sam has learned in all the time he's been on the force. I'm wondering if it might not be a good idea. I think that it could be done in such a way, that Bill brought up a few times up here, that he's maybe saved somebody's ass, or maybe saved some policeman from getting the grease by very tactfully and unnoticed

---

[33] Ibid., pp. 60–61.

grabbing some guy and getting him the hell away from there. We make mistakes; I've made mistakes; everybody here has. Just like Sonny Barger said, the whole Hell's Angels group has to suffer because of one man's mistake. We have to suffer if I get in the shit, and Sam and Bill have to come in and bail me out, they're not going to be happy if I'm wrong; then they have to ride my heat too. We brought it up, but it's something to think about.[34]

The stimulus to the panel idea in the second-generation group was an interview the group conducted with one of its members, at his own request. The member (Jones) had experienced an incident that left him puzzled and upset. The interview was animated, and the group's leader (our ex-subject) formulated some hypotheses about the incident's dynamics:

Leader: I think what we're interested in is the sequence of events, and Joe was trying to sort of draw a diagram of what was happening between you and this guy when you were alone with him; of him ignoring you, a feeling that you would have that would control your next move which is, One, you're apprehensive about him because you've arrested people that have used drugs before, and they have always resisted. Or you've always had a problem with them. So, this guy is going to give you a problem. Two, you were expecting him to make a move toward you although we brought out that there were really no signs or cues that gave you that reason, merely because this has happened before. So these two cues that you have, rather unconsciously on your part, are going to govern what you do next. Officer Two drives up. You try and tell him the guy is high, but he doesn't catch it. He doesn't talk to you, so there's no consultation. You haven't gotten rid of your uptight feeling about this thing, you know, in talking to the other guy about it. You kind of feel like you might have to handle this whole thing yourself,

---

[34] Ibid., p. 41.

because the other buy isn't aware of how dangerous this man is. This is probably what you were thinking.

Jones: Yeah.

Leader: When he shines the light to check his eyes and the guy says "keep the light out of my eyes," maybe he moved the flashlight away and all your expectations have at last been fulfilled. This guy moved and showed that he's done what you expected him to do. That would cover your maybe hasty move in grabbing him around the neck. . . .

Jones: Yeah.[35]

Two sessions later, the interviewee himself returned to the subject. He said that an officer could learn a great deal from an experienced fellow-officer at key junctures of his career. This casual remark inspired another officer—a brilliant young man who became our project theorist—to start planning the Review Panel. The officer himself described the birth of the idea as follows:

And about here I started scribbling. . . . And I started making little notes about maybe coming up with trying to work up some sort of system where we can have line patrolmen or the peer group meet in some sort of order review or some sort of review unit where you can analyze the problems that the specific officer might be having on the street when it becomes apparent. Recommendations from superior officers, numerous trips up to Internal Affairs, just numerous violent incidents on the street. This would not be a disciplinary unit or anything like this and it wouldn't really come up with any particular findings pro or con about the officer's actions.[36]

The panel idea became accepted by the group as they rehearsed interviews with each other and officers from outside the project. Time after time, clear patterns seemed to emerge

---

[35] Ibid., pp. 105–106.
[36] Ibid., p. 114.

as arrest reports were reviewed, and these patterns made sense to the interview participants. The officers even speculated about patterns that might cut across patterns, as in the following dialogue:

Jones: This reminds me of this incident that we've got on tape that I went over. Remember when I snatched the guy when he swung? This is probably the same type of thing that we're talking about here. I reacted so fast because of apprehension, fear of what might happen.

Graham: Do I really need to prove myself when I go through the door, or is it because—well, I find that hard to believe about me. . . .

Officer: You know, in your character, in your ideas about fear, you've rationalized in your own mind that you've cor-ralled fear and you're able to rationalize any incident that comes about where fear should be a part of it. . . .

Graham: Well, there were two incidents like that. . . . I mean I was already ready to pick myself up from the sidewalk and fly through the window.

Graham: Why don't you expound on this fear thing? The group mentioned this as an observation about Beam. And then I just took it like an explanation. And now Kent is actually making a kind of theory out of it. And I don't know how you're bringing in fear, but I'm having a hard time imagining policemen out in the street afraid.

Bill: You've never been afraid?

Graham: Not as a running emotion, as constant a factor as this theory suggests.

Officer: Everytime I get in the car I've got it.

Graham: Well, on a particular incident, yes, but I find the theory being presented as a constant.

Bill: Could the fact that an officer could or could not act out of fear be because he's in a position where he can't make an exit? I would say that if a person was in fear or afraid other than a policeman it's obviously possible for him to get the hell away. A cop can't do that; he's got to stay there, although he feels that fear. Which makes him act out of that fear. You can't leave the scene like a truck driver or a banker or an insurance salesman or anybody else. You've got to stay there; that's your job. It makes it pretty goddamn awesome at times.

Graham: At times, but no one answered this question about the fear as a constant.[37]

Did The Review Panel Work?

The panel was instituted in June 1970, and the results were first examined two years later. Tables 7.1 and 7.2 depict the outcome of this assessment.[38] Table 7.1 covers Panel members and Panel subjects. Table 7.2 excludes officers who served as Panel members only—whose activities were not being reviewed.

Table 7.1

Average Monthly Citizen–Officer Conflicts Before and After Panel Participation: Participants vs. Nonparticipants

Review panel	Before	After
Participants (n = 88)		
Average	0.37	0.16
Variance	0.13	0.02
Nonparticipants (n = 434)		
Average	0.10	0.08
Variance	0.03	0.02

Note: Time before and after participation varied for each participant. Actual months on the street before and after participation were used to determine monthly averages.

Time is controlled for the nonparticipants by proportional random assignments, to correspond to the monthly proportions of participants.

---

[37] Ibid., pp. 260–261.
[38] Ibid., pp. 326–327.

Table 7.2

Average Monthly Citizen–Officer Conflicts Before and After Review Panel Participation: Subjects vs. Nonsubjects

Participants	Before panel	After panel
Subjects (n = 37)		
Average	0.63	0.21
Variance	0.13	0.03
Nonsubjects (n = 485)		
Average	0.11	0.08
Variance	0.03	0.02

A covariance analysis shows differences among averages in these tables to have less than a .01 probability (Table 7.1) and a .05 probability (Table 7.2) of occurring by chance. But more work was clearly needed, and several officers would return as panel subjects later.[39] Collinearity is also an issue. The Department was experiencing change and was moving toward a more community-oriented philosophy of police work. A continuation of the trend would have made it less likely that new Violent Men might arise to take the place of officers reformed by the Panel.

We can see that individual change can go hand in hand with group-based change and organizational change, and even with community change. Our groups were a combinatory strategy, in which the officers tackled an organizational problem (in the process, evolving a positively oriented subculture) and created a solution that centered on individual change. Other programs the groups proposed were differently targeted, and they were all part of an overall strategy of reorienting the police department to be more responsive to the community. There are obviously other roads to Rome. But the point is to make reha-

---

[39] The Action Review Panel accommodated recidivism, with provision for "stress panels" to be run where regular panels had failed to impress subjects. Stress panels were panels that included supervisory officers.

bilitation more than "therapy" in which clients are passive recipients of services. Such strategies not only offer more dignity to participants, but are likely to be more effective than a pure treatment model.

Implications of Our Research Strategy Involving Offenders

We mentioned at the beginning that ours was a unique venture. We approached Violent Men for candid accounts of violence and we did so with colleagues who could penetrate their strange world with ease and familiarity. Our nonprofessional associates were persons we could rely on and whom our subjects could trust. As a result, we secured new types of data, some of which we have presented here. Our experience is susceptible to duplication, not only in research but in operational settings such as probation offices, judges' chambers, and penal institutions. Naturally, it must be made clear that adverse decisions could not follow from interview results; this framework is necessary to maintain the trust of interviewers, as well as of respondents. Another requisite for success is that the professional's premises must be shared with his nonprofessional associates.

Kinsey and his collaborators, among others, have demonstrated that information about controversial areas of human experience can be readily obtained by middle-class interviewers. We could add a footnote asserting that similar results can be secured in various contexts with appropriate personnel. This conclusion is not limited to inmates and parolees; our police researchers were able to document serious problems in situations where the average outsider would be faced with assurances that the system was perfect.

To be sure, appropriate questions must be posed. The closer we stay to actual experience, the more uncontaminated the reports we can expect. Validity is assured if each respondent knows that we are trying to view his actions from his point of view. And the subject's own descriptions of conduct and perception can then be placed in context to arrive at more general characterizations of human personality.

The use of nonprofessional research personnel such as inmates offers new career possibilities for nonprofessionals, as well as advantages to the researcher. It has been argued that technological unemployment must be alleviated by expanding careers in the people-processing professions.[40] This imperative, as we see in the case of research, coincides with personnel needs in the field. For instance, when social scientists take increasing interest in social change, they must rely on linkage personnel to obtain meaningful information from the disadvantaged. And, clearly, penology stands in need of new approaches to persons who are currently stored in correctional institutions. Research participation can easily and cheaply serve rehabilitative goals. (The chances of recidivism among several of our associates was originally very high; instead, some of these persons today occupy responsible positions in the human services industry.)

Needless to say, the benefits of converting inmates into researchers are not automatic and free of risk. Like professional workers, nonprofessional participants in research must be selected with care. Unintelligent or completely illiterate persons are of limited use, as are social isolates. A cynical, exploitative, or immature outlook can create a poor prospect for programs that have the usual training resources. This is also true of rigidly held preconceptions, though to a lesser extent.

On the other hand, too close attention to selection criteria can produce a staff of quasi-professional nonprofessionals, who may be rejected by research subjects and even be considered a species of Uncle Tom. Not being trusted, they may have relatively limited useful knowledge or insight, contribute little, discover they are marginal members of the team, and develop poor motivation.

Even careful selection will not altogether eliminate these possibilities. The nonprofessional must get training that is not only directly related to research but also can provide him with incentives, support, and a meaningful self-concept. Some of this training may be of the sort routinely encountered in grad-

---

[40]A. Pearl and F. Riessman, *New Careers for the Poor: The Non-Professional in Human Service* (New York: Free Press, 1965).

uate schools; some may be more characteristic of social movements. The nonprofessional researcher must be, in a sense, a "convert." He must acquire a new role, a new set of values, and new models and friends while remaining in close touch with his old associates. The professional merely places others under the microscope; but the nonprofessional must convert his own life experiences into data. While the rest of us can view research as a job, the nonprofessional must see his involvement as a mission or a crusade—or he will have trouble playing the role.

A Final Word

Our view of violence is not fatalistic or suffused with hope. It promises that Violent Men can be assessed and understood, and that they can, in time, be regenerated. And it assumes that the games played by Violent Men need not end in tragedy. By the same token, a certain amount of tragedy seems inevitable. If Violent Men come to light through violence, their classification and rehabilitation must always follow in the wake of some personal and social harm.

What of prevention? Ultimately, nonviolence presupposes opportunities shared by all, and material progress matched by advances in interpersonal conduct. Our observations suggest the importance of civilized child-rearing, of education that stresses selflessness and self-confidence and that leads to positive communication. Our Violent Men, after all, are basically children who have learned to use force as a compensatory tool.

We presume that a nonviolent society has no room for agencies that profit from the exercise of destructiveness, nor for persons who direct its large-scale use. Men who press explosive buttons or who sign bloodthirsty orders are entrepreneurs of violence, and they set the stage for lone operators. The same holds for individuals who coldly plan for inconceivable contingencies, or who produce and disseminate means of destruction. When the roles exercised by such persons have been eliminated from the games societies play, we can attend to our Violent Men with a clearer conscience and a more unambiguous mandate.

Appendix

Code for Interpersonal Situations Resulting in Violence Against Police Officers

General Instructions

For each incident, one category is coded as "primary," which means that it most directly or immediately leads to the main act of violence.

Parenthetically noted are all other categories which apply to the same assailant in the same situations. (This includes all moves which lead to the violence, and all occasions for subsequent violence by same person.)

Categories applicable to other assailants are separately coded.

Code

A   Perseverance in—or transfer or extension of—violence
    The instances denoted here are situations in which the person is engaged in assaulting others when the prospective victim arrives on the scene, and in which *the violence is simply extended to the victim* (officer),

    A1   As a reaction against interference with, or interruption of, violent actions

    A2   Because new victim is seen as siding with current victim

    A3   Because violence is viewed at the time as appropriate behavior

An   Other or Ambiguous

B   Defense of Personal Autonomy
These are situations in which the individual appears to *react to actions by the victim which make him (the aggressor) an object of undesirable manipulation.*
B1   Violence as a reaction to touching or other bodily contact
B2   Violence as a reaction against orders or instructions
B3   Violence as a reaction against uninvited entry in home, or other trespass on self-defined area of jurisdiction
B4   Violence as reaction to being disturbed or awakened
Bn   Other

C   Protection against Concrete Danger
These are situations in which the person sees the victim as an instrument to impending doom, and reacts *in an effort to avoid or retard danger,* or to prevent being subjected to it without a fight.
C1   Violence in an effort to flee or escape arrest
    C1a   After having assaulted officer physically or verbally, and being arrested for this fact
    C1b   After being arrested or subject to arrest for violence against others
    C1c   After being arrested or subject to arrest for action not related to violence
    C1d   Without prior arrest
C2   Violence in an effort to prevent being transported or moved after being arrested
    C2a, b, c (Same as above)
C3   Violence in an effort to avoid discovery of evidence which would lead to arrest or other unfavorable action
C4   Violence as a manifestation of displeasure with arrest
    C4a, b, c (Same as C1 and 2)
Cn   Other

D   Defense or support of others
In these situations the person *takes the part of others* whom he views as requiring or deserving aid. The person uses violence in an effort to rescue or to increase the effectiveness of "significant others" who are objects of aggression or incursion.

D1   Violence in defense of other persons engaged in physical struggle or being physically subdued

D2   Violence in defense of others who are being—or have been—arrested

D3   Violence in defense of others who are subjected to perceived threat or danger

Dn   Other

E   Violence as an expression of contempt or disapproval
These are situations in which the victim merely serves as a negative stimulus by virtue of his identity and physical presence. Violence here serves *as a manifestation of disapproval* or to assert the person's status vis-à-vis the victim.

E1   Violence to reinforce challenge to a duel

E2   Violence following verbal threat to victim

E3   Violence following verbal abuse or expression or contempt

E4   Unannounced and spontaneous violence

En   Other

X   Unclassifiable
These situations comprise those in which there is insufficient information available for a judgment. Those which are merely ambiguous are to be coded in terms of applicable alternatives.

Illustrative Incidents (Oakland, 1963 and 1964): Excerpts From Police Reports

Code

We responded to the apartment and were confronted with a man and woman fighting on the bed over a long barreled gun. . . . We reacted by attempting to separate the combatants. . . . Officer M. told the defendant to calm down and to give him the gun; Officer C. attempted to pull the gun from the defendant all the while she is struggling and holding on to the weapon, kicking, scratching and yelling profanity. Officer M. attempted to pull the defendant's hands

A1   from the weapon so Officer C. could secure it and in doing so the defendant bit Officer C. on the wrist and forearm. Once the weapon had been obtained by Officer C. who broke it open and removed a live round . . . the defendant then directed her attack upon Officer M. by kicking him in the groin area, and biting his finger (right forefinger); when he clutched at his hand the defendant slapped Officer M., inflicting two large scratch marks, ripped off his tie, called him a "no good mother-fucking cop," choked him and kneed him in the groin area during the ensuing struggle. . . . As the defendant was being (C2a,b) directed to the police vehicle she kicked and struggled despite efforts to calm her which required her to be carried and dragged to the police vehicle. After the defendant was removed from the police vehicle a white handled 4½" blade steak knife was found in the front seat. . . .

Susp. #1 was brought in by ambulance claiming to have been assaulted by persons unknown, Susp. #1 was not visibly injured, since arriving had pushed Dr. S. and nurses around and using vile and profane language. C1P observed Susp. #1, in corridor, pushing Susp. #2 around who was trying to quiet Susp. #1 down. Suspect #1 was calling everybody a motherfucker, white son of a bitches, cock suckers, etc. C/P approaches Susp. #1 and told him to quiet down and asked him what was wrong. He said "Fuck A3 You" and at that struck C/P in face with fist. . . .Wit.s' stated Suspect #1 "blew up" for no apparent reason. Susp. #1 sent to ward D-1 ACH. as Poss. 5050 but, he was refused admittance as drs. stated he would not rightly classify as 5050 and that apparently he didn't like the fact that the police officers (C/P and (E3) wit. #1) were caucasian and this was the reason for the assault.

R/O's called to above address by wit. (susp's wife) because she stated her husband was drunk and insulting her guests. R/O's took wit. outside to explain to her, her rights in such a matter and susp. came to door and started to call out. R/O's went in to quiet

A2 susp. and while talking to him—susp. swung at comp. and reached for R/O's neck ripping his tie off.

A3 A/O heard a loud splash of glass hitting the pavement. Wit #1 approached the A/O and said his woman, the suspect, was mad at him and he couldn't calm her down. Just then two more bottles came flying through the air and one landed just inches from the patrol car. . . . As this officer started into the apartment, a drinking glass was seen to be thrown by the suspect at the A/O. This glass struck the door frame and shattered upon contact, over the A/O. A/O chased the suspect across her living room to the kitchen area and he grabbed her about the arms as she was reach-

(A1) ing for another glass. Suspect began kicking and trying to free herself from the A/O's grasp. It was necessary for the A/O to subdue the suspect by placing her face down on the couch and handcuffing her arms behind her back. . . . Several months ago the A/O investigated where she was the suspect in a child beating offense.

(C1c) Placed subject under arrest and then with that subject started to walk away. Sgt. C. took hold of his arm

B1 and then the subject went violent, jerking Sgt. C. around in front of him and both of them down to the street with reporting officer then attempting to hold subject. Sgt. C. had subject's right arm and both officers attempting to put handcuffs on. . . . The sub-

(C1a) ject was very violent and then kicked Officer B. on the left side of face and neck, throwing him backward to street behind. Additional force, club used on subject's left arm area, 1 stroke and with no results a second swing was attempted to slow subject down and his writhing, twisting, kicking, etc. Subject was struck glancing blow on left side of head. Subject was in a violent berserk condition using all the vile language at his command. . . . While at hospital on Guerney, subject again threatened to get Officer B.,

(E2) "I'll get you one of these days I'll get you good" . . .

finally shook hands with all concerned with "I'm not such a bad guy, really not such a bad guy."

(B1) The reporting officer approached the suspect and since he wasn't looking tapped him on the shoulder and told him to quit blocking the exit. The suspect immediately whirled around and said "don't touch me" and shoved the officer backwards with both hands. The suspect then grabbed the officer by the
(C2a) tie and threw him off balance. . . . The suspect was
(C4a) taken to the patrol wagon—fighting all the way and placed in it. The suspect got one arm free as he entered the wagon and turned to fight. Force was again used to place the suspect in the wagon.

(B2) Off. C. asked susp. #1 for his name and he walked
(C1c) off towards the Telegraph exit. Off. C. repeated the question and susp. #1 kept walking, so Off. C. grabbed
B1 susp. #1 right jacket sleeve and then susp. #1 spun around and swung at Off. C.'s head. Off. C. grabbed susp. #1 and susp. #1 grabbed and tore Officer C.'s
D1 shirt . . . susp. #1 was kicking, swinging his arms and using loud profanity. While Susp. #2 went to his brother's assistance using loud profane language. Susp. #2 was apprehended by Off. B. and held bodily, however susp. #2 did kick Wit. #2 a couple of times in the stomach. . . . While susp. #1 was being
(E4) escorted from the dept. store he yelled profanity to the crowd which had gathered, he yelled out "You white mother fuckers." The crowd consisted of men, women and children.

Comp. again identified himself as a police officer, asked if she was O.K. and was she awake now. Comp. assured the Officer that she was, asked what he wanted and the Comp. then explained the situation concerning the next door neighbor. Defendant replied "Why that Black nigger bitch is out to get me" and made several other remarks concerning neighborhood problems. The defendant then directed her verbal attack on the Comp. and asked just what he wanted—to get out and that he had no right to be in her house. With that the defendant picked B3 up a phone lying on the floor and struck the Comp. with it inflicting a 2" diameter bruise on the left cheek below the eye and in doing so knocked Comp. to one side. She then pushed and tore at the Comp. ripping off his necktie in an effort to get him out the front door and telling him he was just "an asshole little boy trying to play Police Officer.". . . The Comp. attempted to calm the Defendant down, explaining he was a police officer in the performance of duty and to exhibit some demeanor and respect, all the while which the defendant insisted on directing pro-fanities, and insults and pushing and tearing at the Officer's shirt and badge knocking off his hat and glasses. When the matter grew impossible to deal with verbally, Comp. informed the defendant she was under arrest for battery and proceeded to hand-(C2a) cuff the Defendant after another struggle, then after great difficulty the defendant was carried, dragged and supported in every manner in an effort to place same in the patrol car . . . was finally placed into the car by the Comp. after being kicked several times in the groin area. . . . When the Wagon Officers arrived defendant was placed into the Wagon but not with-out a great struggle in which she kicked the four arresting officers, grabbing and tearing at the Comp. shirt and badge, and in doing so bent Wit. #2's badge and inflicting several scratches on Comp.'s hand (backside).

Susps. were walking through the park drinking "Old Chateau and Greystone Wine." Susps. were with a large group of MN Teenagers. They broke off top of (A3) light pole #0180. They started throwing garbage cans in the Lake and using Loud and Boisterous Language near the concessions, Susps. entered a newly re-decorated washroom and tore all the dispensers from the wall and broke everything in view. In general the place was a shambles. When Police arrived this gang split up and ran. Above two susps. . . . finally spotted hiding in bushes. Off. L. told susp. #1, "Come out." Susp. #1 started to run. When Off. L. grabbed him susp. spun around and hit Officer in forehead.

C1b   Susp. was finally subdued after he put up a violent struggle.

Comp. observed susp. running through creek bed, and recognized susp. as one of the juveniles being in the yard at L.S.'s. Comp. called to susp., and susp. walked to within 20 feet of comp. Comp. advised susp. he was under arrest, and to come along with comp. Susp. ran into the creek bed where he was

C1c   apprehended by comp. (148P.C.Resis.) Susp. began kicking comp. and pulling comp.'s shirt and tie. Susp. attempted to bite comp. in the leg, then kicked comp. in the face (243P.C.) Officer A. assisted comp. to

(C2a)   place susp. in patrol car, where susp. kicked and broke the glass partition over rear of the front seat.

R/O observed 2 MW 16–18 years. . . . Both appeared to be unsteady on their feet and possibly drunk. R/O pulled his car alongside and while stepping out

(B2)   of the car said "Come here fellas." Both continued walking. R/O said louder "I said come here now hold it," whereupon the suspect ran north. . . . R/O pursued suspect and caught him as he was going over the railing of a witness' back porch. As R/O grabbed

C1d   suspect, the suspect turned and swung at R/O with his right fist. R/O struck suspect twice with baton to subdue him and had to continue to struggle to get

(C4a)   suspect handcuffed.

The above named susp. was being booked for violation of parole . . . as the report was being made the susp. started running down the hall toward the exit of this division. The susp. was told to stop on several occasions but he continued to try and evade the officers. The susp. ran to the East end of the

Police Building where he ran into a dead end. The susp. ran into the bathroom and Off. D. followed him. Off. M. was stationed at the alternate exit and the susp. came out this exit and the attempt was made at this time to take the susp. into custody. The susp. at this time started fighting Off. M. and struck

C1c him with his fist and knee. Necessary force was used to subdue the susp. at this time. Off. M. and D. restrained the susp. and handcuffed him, the susp. was still belligerent and attempted to kick both officers while being taken back to Vice Control Division.

While Officers were waiting, Susp. returned and started arguing with complainant, Mrs. H. After several minutes it was determined that the Susp. was under the influence (647FPC) from the following reasons. Susp. was loud and using profanity. Susp.'s speech was thick. Susp. smelled very strongly of an intoxicating beverage. Susp. was then informed that he was under arrest for 647FPC "under the influence." . . . Susp. was very uncooperative, refused to get in the back seat of the patrol car to await the arrival of the Police Wagon. Upon arrival of the Police Wagon susp. refused to get out of the police car and had to be coached. When susp. finally got out of the police car

C2c he then refused to get in the wagon, and had to be helped in. Once in the wagon susp. suddenly turned and kicked the wagon doors open. Susp. then continued kicking at Complaint. and Wit. (Wagon Officers) Susp. kicked comp.'s hat off his head. Susp. grabbed comp. by the shirt front and pulled him into the wagon. Susp. kicked comp. on the knee cap and leg. Wit. went into the wagon to aid comp., then resorted to use of baton to defend himself and comp. and subdue the susp.

Went to the suspect's residence and identified themselves as police officers, stating that they were in possession of a search warrant for the suspect's dwelling. . . . She ran from the door toward the interior of the house yelling at the top of her voice "Joe, Joe, it's the police." At this point susp. G. ran

C3 to a gun locker which contained 3 rifles and 1 shotgun. . . . Officers used necessary force to enter the suspect's dwelling and seized susp. G. J., who was attempting to load the 12 ga. shotgun. When officers

(B3) approached susp. G. J., he as yet had not loaded the shotgun and using same as a club struck State Agent W. across the left temple with the barrel of the gun, until handcuffed was resisting violently.

A male negro holding a hunting knife in his hand had crossed Foothill Boulevard near 46th ave. While crossing the street this suspect was brandishing the knife and making swiping motions with the knife at passing cars and a bus . . . had broken a window

(A3) out of room 106 at Freemont High and directed profane language and threats at Mr. R.B. . . . Officer B. noticed the handle of a knife protruding from the belt of the suspect's right side. When the suspect got on the sidewalk Officer B. approached him to inquire about the knife he was carrying on his person. At this time the suspect pulled out the knife, pointed it directly at the Officer and said "You mother fucking

C3 cop you can't take this from me, I'll kill you." Then
(A1) the suspect started advancing toward Officer B. and
(E1) a struggle ensued involving Officer B., Officer C. and the suspect. . . . The suspect was informed that he was under arrest and he pushed and struck at both Officer C. and B. While the Officers were attempting to remove him from the scene to the Police

(C2a) Vehicle, the suspect grabbed, hit, scratched, kicked, and bit Officer C. The suspect choked, hit, and kicked Officer B. During the struggle the knife disappeared and at this time has not been located. Further during the struggle the suspect deliberately grabbed Officer C's. watch, broke the band and threw it on the ground. The watch was later located in three parts, some of the parts are missing and the watch is not functioning. Also during the struggle Officer C's. sport coat was torn at all three pockets and apparently not repairable. Officer B. suffered damage on both arms of his rain coat. . . . The reporting officers gained control and were restraining suspect T. in the street in front of 4605 Foothill Boulevard, when Suspect H.

D1 approached from their rear and began kicking and kneeing both Officer B. and Officer C. At this time Sgt. B.M. arrived and while restraining and taking into custory Suspect H., suffered damage to the right knee of this uniform pants.

Comp. asked the suspect to accompany him outside to discuss the matter. The suspect followed comp. to the front door and stopped. Comp. told the suspect that he had been accused of bothering the other

C3 customer. The suspect grabbed comp.'s shirt, pulling off the flap of the left pocket. Comp. told suspect at

(C2a) this time that he was under arrest. Suspect then struck the comp. in the chest and kicked him in the shins. Comp. then struck the suspect several times with his baton knocking him to the floor and suspect then grabbed comp.'s legs and hung on.

After the driver had been asked to get out of the vehicle, officer M. attempted to drive it into the shoulder. Subject stated Officer M. couldn't move the vehicle and threatened to "Get Him" if some-

(E1) thing happened to the vehicle, if it was moved. Subject was asked to get out of the vehicle to determine his sobriety and started interfering with the sobriety tests being given by Officer T. to the driver. At this time he told Officer M. to remove his gun, and the subject would "beat the shit out of him." The subject was repeatedly told to get back into the vehicle and

(B2) he refused, stating we "couldn't tell him what to do." Officer T. took the subject by the arm and started to lead him to his vehicle. The subject jerked away

C4 again stating he couldn't tell him what to do. Subject was placed under arrest. Both officers at-

(C2a) tempted to hand-cuff the subject, but the subject resisted. . . . After the subject was hand-cuffed, he kicked Officer T. in the middle while he was being placed in the patrol vehicle. At the jail he again refused to walk and had to be forcibly brought into the booking room. During this time the subject kicked Officer M. in the left eye.

Def. then asked A/O "do you want to play . . . The def. said they should go into the restroom because the police patrol the park and have arrested people there. The def. then checked the women's restroom for occupants and then went into the men's restroom. The A/O followed and upon entering saw the def. on the right with his pants zipper open and his penis sticking out. . . . A/O then displayed his police star and said police. Def.'s eyes widened then lunged at

D2 the A/O striking him in the face. Def. and A/O struggled and the def. broke away but was immediately confronted by a second officer and submitted to arrest.

During the discharge of duties by the COMPLAINANT's in which two male Negro suspects were being placed under custody for 484 PC (Shoplifting) the suspect approached and demanded that they be released, that they were with him and that they had not did anything. Suspect positioned himself in such a manner that it enabled the #1 484 PC suspect to escape; #2 484 suspect was placed in the patrol car during which time suspect interfered in a loud boisterous voice directing abusive language at the Complainants. . . . At this time suspect began to physically

C4 attack Complainants by grabbing at Officer D.'s tie and shoving Officer C. to the side. Suspect took several swings at the Officers, striking them about the body. At this point Officer P. arrived and suspect was placed under arrest for assaulting a police officer.

(C4a) It was necessary to meet his force with physical restraint in which patrol car aerial was torn off by suspect. When he was placed up against the patrol car, he was told in no uncertain terms he was under arrest. He continued to direct his physical attack against arresting officers. When an attempt to restrain suspect became fruitless, it became necessary to place handcuffs on suspect, all the time which he continued to struggle. Complainants failed to get suspect handcuffed and he was threatened with the use of the police baton. He continued his attack and it became necessary to strike the suspect several times with the baton.

D2   When he was told he was under arrest (his girlfriend) kicked this officer on the left leg and yelled arrest me too. Susp. was wearing heels with sharp pointed toes. A/O suffered injury to shin of left leg— laceration and bruise.

(C3)

(E3)

E2   Suspect #1 stated "I don't have to show you my license because I haven't done anything wrong, and I think this is pretty God Damned ridiculous to go stopping people and trying to give tickets during the Christmas Season. Comp. Informed Suspect #1 that he was required by law to submit his license to a police officer on request, and failure to do so shall result in arrest. Suspect #1 then submitted license to comp. and stated "Where am I living, in some Communist Country? You're just a snot nosed brat in a blue jacket." At this time rather than take more oral abuse from suspect, comp. returned to patrol car to write citation in peace. Comp. was only a short ways through the citation when Suspect #1 came back to comp's. patrol unit. . . . Comp. ordered suspect back to his vehicle. Suspect refused stating you don't tell me what to do you little bastard. I am going to get your badge number and fix you. Suspect #1 reached in my window and grasped my badge, and comp. stated "get your hands off of me!" Suspect #1 then stated "Oh yea." and grabbed my badge trying to rip it off and half pulling comp. out of patrol

D2   car. Comp. lifted door handle and kicked open door knocking Susp. #1 to ground. At this time wit. #1 arrived and helped Comp. put cuffs on Suspect #1. While doing this Comp. was attacked from behind by Suspect #2, who was cuffed immediately.

E3   A/O's S. and P. were patrolling N/B on Market St. and observed 3 M/Ns (the suspect being one of them) standing on the N/E corner. . . . Suddenly the suspect yelled out, "You rotten mother fucker white cops." He shouted this several times at the A/O's. . . . Officer S. got out of the car and approached the suspect. The suspect turned and started away from the officer. The Officer told the suspect to stop and that he wanted to talk to him. As Officer S. approached, the suspect swung around and struck Officer S. on the face. As Officer S. staggered back, the def. swung his umbrella at the Officer and missed. Officer S. stepped in and grabbed the suspect by his sport coat and the suspect stepped out of the coat and started running. . . . Sgt. P. observed suspect in a bar at 16th and Market. As Officers converged on the bar and the suspect ran out the rear door. The

(C1a)   suspect fell down and as Sgt. P. and Officers W. & S. converged on him the suspect kicked out, striking Officer W. in the left knee. He slipped out of the grasp of the Officers and ran down. . . . Suspect was finally stopped on 18th Street by Lieutenant H. and Officer R.O. The suspect continued to struggle and fight and Officer W. joined the Lt. and Officer and the 3 officers finally subdued the suspect and he was handcuffed. The Suspect continued to struggle, and kick and scream invectives at the Officers and was transported to Headquarters. The Suspect was put in the rear of a patrol wagon to await the arrival of reports and he again started to kicking and screaming. He kicked another prisoner and swore at him. . . .

Def. was in the bar creating a disturbance. . . . Def. had strong odor of alcoholic beverage. Eyes bloodshot, speech slurred. . . . Def. placed in rear seat of patrol car and wagon called . . . had to be transferred from K's car to R's car. A/O's opened door and def.

(E3) got out and told A/O's that they were "fucking punks" "cocksuckers" and "assholes" and that he was going to "kick the shit" out of them. With this def. took a

E2 swing at A/O R. Necessary force used to subdue def. Def. kicked A/O K. Def. pulled both officers' ties off. Def. was handcuffed and placed in patrol car. Def. sat there calling A/O's profane names: ex: cocksuck-

(C4a) ers, fucking punks, cunts, chicken shit, sons of bitches. Def. threatened A/O's several times saying if we would take the handcuffs off he would kick our asses, etc.

(E1) When wagon officers arrived, def. said all 4 officers were fucking punks and that he would take all 4 of us at once if we would take off the cuffs.

References

Agee, V. L. (1979). *Treatment of the violent incorrigible adolescent*. Lexington, MA: Heath.

Aichhorn, A. (1955). *Wayward youth: A psychoanalytic study of delinquent children, illustrated by actual cases studies*. New York: Meridian Books.

Allport, G. W. (1961). *Pattern and growth in personality*. New York: Holt, Rinehart & Winston.

Apter, S. J., & Goldstein, A. P. (Eds.). (1986). *Youth violence: Programs and prospects*. Elmsford, NY: Pergamon Press.

Bandura, A. (1973). *Aggression: A social learning perspective*. Englewood Cliffs, NJ: Prentice-Hall.

Bandura, A. (1979). The social learning perspective: Mechanisms of aggression. In H. Toch (Ed.), *Psychology of crime and criminal justice*. New York: Rinehart & Winston.

Bandura, A., & Walters, R. H. (1959). *Adolescent aggression*. New York: Ronald Press.

Bensing, R. C., & Schroder, O. (1960). *Homicide in an urban community*. Springfield, IL: Charles C Thomas.

Berdie, R. F. (1947). Playing the dozens. *Journal of Abnormal and Social Psychology, 42*, 120–121.

Berne, E. (1964). *Games people play*. New York: Grove Press.

Bettelheim, B. (1955). *Truants from life: The rehabilitation of emotionally disturbed children*. New York: Free Press of Glencoe.

Bittner, E. (1970). *The functions of police in modern society*. Washington, DC: National Institute of Mental Health.

Campbell, A., & Gibbs, J. J. (Eds.). (1986). *Violent transactions: The limits of personality*. London: Basil Blackwell.

Chaiken, M. R., & Chaiken, J. M. (1984). Offender types and public policy. *Crime and Delinquency, 30*, 195–226.

Chevigny, P. (1969). *Police power*. New York: Pantheon.

Conot, R. (1967). *Rivers of blood, years of darkness*. New York: Bantam Books.

Cressey, D. R. (1955). Changing criminals: The application of the theory of differential association. *American Journal of Sociology, 61*, 116–120.

Dollard, J., Doob, L., Miller, N., Mowrer, O., & Sears, R. (1939). *Frustration and aggression*. New Haven, CT: Yale University Press.

Fannin, L. F., & Clinard, M. B. (1965). Differences in the conception of self as a male among lower and middle class delinquents. *Social Problems, 13*, 205–214.

Feshbach, S. (1964). The function of aggression and the regulation of aggressive drive. *Psychological Review, 71*, 257–272.

Fromm, E., & Maccoby, M. (1970). *Social character in a Mexican village*. Englewood Cliffs, NJ: Prentice-Hall.

Grant, J. (1965). The industry of discovery: New roles for the nonprofessional. In A. Pearl & F. Riessman (Eds.), *New careers for the poor*. New York: Free Press of Glencoe.

Greenwood, P. W. (1982). *Selective incapacitation*. Santa Monica, CA: Rand Corporation.

Hampden-Turner, E. (1976). *Sane asylum*. New York: Morrow.

Hannerz, U. (1969). *Soulside: Inquiries into ghetto culture and community*. New York: Columbia University Press.

Hemingway, E. (1927). *Men without women*. New York: Scribner's.

Hersey, J. (1960). *The war lover*. New York: Bantam Books.

Howells, K. (1976). Interpersonal aggression. *International Journal of Criminology and Penology, 4*, 319–330.

Huesman, L. R., Eron, L. D., Lefkowitz, M. M., & Walder, L. O. (1984). *The stability of aggression over time and generations*. Victoria, British Columbia, Canada: International Society for Research on Aggression.

Independent Commission on the Los Angeles Police Department. (1991). *Report of the Independent Commission on the Los Angeles Police Department*. Los Angeles: Author.

Jones, M. (1949). Acting as an aid to therapy in a neurosis centre. *British Medical Journal, 1*, 756–758.

Jones, M. (1956, March 31). Work therapy. *The Lancet*, pp. 343–344.

Katz, J. (1988). *Seductions of crime: Moral and sensual attractions in doing evil*. New York: Basic Books.

Lochman, J. E., Burch, P. E., Curry, J. F., & Lampon, L. B. (1984). Treatment and generalization effects of cognitive–behavioral and goal-setting interventions with aggressive boys. *Journal of Consulting and Clinical Psychology, 52*, 915–916.

Lochman, J. E., & Lampon, L. B. (1988). Cognitive–behavioral interventions for aggressive boys: Seven month follow-up effects. *Journal of Child and Adolescent Psychotherapy, 5*, 15–23.

Lorenz, K. (1966). *On aggression*. New York: Harcourt Brace Jovanovich.

Los Angeles Police Department, Administrative Research Unit, Planning and Research Division. (1966, April 18). *Attacks on Los Angeles police officers* [Mimeographed report].

Luckenbill, F. (1977). Criminal homicide as a situated transaction. *Social Problems, 25*, 176–186.

McNamara, J. H. (1967). Uncertainties of police work: The relevance of police recruits' background and training. In D. J. Bordua (Ed.), *The police: Six sociological essays*. New York: Wiley.

Megargee, E. I. (1966). Undercontrolled and overcontrolled personality types in extreme antisocial aggression. *Psychological Monographs, 80*(3, Whole No. 611).

Miller, W. B., Geertz, H., & Cutter, H. (1961). Aggression in a boys' street-corner gang. *Psychiatry, 24*, 283–298.

Morris, N. (1974). *The future of imprisonment*. Chicago: University of Chicago Press.

Mowrer, O. H. (1964). *The new group therapy*. Princeton, NJ: Van Nostrand.

Moyer, K. E. (1987). *Violence and aggression: A physiological perspective.* New York: Paragon House.

Mueller, P. C., Toch, H., & Molof, M. (1965, August). *Report to the Task Force to Study Violence in Prison.* Sacramento: California Department of Corrections, Research Division. (Mimeographed)

Niederhoffer, A. (1969). *Behind the shield.* New York: Doubleday Anchor.

Novaco, R. W. (1975). *Anger control.* Lexington, MA: Heath.

Olweus, D. (1979). Stability of aggressive reaction patterns in males: A review. *Psychological Bulletin, 86,* 852–875.

OSS Assessment Staff. (1948). *Assessment of men.* New York: Rinehart.

Parsons, T. (1947). Certain primary sources and patterns of aggression in the social structure of the western world. *Psychiatry, 10,* 167–181.

Pearl, A., & Riessman, F. (1965). *New careers for the poor: The non-professional in human service.* New York: Free Press.

Peterson, M. A., & Braiker, H. (1981). *Who commits crime: A survey of prison inmates.* Cambridge, MA: Oelgeschlager, Gunn & Hain.

Quay, H. C. (1984). *Managing adult inmates: Classification for housing and program assignments.* Washington, DC: American Correctional Association.

Quinsey, V. L. (1977). Studies in the reduction of assaults in a maximum security psychiatric institution. *Canada's Mental Health, 25,* 21–23.

Quinsey, V. L., & Varney, G. W. (1977a). Characteristics of assaults and assaulters in a maximum security psychiatric unit. *Crime and/et Justice, 5,* 212–220.

Quinsey, V. L., & Varney, G. W. (1977b). Social skills game: A general method for modeling and practice of adaptive behavior. *Behavior Therapy, 8,* 279–281.

Rapoport, A. (1960). *Fights, games and debates.* Ann Arbor: University of Michigan Press.

Redl, F., & Wineman, D. (1952). *Controls from within: Techniques for the treatment of the aggressive child.* New York: Free Press.

Redl, F., & Wineman, D. (1962). *Children who hate: The disorganization and breakdown of behavior controls.* New York: Collier Books.

Reiss, A. J. (1968). Police brutality: Answers to key questions. *Trans-action, 5,* 10–19.

Reiss, A. J., Jr. (1971). *The police and the public.* New Haven, CT: Yale University Press.

Report of the National Advisory Commission on Civil Disorders. (1968). New York: Bantam Books; Dutton.

Rice, M. E., Harris, G. T., Varney, G. W., & Quinsey, V. L. (1989). *Violence in institutions: Understanding, prevention and control.* Toronto: Hogrefe & Huber.

Robins, L. N., & Braroe, N. W. (1964). The lay interviewer in research. *Journal of Nervous and Mental Disease, 138,* 70–78.

Rothman, D. J. (1980). *Conscience and convenience.* Boston: Little, Brown.

Schelling, T. C. (1963). *The strategy of conflict.* Cambridge, MA: Harvard University Press.

Schultz, L. G. (1960). The wife assaulter. *Journal of Social Therapy, 6,* 103–111.

Schwitzgebel, R. (1954). *Streetcorner research: An experimental approach to juvenile delinquency.* Cambridge, MA: Harvard University Press.

Short, J. F., & Strodtbeck, F. L. (1965). *Group process and gang delinquency.* Chicago: University of Chicago Press.

Shubik, M. (1964). *Game theory and related approaches to social behavior.* New York: Wiley.

Sigurdson, H. R., Dodge, D. G., Gromfin, A., & Sanfilippo, R. (1964). Community education for delinquency prevention: Santa Monica Community Study. In *Corrections in the community: Alternatives to incarceration* (California Board of Corrections Monograph No. 4). Sacramento: California Board of Corrections.

Spencer, C. (1966). *A typology of violent offenders* (Research Report No. 23). Sacramento: California Department of Corrections, Research Division.

St. Thomas Psychiatric Hospital. (1976). A program for the management and prevention of disturbed behavior. *Hospital and Community Psychiatry, 27,* 724–727.

Stürup, G. K. (1968). *Treating the "untreatable."* Baltimore: Johns Hopkins.

Szasz, T. (1989). *Insanity: The idea and its consequences.* New York: Wiley.

Toch, H. (1965). *The social psychology of social movements.* Indianapolis, IN: Bobbs-Merrill.

Toch, H. (1976). *Peacekeeping: Police, prisons and violence.* Lexington, MA: Heath.

Toch, H. (1980). *Therapeutic communities in corrections.* New York: Praeger.

Toch, H. (1983). The management of hostile aggression: Seneca as applied social psychologist. *American Psychologist, 38,* 1022–1026.

Toch, H., & Adams, K. (1989a). *Coping: Maladaptation in prisons.* New Brunswick, NJ: Transaction.

Toch, H., & Adams, K. (1989b). *The disturbed violent offender.* New Haven, CT: Yale University Press.

Toch, H., & Grant, J. D. (1991). *Police as problem solvers.* New York: Plenum Press.

Toch, H., Grant, J. D., & Galvin, R. T. (1975). *Agents of change: An experiment in police reform.* Cambridge, MA: Schenkman.

Toch, H., & Redl, F. (1979). The psychoanalytic perspective. In H. Toch (Ed.), *Psychology of crime and criminal justice.* New York: Holt, Rinehart & Winston.

Travis, C. (1982). *Anger: The misunderstood emotion.* New York: Simon & Schuster.

Turner, R. H. (1964). Collective behavior. In R. E. L. Faris (Ed.), *Handbook of modern sociology.* Chicago: Rand McNally.

Von Hentig, H. (1967). *The criminal and his victim.* New York: Anchor Books.

Wertham, F. (1967). The function of social definitions in the development of delinquent careers. In *Juvenile delinquency and youth crime* (President's Commission on Law Enforcement and Administration of Justice, Task

Force Report; pp. 155–170). Washington, DC: U.S. Government Printing Office.

Westley, W. A. (1970). *Violence and the police.* Cambridge, MA: MIT Press.

Wolfgang, M. E. (1958). *Patterns in criminal homicide.* Philadelphia: University of Pennsylvania Press.

Wolfgang, M. E., & Ferracuti, F. (1967). *The subculture of violence: Toward an integrated theory of criminology.* London: Tavistock.

Wolfgang, M. E., Figlio, R., & Sellin, T. (1972). *Delinquency in a birth cohort.* Chicago: University of Chicago Press.

Wolfgang, M., Thornberry, T., & Figlio, R. (1987). *From boy to man, from delinquency to crime.* Chicago: University of Chicago Press.

Wolfgang, M. E., & Weiner, N. A. (Eds.). (1982). *Criminal violence.* Newbury Park, CA: Sage.

Wright, R. (1949). *Native son.* New York: Harper.

Yablonsky, L. (1965). *The tunnel back: Synanon.* New York: MacMillan.

Index

About the Author

Hans Toch is Distinguished Professor at the University at Albany of the State University of New York, where he is affiliated with the School of Criminal Justice. He obtained his PhD at Princeton University and has taught at Michigan State University and Harvard. Toch is a Fellow of the American Psychological Association and the American Society of Criminology. He is a recipient of the Hadley Cantril Memorial Award and has served as a Fulbright Fellow in Norway.

Among Toch's recent books are *The Disturbed Violent Offender* (1989) and *Coping: Maladaptation in Prisons* (1989) with Ken Adams, and *Police as Problem Solvers* (1991) with J. Douglas Grant. One of Toch's early books was *The Social Psychology of Social Movements* (1965); his first interests included problems of public opinion, perception, and social perception, but he has a longstanding concern with the psychology of violence. Toch has described himself as "an applied social psychologist" with a "serendipitous specialization" in criminal justice and criminology. The area of specialty evolved during decades of research in California and New York State prisons and in metropolitan police departments. Toch says that his crime-related concerns meant "a bit of innovating, teaching subject matter from a psychological perspective that is the traditional purview of sociologists." Toch describes himself as "an unwitting pioneer" in a "now established interdisciplinary endeavor that has become a growth industry."